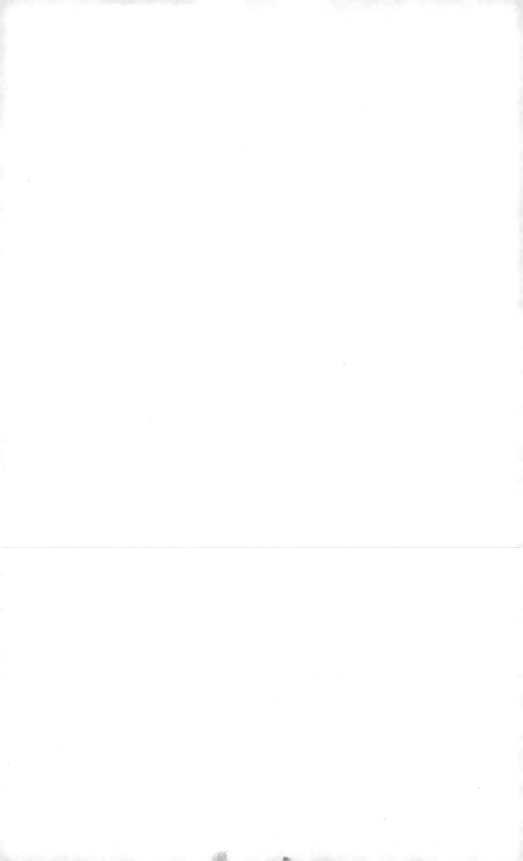

The Smallest Minority

THE SMALLEST MINORITY

INDEPENDENT THINKING IN THE AGE OF MOB POLITICS

REGNERY GATEWAY

Regnery Gateway™ is a trademark of Salem Communications Holding Corporation; Regnery® is a registered trademark of Salem Communications Holding Corporation

Cataloging-in-Publication data on file with the Library of Congress

ISBN 978-1-62157-968-7
e-book ISBN 978-1-62157-977-9

Published in the United States by
Regnery Gateway, an imprint of
Regnery Publishing
A Division of Salem Media Group
300 New Jersey Ave NW
Washington, DC 20001
www.RegneryGateway.com

Manufactured in the United States of America

10 9 8 7 6 5 4 3 2 1

Books are available in quantity for promotional or premium use. For information on discounts and terms, please visit our website: www.Regnery.com.

A NOTE FROM THE AUTHOR:
I took the title of this book from Ayn Rand.
I took it from her because she doesn't deserve it.

History has thrown up a character whom we are accustomed to call the 'mass man.' His appearance is spoken of as the most significant and far-reaching of all the revolutions of modern times. He is credited with having transformed our way of living, our standards of conduct and our manners of political activity. He is, sometimes regretfully, acknowledged to have become the arbiter of taste, the dictator of policy, the uncrowned king of the modern world. He excites fear in some, admiration in others, wonder in all. His numbers have made him a giant; he proliferates everywhere; he is recognized either as a locust who is making a desert of what was once a fertile garden, or as the bearer of a new and more glorious civilization.

—*Michael Oakeshott, "The Masses in Representative Democracy," 1961*

Contents

Foreword

Liberal education is liberation from vulgarity. The Greeks had a beautiful word for "vulgarity"; they called it *apeirokalia*, lack of experience in things beautiful.

—*Leo Strauss, "What Is Liberal Education?" 1959*

I used to work not far from a temple in New Delhi dedicated to Hanuman, the monkey-faced Hindu deity who is the patron of the capital city—a 108-foot tall[1] statue of him looms over the Jhandewalan metro station. Monkeys are a problem. Basically, you can't fuck with a monkey in Delhi, for religious and civic reasons, so there's a plague of the things all over the city but especially in the temple precincts. They are basically high-IQ New York subway rats with opposable thumbs. It's not good.

The pilgrims come to seek Hanuman's blessing, and they feed the monkeys—feeding the plague. The amateurs bring them bananas and fruit and such, but the real pros—the Hanuman-worship insiders—bring the monkeys what they really like: McDonald's.

They're lovin' it.

The monkeys in India are a gigantic pain in the ass and a genuine menace, too: Every now and then, they kill somebody, or maim

---

1 A number of great significance in the Dharmic religions.

somebody pretty good. I once made the mistake of walking home to my apartment in Delhi after dark with a bag of kebabs for dinner, and by the time I got to my place I was being chased by about forty mangy and scrofulous dogs who were keenly interested in my take-out. (From Karim's, of course: world's best.) Dogs you can deal with. Imagine if it had been monkeys.

Working for *The Atlantic* was kind of like that.

If you've ever been to the monkey house in one of those awful downscale zoos that smell very intensely the way you imagine that Bernie Sanders probably smells faintly, you know what monkeys—these particular monkeys—are like: They jerk off and fling poo all day, generally using the same hand for both, and they don't do a hell of a lot else, unless there's McDonald's. All day: jerk off, fling poo, jerk off, fling poo, jerk, fling, jerk, fling.

Twitter, basically.

And after about 300,000 years of anatomically modern *H. sap.*, here we are again: monkeys, albeit monkeys with wifi. You could try being human beings. You could. You could try a little freedom on for size, and see how it fits and feels. You aren't going to. We both know that.

Jerk off, fling poo, jerk off, fling poo, jerk, fling, jerk, fling.

I hate monkeys.

This is their story.

CHAPTER ONE

A Volscian Commission

A s a matter of contemporary etiquette, we writers and talkers are not supposed to call ourselves "intellectuals." It sounds like bragging, and we can't have that—we are supposed to rely on mediating irony and moral mumbling, lest we stumble into the great error and great sin of Trying Too Hard. We all know what happens to the tallest poppy. It's strange: If I were an unusually tall, green-eyed, Flemish-American hermaphrodite running for Congress as a Republican—and the Republicans should be so lucky!—the convention would be for me to begin every third sentence, "As an unusually tall, green-eyed, Flemish-American hermaphrodite, I believe that…" or, "If elected, I will be the first unusually tall, green-eyed, Flemish-American hermaphrodite elected to the House as a Republican," or, "In America, an unusually tall, green-eyed, Flemish-American hermaphrodite can grow up to be anything, even another asinine, useless, beef-witted politician, one who is blessed to have been born in this great country with two distinct sets of sex organs and a burning desire to put them to work for America—for We the People."

Intellectuals. You can practically see the foamy little green drop-lets of contempt running off the word. And so the intellectuals have, for some time, been obliged to pretend to be something else: your friend, the tribune of the plebs, the advocate of the common man, or, worst of all, the "realist," the one who wants to use "common sense" on behalf of "ordinary folk" in the pursuit of "what works."

Clever little monkeys, in their way. They seem almost human at times.

You know the type: I was once on a panel with Cleta Mitchell, one of those gold-plated Republican populists who is always going on and on about the Washington Establishment and "insiders." I told her I thought she was more or less full of it, and—we were in front of an audience of conservatives—she raged that I was an example of "inside-the-Beltway Establishment thinking." I am a writer who lives in Texas and who is not even a member of the Republican party, much less part of its "establishment." Cleta Mitchell *literally* works inside the Beltway—the asphalt one, in Washington, D.C., not a metaphorical one—at the politically connected law firm of Foley & Lardner, right there on Washington Harbor, where she…oh, here's a bit of her official firm biography: "Ms. Mitchell represents numer-ous candidates, campaigns and members of Congress, as well as state and national political party committees. She has served as legal coun-sel to the National Republican Senatorial Committee and the National Republican Congressional Committee." She is such an out-sider that she appears on a Fox News program called *Insiders*, and she—you could not make this up—literally wrote the book on being a lobbyist in Washington: *The Lobbying Compliance Handbook*.

"Establishment." "Inside the Beltway." That rotten, fruity lan-guage—that utterly nonsensical adolescent horseshit—just comes naturally to some people. I once had a state Republican party chair-man tell me that "the Establishment in my state hates me." I asked him who, exactly, composed this Establishment, if not the chairman of the goddamned party? He looked at me as a goldfish would if it saw a strange new underwater castle. It took me a long time to decipher what that look means. It means: "But I thought we were friends!"

The original sin of the American intellectual is his desire to be popular.

And not just popular, but popular in the way politicians are popular: a man of the people—but a man of the people to whom the people must defer and pay tribute, because he wields power over them. Everyone whose career has a public aspect is conscious of reputation, but there are different classes of reputation; American journalists in particular do not seem to know what it is they are here to do. Journalists in the United Kingdom understand themselves to be part of the world of literature, broadly defined, while journalists in the United States understand themselves to be part of the world of *politics*. (The observation is not original to me.) You can see it in the lawyerly prose of American journalists, which is so much more careful and so much less interesting than that of their counterparts overseas. They go on television and speak like men who are running for an office; their approach to their adversaries and rivals has less the character of argument than of opposition research—where there should be conversation, they can offer only *indictment*. The mind of the American political journalist is, in its contemptible union of neediness and arrogance, a study in miniature of the mind of the man with whom American journalism imagines itself to be locked in eternal moral combat: Richard Nixon.

Nixon won forty-nine states in 1972. But that is a different kind of popularity. The intellectuals who are after that kind of popularity do not know what it is they are supposed to be doing.

I get that we writers and commentators and political hustlers have to make a living somehow, the times being what they are, and

I do hope that this book sells a gazillion copies. By the time you are reading these words, I will very likely have been on sixty or seventy talk-radio shows and a few television programs, and I will flog the Schumer out of it. Like Don Corleone, I don't judge a man for how he makes his living. What I judge a man for is something else: Not the desire to have an audience, to make money, all that sort of thing, but the abject, craven, humiliating need to be loved by strangers. I mean the emptiness that a certain kind of man or woman tries to fill with adulation, characteristic of the man who cannot stand in front of a crowd without being possessed to deliver corny prepackaged applause lines, who will kiss the collective ass of the mob—and any mob will do—because that mob ass simply must be kissed. There are many problems with that kind of character in a writer, the main one of which is that it keeps the writer from doing his job.

I'm not your friend, your advocate, or your tribune, and I am not trying to get anybody elected to any office—much less myself. That is not what I do. There are many people who do that. The world really does not need another, especially one who is not committed to that profession and who almost certainly would not be any good at it.

Caius Marcius, the legendary Roman soldier, is Shakespeare's greatest tragic hero. After his reputation-making military victory, he declines the offer of an enormous financial reward—a tenth of the loot he brought home to Rome—saying:

> I thank you, general;
> But cannot make my heart consent to take
> A bribe to pay my sword: I do refuse it.

The cheers of the great masses he holds in similar contempt.

Your affections are
A sick man's appetite, who desires most that
Which would increase his evil. He that depends
Upon your favours swims with fins of lead
And hews down oaks with rushes. Hang ye! Trust ye?
With every minute you do change a mind,
And call him noble that was now your hate,
Him vile that was your garland.

The only extraordinary honor he accepts is the agno-men "Coriolanus."

But his pride ultimately gets the better of him. In an act that goes against his character, he decides to seek political office, not for the love of acclaim but in order to satisfy his sense of honor, which, because he was a civilized man, is founded on his understanding of his duty as a citizen. But there is no seeking office without bending over for *Homo bolus*, which Coriolanus cannot do as long as he remains Coriolanus. There is a wonderfully funny scene in which he talks himself into—and then immediately out of—making a ritual curtsy to the plebeians.

Well, I must do't:
Away, my disposition, and possess me
Some harlot's spirit! my throat of war be turn'd,
Which quired with my drum, into a pipe
Small as an eunuch, or the virgin voice
That babies lulls asleep! the smiles of knaves
Tent in my cheeks, and schoolboys' tears take up
The glasses of my sight! a beggar's tongue
Make motion through my lips, and my arm'd knees,
Who bow'd but in my stirrup, bend like his
That hath received an alms! I will not do't,

Lest I surcease to honour mine own truth
And by my body's action teach my mind
A most inherent baseness.

You'll notice that Coriolanus here knows that to do what is expected of him, he would have to first become someone else: the harlot, the eunuch, the virgin, the schoolboy, the beggar—anything but the man he is.

Somebody forgot to tell him that elections are "binary." *Anything to keep the plebs out of power, what with the upcoming vacancies on the quaestorship that need to be filled by the right kind of people and the partisan fight over reforming the Licinian Rogations coming up in the next session.*

And so, of course, things go badly for Coriolanus. He ends up spitting blue fire at the very rabble he was supposed to be courting. The plebeians try to banish Coriolanus. Coriolanus will not have it. He banishes them:

You common cry of curs! whose breath I hate
As reek o' the rotten fens, whose loves I prize
As the dead carcasses of unburied men
That do corrupt my air, I banish you;
And here remain with your uncertainty!
Let every feeble rumour shake your hearts!
Your enemies, with nodding of their plumes,
Fan you into despair! Have the power still
To banish your defenders; till at length
Your ignorance, which finds not till it feels,
Making not reservation of yourselves,
Still your own foes, deliver you as most
Abated captives to some nation

That won you without blows! Despising,
For you, the city, thus I turn my back:
There is a world elsewhere.

    The glory of the play is its austere language. Shakespeare at his most mature felt very little need for adornment; what he offers is compact and modern. There is much in the play that feels contemporary. Even the mechanics of the politics—the pageantry of "the Resistance"—remain fresh, with a touch of identity politics.

Ædile: He's coming.

Brutus: How accompanied?

Ædile: With old Menenius, and those senators
That always favour'd him.

Sicinius: Have you a catalogue
Of all the voices that we have procured
Set down by the poll?

Ædile: I have; 'tis ready.

Sicinius: Have you collected them by tribes?

Ædile: I have.

Sicinius: Assemble presently the people hither;
And when they bear me say 'It shall be so
I' the right and strength o' the commons,' be it either
For death, for fine, or banishment, then let them

If I say fine, cry 'Fine;' if death, cry 'Death.'
Insisting on the old prerogative
And power I' the truth o' the cause.

It is not very difficult to imagine the foregoing happening on Twitter rather than in the Forum.

My subject here is individuality, not in the silly and negative adolescent sense of "individualism" grossly construed—not "the moral and legal conception of the individual as that which is isolated, [but] a more concrete conception which takes him to be that which is complete," as the English philosopher Michael Oakeshott puts it in "The Authority of the State." In the context of our political discourse—and this is as true for the citizen who takes his citizenship seriously as it is for the professional writer and critic—the individual is the one who can stand at least partly away from the demands of his tribe and class and try to see things as they are, and shout back over his shoulder what he sees. He is neither the Cavalier on the inside peering carefully out over the parapet nor the Roundhead on the outside looking suspiciously in—he is on the outside looking *out*.

I start here with Coriolanus. I end with Lucifer. There's a lot of Twitter in-between. I trust I make myself understood.

CHAPTER TWO

The Road to Smurfdom

Bid them wash their faces and keep their teeth clean.

—*William Shakespeare, Coriolanus, Act I, Scene 3*

The story I am telling here is not a new one. The social, economic, and political factors contributing to our current politics of mob madness, mass hysteria, and vicious tribalism—under the influence of a psychotic political pseudo-culture that regards intolerance as a *virtue*—have combined in similar ways before, with similar results. These episodes amount to a periodic and sometimes bloody illustration of Reinhold Niebur's maxim: "The society in which each man lives is at once the basis for, and the nemesis of, that fulness of life which each man seeks."[1]

The most illuminating point of comparison for my purposes in this book is the political culture (which was also the religious culture, by necessity) of Europe at the end of the Middle Ages and the beginning of the Renaissance. As the Marxist-Freudian social critic Erich Fromm tells the story in his *Escape from Freedom*, the emergence of a primitive form of capitalism at the end of the medieval period upset

---

1 *Moral Man and Immoral Society: A Study in Ethics and Politics*, 1932.

9

not only the economic order of the societies it was beginning to transform but also the *social* order, which was under stress as traditional sources of status and meaning were, to use the word of our moment, *disrupted*. The medieval social order, Fromm argues, may have been poor in strictly material terms, but it was stable and predictable, with serf and lord alike secure in his place in the world—in this kingdom and in the Heavenly Kingdom. The economic changes brought by capitalism left them free, but also alone. They became instances of what Michael Oakeshott describes as the "individual *manqué*,"[2] botched individuals who suffer from an "incapacity to sustain an individual life," who therefore experience modern individualism as a burden rather than as an opportunity—much less as a joy. When progressives lampoon conservatives as being the party of "you're on your own," and when conservatives propose measures to "protect" their constituents from ordinary social and economic change, these are the people they are addressing.

The deracinated citizen-subjects of the emerging primitive capitalist world sought out new sources of meaning and a new kind of lordship to which to submit themselves and thereby be relieved of the terrible burden of individuality. What they settled on was Protestantism, which grew in the same garden as capitalism: among the urbanizing populations of the Low Countries and England. Fromm in essence sets Max Weber's thesis in *The Protestant Ethic and the Spirit of Capitalism* on its head: Protestantism did not create capitalism—capitalism created Protestantism.

---

2 *Rationalism in Politics*, 1962. From the misery of the aborted individual, who feels himself morally and intellectually unsuited to the tasks put before him by the times in which he lives, arises "the impulse to escape from the predicament by imposing it upon all mankind. From the frustrated 'individual *manqué*' here sprang the militant 'anti-individual,' disposed to assimilate the world to his own character by deposing the individual and destroying his moral prestige."

Deracination, crisis, fanaticism—the pattern is general enough to be detected in many other societies at many other points in history. A similar vector leads from the failure of the Great Leap Forward to the fanaticism of the Cultural Revolution. China is arguably going through another such episode right now, with the end of orthodox Communism, the great migration to the cities, and the emergence of what Yasheng Huang wittily christened "Capitalism with Chinese Characteristics" having overturned many of the governing assumptions of that enormous and remarkable country and left the social status of 1.4 billion people up for grabs. The authoritarian regime in Beijing has offered up a new and updated version of fanatical nationalism in the hopes of filling that void. But such transitions cannot be planned or managed, even by the worst of despots. That is the joy—and, sometimes, the terror—of our unruly and increasingly liberated world.

In our own context, globalization has led to the emergence of a new kind of capitalism, one that is based on the first effectively universal market in human history and made dynamic by specialization, division of labor, and social cooperation on a scale that would have been considered beyond the dreams of Utopia a generation ago.

These are the best of times, not the worst. That is true by almost any measurable standard: severe poverty has declined steeply for two decades around the world, fewer people are dying in wars (in 1950, 546,501 people died in battle worldwide; in 2016, that number was fewer than 90,000[3]), fewer people are dying from easily preventable diseases, etc.

The masses never hard it so good. This is the golden age of *Homo bolus*.

---

3 "Battle deaths in state-based conflicts since 1946 by region," Max Roser, Our World in Data, 2018.

But the masses are not happy. They are miserable. They are masses; misery is what they do. It does not matter whether they have anything to be miserable about. If they want something to make them feel miserable, they will discover or invent it.

In the United States, two competing strains of angry populism are locked in a cold civil war over the same piece of psychic real estate, and almost every public conversation is dominated by what Georges Sorel might very well have described as "the superb blond beast wandering in search of prey and carnage,"[4] had he lived into our era. Things are at least equally grim, and in many cases much worse, abroad: India is wracked by a newly militant and fanatical *Hindutva*, Hungary groans under the corrupt strongman rule of Viktor Orbán, Venezuela reels in the hangover from the leftist strongman rule of Hugo Chávez and the persistent tyranny of his heirs, angry populist movements of both the Left and the Right have brought political violence and the threat of such violence to Europe, the United Kingdom, the United States, and elsewhere. Our politics have not only become more polarized but also more expansively fanatical, with the political battleground extending to the classroom, the place of employment, the church, and any other host within reach of this parasitic pestilence.

We are undergoing a process that is in some ways parallel to what medieval Europe went through with the disruptive emergence of primitive capitalism. Globalization has brought wealth and cooperation, but it also has disturbed longstanding modes of life and upended communities, especially those affected negatively[5] by outsourcing and offshoring, changes in the nature of work which are

---

4 A strange kind of blond beast, one that enjoys being the center of attention. A genuine beast would not care who was looking.

5 When is the last time you read about one of the many communities positively affected— indeed, blessed—by offshoring?

themselves the misunderstood and ignorantly hated manifestations of the integration of global supply chains and other deep economic changes that are, gradually, making the world a radically better place.

Some communities have lost political influence; others, especially the coastal cities, believe that they have not gained enough. Changes in the patterns of family life have left many men—especially those who are not economic high-achievers—devoid of sources of status and social fixedness, and have frustrated many women's pursuit of marriage and motherhood. The quality of material life in the United States has improved radically across the board since the 1980s, but the profits of globalization have accrued disproportionately to a relatively small group of entrepreneurs and high-tech workers, along with those in related fields such as finance and, inevitably, government. Americans are as a whole better off in most of the things that can be measured, but the story grows more complex the finer you cut it. For example, the life expectancies of non-college-educated white men are declining while those of most other groups rise, and the cause of the decline is the disease of despair in different manifestations: overdoses and other drug-related deaths, deaths from alcohol-related causes, and suicide.

This exudate of outrage and dread has arrived together with the rise to prominence of social media and other instruments of communication that not only are better-suited for emotional outbursts than for reasoned discussion, but which, as a consequence of their basic social architecture, reward rage, extremism, and hostility while they suffocate intelligence, charity, and gentleness. Communication is only *incidental* to social media. Social media is not a platform for publishing but a means of seeking human connection, not communication but communion, or at least a simulacrum of it. Social media is not the second coming of the eighteenth-century pamphleteer; it is *Homo bolus* at prayer—to himself, of course.

Social media is based on a simple economy: *Outgoing* attention is the *labor* that social media requires of its proletariat; *incoming* attention is the *wage* it pays them. The group dynamics in this economy of little Willy Lomans all but ensure that the majority of the ordinary person's social-media interactions are with like-minded people and that these groups of like-minded people self-radicalize in the way most like-minded groups do, a pattern that has long been familiar to scholars of deliberation and group psychology.

Social-media mobs provide a partial substitute for the sense of identity and belonging that disruptive global capitalism has taken away from many people, especially the upper degrees of the middle class, a group whose domination of Twitter has transformed the platform into a kingmaker-executioner in spite of its relatively tiny user base, which amounts to only about 14 percent of Facebook's active user population. Twitter is the theater of what F. A. Hayek called "second-hand dealers in ideas"—journalists, mid-level academics, political operatives, leaders of civic groups, and the like. They are, in fact, the very people whom Robert Putnam and other chroniclers of civic disengagement would expect to be community leaders and conduits of information and engagement.

Which they are. That's the problem.

As the Buddhist scripture says: "I do not dispute with the world; the world disputes with me."

Funny thing about this book: I had begun shopping around the proposal for writing it long before my brief period of employment with THAT AUGUST JOURNALISTIC INSTITUTION and the subsequent witless chimp-brained media freak-out and CAFFEINE-FREE DIET MAOIST struggle session that followed and climaxed with my being

fired by editor-in-chief Jeffrey Goldberg on my third day of employment there and after a good deal of stink-eye from some seething
young woman with an unfortunate All-Lesbian World Bowling
Champion haircut loitering glumly in the coffee room. I was, for a
few days, a writer who was much more read about than read. After
the ninth (or so) *New York Times* denunciation of my soul and my
work, my professional dance card began to fill up with pleasing speed.

That's the upside of being in the controversy business: I always
get paid. Hooray for me.[6]

But why was I flogging this book way back *before* I got involved
in what I must with some genuine disappointment characterize as
only the *second*-most-infamous episode involving a shady right-
winger and the Watergate complex?[7] There were good reasons. A
combination of deep stupidity and casual authoritarianism already
had begun to disfigure our public discourse: the firing of Brendan
Eich for his views on marriage, and the IRS's criminal leak of the
National Organization for Marriage's confidential tax documents in
the service of a campaign to harass and attack its donors; the firing
of James Damore for the crime of being stupid enough to believe that
his po-faced ham-souled Caitlyn-haunted superiors at Google were
being anything like halfway serious when they asked for dialogue
about diversity in the firm; the campaigns against Bret Stephens and
Bari Weiss at the *New York Times*; the "de-platforming"[8] of conservatives and other nonconforming voices on social media; the violence

---

6 "...and fuck you." Bad Religion, 1994. "I don't exactly want to apologize for anything."
7 *The Atlantic*'s offices are at the Watergate, and skulking around the premises is always a
bittersweet thing for a man like me.
8 "When you tear out a man's tongue, you are not proving him a liar, you're only
telling the world that you fear what he might say." So goes the wisdom of Tyrion
Lannister. But you can tell what's really on the mind of the pop-literary twenty-first
century by the fact that *Game of Thrones* contains so few tongue amputations and so
many genital amputations.

and firebombings targeting unpopular speakers at Berkeley and other college campuses—and much more. The blackshirts and the American Association of Outrage Professionals were as creepily tumescent as Anthony Weiner cruising a Hello Kitty boutique, but my little book proposal was met with almost no excitement until I became, for a couple of weeks, the headline in the story.

I'll revisit that tawdry little episode in these pages to the extent that it is necessary to the story, but this isn't a memoir.

My subject here is not the life and times of Kevin D. Williamson.[9] My subject is what Coriolanus[10] called "the beast with many heads"— mob politics, on social media and in what passes for real life, which increasingly is patterned on social media—and its effects on our political discourse and our culture. It is the most important political issue of our time. Discourse—the health and character of that discourse—is a force that exists above and outside of the specific policy questions of the day; it is the master-issue that will determine how every other issue is talked about and thought about—and whether those issues are *thought about* at all.

We think in language. We signal[11] in memes. Language is the instrument of discourse. Memes are the instrument of *antidiscourse*, i.e., communication designed and deployed to *prevent* the exchange of information and perspectives rather than to *enable* it, a weapon of mass intellectual destruction—the moron bomb. The function of discourse is to know other minds and to have them known to you; the function of *antidiscourse* is to lower the status of rivals and enemies. Antidiscourse is not a conversation about politics—it *is* politics; it is no more discourse than a "BETO FOR PRESIDENT" yard sign is literature. It is a

---

9 I suppose I'll write a memoir eventually. I think I'll call it *The Gun Didn't Know I Was Loaded*.

10 *Coriolanus*, Act IV, Scene 1. William Shakespeare, c. 1605.

11 Nothing like *signifyin'* in the Henry Louis Gates sense, with its necessarily intelligent playfulness, but something essentially post-literate and cheerless. Something closer to what is commonly derided as "virtue-signaling."

way of holding the conversation captive within politics itself rather than permit it to get partly clear of the wall and examine the questions of the day from the outside with some degree of clarity and independence. Antidiscourse and discourse serve different functions; trying to understand what is going on in political life by relying on antidiscourse is like trying to fuel a Falcon Heavy rocket with Soarin' Strawberry Kool-Aid. Caravaggio didn't paint *The Martyrdom of Saint Matthew* with his dick. And he loved his bony cannelloni—it just wasn't the tool for the job.

War and peace, taxing and spending, crime and punishment, detonating munitions on the heads of goat-bothering savages in Panjshir until all that's left looks like a hot-yoga class following a PTA meeting in Greenwich, Connecticut: None of these can be addressed in a way that does any real political work without a political culture that not only tolerates genuine discourse—meaning genuine *disagreement*—but also comprehends that discourse in its own functional terms apart from petty advantage-seeking, cultural gang-sign flashing, and cheap partisan opportunism. But we do not have that kind of a political culture, or, in some ways, any culture at all, properly understood. What we have is Instant Culture, which is to culture what stevia is to sugar, what masturbation is to sex, what Paul Krugman's *New York Times* vomitus is to journalism, what Monday's dank memes are to the English language: a substitute that replicates the real thing in certain formal ways but that remains nonetheless entirely lacking in the essence of the thing itself. It is the strap-on dildo sitting there dead and plastic and inert where Western civilization used to be.[12]

---

12 Or, as Leo Strauss put it, "Modem democracy, so far from being universal aristocracy, would be mass rule were it not for the fact that the mass cannot rule but is ruled by elites, i.e., groupings of men who for whatever reason are on top or have a fair chance to arrive at the top; one of the most important virtues required for the smooth working of democracy, as far as the mass is concerned, is said to be electoral apathy, i.e., lack of public spirit; not indeed the salt of the earth but the salt of modern democracy are those citizens who read nothing except the sports page and the comic section. Democracy is then not indeed mass rule but mass culture. A mass culture is a culture which can be appropriated by the meanest capacities without any intellectual and moral effort whatsoever and at a very low monetary price." "What Is Liberal Education?" 1959.

And that is why the desire for popularity is the original sin of the intellectual: When he subordinates his independent mind to the demands of the herd, he ceases to perform any useful function. He abandons culture for Instant Culture, discourse for antidiscourse, and truth-seeking for status-seeking.

Culture, as Michael Oakeshott characterized it, is a conversation: "As civilized human beings, we are the inheritors, neither of an inquiry about ourselves and the world, nor of an accumulating body of information, but of a conversation, begun in the primeval forests and extended and made more articulate in the course of centuries. It is a conversation which goes on both in public and within each of ourselves."[13] Because it is characterized by crude signaling rather than by conversation as such, Instant Culture differs from culture properly understood in that it includes no meaningful connections across time, having the character of a spasm rather than that of a continuity. It is the Jacobin herd stampeding through G. K. Chesterton's "democracy of the dead," and like any stampeding herd it is both terrifying and terrified, directionless and hysterical moral panic on the digital hoof.

Language is how we think; culture is where we think. Without culture and language, we are deprived of a means of intellectual and moral orientation and are forced to seek new and necessarily inferior ones, choosing from a New Jersey diner menu of grossness and insipidity: nationalism, racism, tribalism, class solidarity, religious particularism, "intersectionality" (which is only mutant nationalism, the same pre-Oedipal penis-clutching obsession with superficial markers of distinctiveness), ideological fanaticism, shallow partisanship—all of them jumbled together by the instruments of Instant Culture (social media and related Internet phenomena, antidiscourse, memery, the rituals of electronic tribalism) to produce illiterate and unnavigable mess that now passes for our political culture, and our culture at large.

---

13 "The Voice of Poetry in the Conversation of Mankind," *Rationalism in Politics*, 1962.

The question before us is whether American democracy can *think*, which would necessitate the rediscovery of rigorous literary language[14] and political culture properly understood, or whether America democracy will abandon literacy and content itself with *signaling*. "Culture" as such is not something only for the libraries and opera houses—it is life on the democratic street. Modern democracy, as Leo Strauss described it, is only the "hard shell which protects the soft mass culture," and hence "modern democracy stands or falls by literacy," which is "the counter-poison to mass culture."

It will be quite something if we go from John Hancock's extravagant paraph on Thomas Jefferson's concise English masterpiece to signing our names with an "X" in such remarkably short period of time. One thinks of those isolated island-dwellers who discovered and lost and rediscovered barbed hooks and other technologies a half-dozen times over the centuries. Peoples who fail to communicate cannot even defend their own local memory.

This, like much else, was foreseen by George Orwell, who wrote in 1946: "It is clear that the decline of a language must ultimately have political and economic causes: It is not due simply to the bad influence of this or that individual writer. But an effect can become a cause, reinforcing the original cause and producing the same effect in an intensified form, and so on indefinitely. A man may take to drink because he feels himself to be a failure, and then fail all the more completely because he drinks. It is rather the same thing that is happening to the English language. It becomes ugly and inaccurate because our thoughts are foolish, but the slovenliness of our language makes it easier for us to have foolish thoughts."[15] Orwell made these observations about the bad political *writing* of his time—but our subliterate culture is well on

---

14 How many American voters could actually read, say, *Sartor Resartus* or *Moby-Dick*? And by "read" I mean "read the sentences," not "read the words." What proportion of them could meaningfully comprehend the *Federalist Papers*?
15 George Orwell, "Politics and the English Language," 1946.

its way to giving up writing entirely in favor of a crude new Instant Culture mode of semiotic exchange that amounts to a high-tech version of those old Lubang Jeriji Saléh cave paintings. The modern primitive is no less primitive for having a smartphone.

The alternative to political discourse—you know, with sentences and stuff—is a hokey *luchador* wrestling match between the mind-killed partisans, grunting modern primitives, talk-radio hucksters, cable-news hustlers, purveyors of freeze-dried apocalypse lasagnas and mystical doggie vitamins, associate professors of being pissed-off and generally aggrieved, and the sundry other dumbasstical shitweasels[16] who currently dominate our political conversation, a spectacle and a debacle that will go on and on—until it doesn't.

---

16 For "dumbasstical shitweasels" you may read, "ordinary constituent of the *demos*." In much the same way as the patrician was once forbidden by custom from engaging in trade, money-lending, and most kinds of money-making activities, the ancient habit of intellectuals' keeping rah-rah partisan politics at many arms' length helped order society by means of something we do not think very highly of in the age of social media: *hierarchy*. "The modern world has made the intellectual into a citizen, subject to all the responsibilities of a citizen, and consequently to despise lay passions is far more difficult for him than for his predecessors. If he is reproached for not looking upon national quarrels with the noble serenity of Descartes and Goethe, the intellectual may well retort that his nation claps a soldier's pack on his back if she is insulted, and crushes him with taxes even if she is victorious. If shame is cried upon him because he does not rise superior to social hatreds, he will point out that the day of enlightened patronage is over, that to-day he has to earn his living, and that it is not his fault if he is eager to support the class which takes a pleasure in his productions.... Let me add that the modern writer's desire to be a political man is excused by the fact that the position is to some extent offered him by public opinion, whereas the compatriots of Racine and La Bruyère would have laughed in their faces if they had thought of publishing their views on the advisability of the war with Holland or the legality of Chambres de reunion. There again, it was easier to be a true intellectual in the past than to-day." Julien Benda, *The Treason of the Intellectuals*, 1927. Which is to say: The intellectual becomes a plebeian in part because the patricians abandoned their duty. NB: I have taken the liberty here and throughout of rendering as "intellectuals" the "clerks" of the Routledge edition, translated by Richard Aldington. "Clerks," with its Kevin Smith connotations, just seems too weird and jarring to me, and it's always been "intellectuals" in the title. I trust Roger Kimball, who edited that edition, will forgive me.

The problem for mass democracy is that the *demos* does not think. It cannot. It lacks the requisite apparatus.

Groups do not think in any meaningful sense. *People* think—one at a time.

And they *exchange thoughts*, to use one of those expressions so common and shopworn that we have forgotten what it means. The value of such exchange is detectable in its absence. Once, not long ago, the morning headlines were full of "Jon Stewart destroys…" whatever the target of the comedian had been the night before. Stewart is gone now, having grown out his beard and gone off into the wilderness to feed on locusts and wild honey. But there are others. The Destroyer remains always with us.

> The ascent is easy, then;
> The event is feared! Should we again provoke
> Our stronger, some worse way his wrath may find
> To our destruction, if there be in Hell
> Fear to be worse destroyed! What can be worse
> Than to dwell here, driven out from bliss, condemned
> In this abhorred deep to utter woe;
> Where pain of unextinguishable fire
> Must exercise us without hope of end
> The vassals of his anger, when the scourge
> Inexorably, and the torturing hour,
> Calls us to penance? More destroyed than thus,
> We should be quite abolished, and expire.[17]

Culture is the context in which we think and share our thoughts. It is what makes William Shakespeare or John Milton or Thomas Jefferson *alive* to us, one unique human mind reaching out to another

---

17 *Paradise Lost*, Book 2. John Milton, 1667.

unique human mind through time through the medium of English sentences. Something just short of the entirety of popular American political discourse in our time consists of only two primitive sentences: "I affiliate with this," "I disaffiliate from that," translated into various kinds of social-media idiotgrams and postliterate *chengyu*:[18] "So much this!" "lol wut?" That supercut gif of Ray Liotta laughing or a pic of Side-Eying Chloe or the U Mad troll or Trigglypuff when words themselves, however jumbled and dyspeptically yawped, become too much work for the unsteady minds and deformed souls of twenty-first century mass so-called culture.

To these rapidly devolving human-shaped things, it's a world of black hats and white hats. The excitable boys and girls on the radio went on and on about how the presidential election in 2016 was "binary," which is a way of attempting to sound smart while saying "Shut the fuck up and get in line, boy!" and simultaneously being dumb as hammered goose shit. In reality, it is Instant Culture, our debased substitute for culture itself, that has become neatly binate,[19] being as it is only an instrument in the service of status-seeking, with the demands of tribalism everywhere debasing and

---

18 Like the idiomatic Chinese expressions, social-media *chengyu* are highly context dependent and assume intimacy with a certain culture—in the case of social media, that's roughly the culture depicted in Mike Judge's prophetic *Idiocracy*. Social-media memes are in this sense the *chengyu* of an inferior literary tradition, a system of literary and historical allusions for people without a literature or history.

19 E.g., the symbiotic relationship between Antifa and Proud Boys is identical to that of the Democratic party and the Republican party in its dynamic, each faction providing the other the one thing whose absence would rob the opposite party, and hence the entire symbiotic relationship, of its coherence: a mortal enemy. The Proud Boys and Antifa are playing the same game of make-believe. They are not seriously competing for political power: They are playing with each other, just as if they were playing softball or tiddlywinks. You will remember that energetic partisans Left and Right in 2016 reserved their bitterest invective for those who declined to choose between the salted and unsalted shit sandwich and subordinate themselves to one faction or the other with the appropriate gusto. *Tribal opposition* is part of the game; *independent criticism* is not.

squandering the only asset this country—this world—has: the functioning *individual* mind.

The next part of this book may strike you as being unnecessarily and maybe even pretentiously recondite, but the subject matter is both necessary to understand and interesting, if you are the sort of person who is interested in things. The political and moral bases for twenty-first century mob politics did not arrive on the world's intellectual doorstep *ex nihilo* or with the advent of Facebook.

Ochlocracy—periodic and desultory mob rule effected through the exploitation and domination of both public and private centers of power—is an ancient problem, considerations of which go back to ancient Greece and beyond. The ochlocratic tendency has in our time interacted with a relatively new idea, *streitbare Demokratie* (militant democracy), a concept associated with postwar Germany whose adherents hold that liberal democracies must sometimes resort to illiberal and antidemocratic techniques, such as suppressing certain kinds of political speech or prohibiting certain political parties, as a form of self-defense against profounder and more ruthlessly scrotum-punching assaults on liberalism and democracy. Militant democracy is an operative constitutional and political doctrine in Germany and in many other European countries, and it provides the legal foundation for acts that would be alien to the American tradition, such as locking human beings in penal cages for the possession of banned books.

That kind of suppression is not entirely unheard-of in American political history—Woodrow Wilson's proud boys did things to meddling newspaper editors that reality-show tough guy Donald Trump wouldn't dream of doing to RealDoll's silicon facsimile of Stormy Daniels (MSRP $6,499.99)—but the First Amendment and our classical-liberal political culture have, for the most part, protected us from the worst of that particular kind of authoritarianism. Or they had. As of this writing, American politics (and politics around much of the rest of the world) is dominated by two rival populisms, each deeply and aggressively illiberal in its own way and both interested in putting public discourse under political discipline. They agree in broad terms about censorship[20] in principle: They disagree about whom to censor.

The German philosophical tradition that so deeply informed the outlook of American reformers and intellectuals such as John Dewey and Theodore Roosevelt has in our era split into mutually hostile progressive and nationalist camps that are, in these illiterate times, incapable of understanding the significance of their common intellectual patrimony.[21] But the fact that the lame pudwhackers marching around Portland in black masks and carrying tiki-torches through Charlotte are too bone-deep stupid to appreciate this doesn't mean that you, dear reader, must choose to be as well.

Concepts such as ochlocracy and *streitbare Demokratie* are remote intellectual abstractions in the sense that the people who want to banish Sarah Jeong or Charles Murray—or me—from the public square or throw us into prison do not first hold salons at which they discuss Karl Loewenstein's thoughts on militant democracy or read up on the intellectual history of Austrian election law. Some of them will sometimes say something about "Shouting 'Fire!' in a crowded theater" without knowing what Oliver Wendell Holmes was up to when he wrote that famous phrase, or, indeed, that it was Oliver Wendell Holmes who wrote it or that the controversy that provoked it

---

20 Throughout, I have reserved the word "censorship" for state action. One of the unpleasant features of ochlocracy is that it commandeers private organizations for political purposes, but it does matter, for the sake of understanding the phenomenon if not for moral reasons, whether a given actor is the agent of a state.

21 My friend Jonah Goldberg tried to explain this to a great many mental defectives and intellectually dishonest frauds who could never get past *Liberal Fascism*'s title and cover art.

involved imprisoning war protesters. But even the ascendant moral illiterates and ordinary functional illiterates in the English-speaking world operate in the remains of a culture (and, hence, in a perverted political discourse) shaped by Shakespeare and the King James Bible, by the English common law and the Declaration of Independence— and by Karl Marx and *The International Jew*, too. People do not have to be conscious partisans of ideas to be beneficiaries of them—or victims of them. In fact, most of the most hapless and pathetic victims of destructive political ideas are almost entirely unaware of what their political ideas are or that they even have any. They insist that they are "pragmatists" or "realists," and their universal belief is that the nation at large and their political faction in particular suffers from a deficit of viciousness in its pursuit of its goals. The fact that they do not understand their political priors does not mean that they do not have any or that these are not consequential. It will not surprise you to learn that these imbeciles in particular do *not* appreciate having this situation explained to them. They kind of resent it, in fact.

These intellectual currents interact with one another, and they interact in a spectacular fashion—a spectacularly stupid and ugly fashion—with social media and other recent innovations in what we could call "communication" only in a very broad and generous sense of the word. (Disease also is said to be "communicated.") The communication that happens on social media right now has more in common with dogs barking at one another than it does with actual political discourse—and I am not being rhetorical or provocative here; I mean that literally and will explain why—but it is also one of the most important semiotic exchanges of our time. It's one degree removed from "You talk like a fag, and your shit's all retarded!"[22] but it's what we've got.

---

22 When *Idiocracy* was first released, I criticized it as being excessively cruel and cynical. Boy howdy, was I wrong. I would like to formally apologize to the Prophet Mike Judge, PBUH.

The intellectual groundwork for the assault on the individual mind already has been done, and its products have been internalized by the fanatical and the mentally deficient and the rage-addicted and those who are intellectually and morally dominated by the rage-addicted. That having been accomplished, the obvious thing to do was to implement policies based on those ideas at the two most vulnerable and critical choke-points in American life: the university, of course, and, more important, the corporation. Social media and related technologies relate to this implementation in two ways: Social media provides a vector of infection for corporations, but those platforms also are the products and properties of a handful of very sensitive and politically vulnerable corporations: Facebook, Twitter, and Google prominent among them. Analysts of fascism in the twentieth century paid careful attention to its embrace of new communication technologies, especially radio. Our modern ochlocrats are outperforming their spiritual forebears in the 1930s dramatically, which is no small thing considered the radically larger number of channels that they are obliged to control. The flood-the-zone-with-memes strategy is the contemporary equivalent of bombing the radio towers—or burning books. The point of burning books was never really to keep other copies of those volumes from being read but to make a public statement about the work and its author. It is "de-platforming" in a more theatrical form.

In my reading for this book, I was surprised by the remarkably similar conclusions reached by three roughly contemporary writers with very different political allegiances and casts of mind: F. A. Hayek, the classical-liberal economist and political theorist who saw in the rise of salaried corporate employment a threat to the economically and socially independent minds of the propertied classes and the economically independent, whose innovations and experimentations are one critical source of experimental social advancement; William

Whyte, the probing business journalist who in his often-misunderstood opus, *The Organization Man*, considered the ways in which the salaryman and the bureaucrat are conformed to the internal mandates of their corporations and agencies—not through economic coercion but rather *voluntarily* as they come to conclude that organization life and organization thinking are empirically superior to intellectual independence and individualism; and Erich Fromm, the psychoanalyst and social critic whose *Escape from Freedom* analyzed the means by which the citizens of the capitalist world seek out new sovereignties to which to subordinate themselves, dissolving their individualism and relieving themselves of a liberty that they never asked for nor wanted nor knew what to do with.

Hayek worried that we were on the Road to Serfdom, and we are—but it begins with the Road to Smurfdom, the place where the deracinated *demos* of the Twitter age finds itself feeling small and blue.

The mob politics of our time is a political phenomenon, in partial aspect, but it is much more substantially a social phenomenon in which the most coddled, selfish, and pathetically puffed-up collections of *Homo* not quite *sapiens* in human history—the just-slightly-upper-middle-class consumer-voters of the twenty-first century capitalist world—are undergoing a kind of corporate nervous breakdown in public as the mercilessly Darwinian bump-and-grind of Instant Culture forces them to confront the fact of their own eternal insignificance, which is the fundamental truth that their common life has been organized around distracting them from themselves for the past forty years or so.[23] The mob is less an instrument for its members to *get their*

---

23 Education in self-esteem, "everybody gets a trophy," etc. In my own experience as an adjunct professor at The King's College, I concluded that the best kind of education for a student's self-esteem is instruction in *grammar*. When they really start to get it, that's the closest thing to a scales-from-their-eyes experience you will see. The magic of it is, they don't just *feel* smarter.

way in this or that quotidian political matter than it is an instrument for them to *find their way* in a much larger and more meaningful sense, in the endless human quest for connection and significance. The disruption of globalization and the emergence of capitalism in its latest iteration has sundered many traditional relationships and dissolved many longstanding institutions and modes of life. The electronic mob—the virtual tribe—is for a great many lonely and foundering misfits the nearest substitute.

But the sterility and brittleness of social-media relationships—and of the real-life relationships that increasingly are patterned on social-media relationships, i.e. *faux* intimacy—make the stampeding electronic herd an ultimately unsatisfactory source of personal meaning and fulfillment for the lonely, enraged, and bored (bored by themselves above all) castaways and refugees of Instant Culture, who along with have thrown away genuine culture, history, and religion like yesterday's newspapers, not that very many of them remember what a newspaper feels like. The moral ethic of Instant Culture is founded on mutual instrumentalization, a lonely and atomistic condition that necessarily relegates everyone outside the self to the Kantian Kingdom of Means.[24] There can be no friendship among *means*. Decency in government is an impossibility among citizen-subjects who understand one another only as means to some other end rather than as valuable in themselves—valuable *as individuals*.

Hayek considered the relationship between the negation of the individual and authoritarianism in the context of political economy; Whyte examined it at great length in the context of working life; Fromm understood it principally as a psychological phenomenon, a pathology of capitalism resulting in the "alienation" of Marxist jargon. Despite their fundamentally opposed social views and political ideologies, each

---

24 Which is a very mean kingdom, indeed.

of these men was in his way a champion of the smallest minority—the only one who matters: the individual.

Genuine political discourse and political culture are possible only among those individuals with enough regard for their own individuality and sufficient confidence in its value to stand apart from the tribe, however partially or imperfectly, and say what needs saying: *Eppur si muove*, "I will not let anyone walk through my mind with their dirty feet," *We hold these truths to be self-evident*, "Do not be afraid," "The Buddhas only point the way," *Non serviam*.

We need free minds now more than ever. It's like Jeffrey Goldberg and his balls: You'll miss them when they're gone.

CHAPTER THREE

The Pond Moves the Scum, Not the Other Way 'Round

The destructive work of totalitarian machinery, whether
or not this word is used, is usually supported by a special
kind of primitive social philosophy. It proclaims not only
that the common good of "society" has priority over the
interests of individuals, but that the very existence of
individuals as persons is reducible to the existence of
the social "whole"; in other words, personal existence is,
in a strange sense, unreal. This is a convenient
foundation for any ideology of slavery.

—Leszek Kołakowski, "Totalitarianism and the Virtue of the Lie," Commentary,
May 1983

E verybody knows I'm a monster. By "everybody" I mean all
good, decent, serious, newspaper analog–reading people, and
by "all good, decent, serious, newspaper analog–reading people" I mean you sad atavistic masturbatory specimens out there in
the wooly wilds of America, by which I mean pud-pounding nobodies in Brooklyn or Guymon, Oklahoma,[1] depending on your tribe,
obsessively following intra-media squabbles on social media, cheer-
ing for what you imagine to be "your side" like a bunch of marginally
employed and past-their-prime NFL-cheering leg-tattooed

---

1 *De gustibus*, &c., indeed.

douche-rockets at some ghastly exuburban[2] sports bar and enjoying a nice bottle of the warm and comforting illusion of solidarity as though Tom Brady or Le'Veon Bell would have taken a voluminous equine piss on you from a great height if you were smoldering and crackling on the sidelines like a sizzling plate of Kansas City burnt ends.

Everybody knows what I am. But let's not talk about me just yet. We'll get to that later.

Let's talk about democracy.

If you are expecting a rousing paean to democracy here, perhaps with a little liberal nod in the direction of free speech and general toleration and other liberal-democratic pieties that you may imagine to be central to my theme here, then you are going to be disappointed. I come not to praise democracy but to bury it. And I don't mean just the vulgar majoritarianism of the Barack Obama "I Won" variety— the primitive-minded might-makes-right organizing principle of "My Vote Tally Is Bigger Than Yours."[3] No, I mean the basic, fundamental thing: the idea that public institutions approach perfection the more closely they approximate the fickle and ignorant demands of the *demos*, and approach glory in greater degree the more ruthlessly they subject the members of a society to the Rousseauean "general will,"[4] that great fiction that has proved itself such a convenient enabler of savagery, that anybody should give the furry crack of a rat's patootie what blockheads think just because the blockheads exist and walk around on real estate adjacent to our own.

---

2 I have in mind the Buffalo Wild Wings at Monmouth Mall, Eatontown, N.J., if you really want to know.

3 "My tribe, my daddy, my dick is bigger than yours," etc. Everybody is a tallywhacker on Election Day, which of course may be abbreviated E.D.

4 "One of the most sinister and formidable enemies of liberty in the whole history of human thought." Isaiah Berlin, *Freedom and Its Betrayal*, 1952.

When libertarians gag on the name Jean-Jacques Rousseau, we cough up that of John Stuart Mill.[5] We libertarians[6] lean pretty heavily on Mill and his "Harm Principle," which is usually summarized in the cliché: "Your right to swing your fist ends where my nose begins."[7] The Harm Principle is pretty useful, and for many of us generally persuasive, at least as a heuristic to gauge the appropriateness of government actions and the moral limitations on those actions. (There is very little more than that to the most simplistic expression of libertarianism.) The musty ol' Harm Principle is Libertarianism 101: If you aren't willing to stick a gun in somebody's face over the matter, then you probably shouldn't support passing a law against it, because all that means is that you are deputizing somebody else to stick a gun in somebody's face over the issue, i.e. the same old violence at one chickenshit degree of separation, general will be damned.

But there is more to society—and to the politics of a society—than formal government *per se*, and there is a great deal of social space to explore between "legally permitted" and "legally prohibited."[8]

Thanks in no small part to the Supreme Court's recent rediscovery of the First Amendment, there is little active governmental

---

5 Here, the common reader, book editor, or literary agent wondering what exactly it is he's set to get 15 percent of will exclaim: "Jesus H. Christ, Kevin, not another jackass libertarian manifesto that begins with an exegesis of John Stuart Fucking Mill, of whom we all got our fill back when we were undergraduates. Are you really going to invoke the 'harm principle' right here in the opening part of the book?" No, no, just bear with me.

6 Or classical liberals, or right-leaning people understandably embarrassed to call ourselves "Republicans," etc.

7 This expression already was hackneyed by the time Oliver Wendell Holmes got around to invoking it, but neither he nor John Stuart Mill nor Abraham Lincoln nor any of the other famous personages to whom it is attributed coined it. It appears in law articles going back to the dark ages of legal prehistory.

8 Unless you're one of those ants in *The Once and Future King*.

censorship in these United States, and relatively little prospect of it.[9] But, as the late Andrew Breitbart[10] famously put it, "politics is downstream from culture." The explicitly and more robustly *democratic* organs of government, particularly the presidency and the House of Representatives, respond quickly (and, very often, cravenly[11]) to the tiniest variations in the political currents of the hour—it should be understood as axiomatic in democratic politics that the pond moves the scum, not the other way around—but the unelected and theoretically apolitical[12] organs of government are moved by the culture as well. That includes the Supreme Court, and that isn't a concern for the far-off future: The First Amendment says *exactly* what it says, but there's dotty, batty, gimpy old Ruth Bader Ginsburg[13] insisting that the federal government can dictate to us what movies can be shown at the theater—because "democracy" cannot thrive if a couple of vulgar right-wing political entrepreneurs are allowed to show their lurid little movie without permission from the federal government.

Mill was rightly worried about the encroachments of government, about the need for formal limitations on governmental powers,

---

9 The angst and wailing over "Big Money in politics" after the *Citizens United* decision reliably omitted the fact that the case was about the federal government's attempting to tell political activists that they could not show a film critical of Hillary Rodham Clinton during the run-up to the presidential election. Following that decision, Senator Harry Reid, best known today for losing—badly—a fist-fight with a piece of exercise equipment, led every single Democrat in the United States Senate in a vote to gut the First Amendment, which may protect pole-dancing in New Jersey and the late Robert Mapplethorpe's unalienable right to sodomize himself with a bullwhip but was explicitly framed for the protection of political speech, e.g. calling Hillary Rodham Clinton a vicious lying moonbat.

10 It is truly a shame about that ghastly, low, witless, disfigured thing on the Internet that daily brings shame to the name "Breitbart."

11 From the Old French *cravant*, meaning whipped into submission like a bunch of sissies with a terrible gaping existential void where their testicles are supposed to be.

12 As if.

13 "More human than human," © Tyrell Corp., 2019.

the "tyranny of the majority,"[14] and the other inevitable abuses of democracy. But he, like Hayek and Fromm a century later,[15] was also deeply worried about informal illiberalism, the non-governmental suppression of ideas, discourse, and social experimentation by a ruthlessly if unofficially enforced conformism. Hayek, the great champion of the free market, and Fromm, a sometime-doctrinaire socialist, ended up pointing to the same menace threatening the individual and his ability to speak and think for himself: *capitalism*.

For Fromm, the fundamental issue was the Marxist idea of "alienation," which for the Marxist begins with the birth of capitalism at the end of the Middle Ages.[16] Frank Tannenbaum offers a useful summary of the socio-economic scene in his *Philosophy of Labor*:

> Membership in a guild, manorial estate, or village protected man throughout his life and gave him the peace and serenity from which could flow the medieval art and craft. The life of man was a nearly unified whole. Being a member of an integrated society protected and raised the dignity of the individual and gave each person his own

---

14 It wasn't a hoary old cliché back when Mill was writing *On Liberty*.

15 Fromm published *Escape from Freedom* in 1941. Whyte published *The Organization Man* in 1956. Hayek published *The Constitution of Liberty* in 1960. Those decades were a rich time for meditations on the nature and causes of the capitalist world's evolution toward a kind of informal totalitarianism, an autocracy of etiquette.

16 For the sake of simplicity, I am dividing what we call "capitalism" into four eras: Primitive Capitalism beginning in the Renaissance; Industrial Capitalism, beginning with the Industrial Revolution; Bureaucratic Capitalism, beginning in the early 20th century; and Global Capitalism, which is as good a name as any for the famously "disruptive" phenomenon currently under way. I am aware that "bureaucratic capitalism" is a term of abuse in some Communist circles; what I mean by it is the rise to prominence of the bureaucratic corporation as a power in itself rather than a legal instrument attached to some entrepreneur. Procter & Gamble was a different kind of thing in 1860 than it was in 1984.

special role. Each man, each act, was part of a total life drama, the plot of which was known and in which the part allotted to each was prescribed. No one was isolated or abandoned. His individuality and his ambitions were fulfilled within the customary law that ruled the community to which he belonged.[17]

Tannenbaum here is describing something that is familiar to students of twenty-first-century politics, which is dominated by nostalgia for the postwar years, what we might think of as the Eisenhower Settlement. In the postwar years, Democrats retreated a bit from the radicalism of the 1930s and came to focus their domestic agenda on preserving and gradually expanding the New Deal, a position that Republicans grudgingly came around to accept themselves.[18] While there were several postwar recessions, the 1950s and 1960s were a time of significant and steady economic growth, strong employment, security, and optimism. There were relatively broad consensuses on both foreign and domestic affairs. The postwar years were unique in ways that cannot be replicated (US industry was unchallenged at the apex because the other great industrial powers were smoldering ruins, their factories having been repurposed for war or blown to smithereens, their work forces decimated, and their societies turned upside-down) and, even so, our national memory of them is inaccurate and romanticized. Very few Americans in our time would willingly accept a 1957 standard of living if it were offered.

But the myth of the postwar generation—that any man willing to work could go down to the local factory and get a good

---

17 1951.
18 As William F. Buckley Jr. tells the story, it was Republican acceptance of the New Deal, not radicalism on the Left, that inspired the launch of the conservative movement. "Our principles are round," Buckley wrote, "and Eisenhower is square."

manufacturing job that would support his family in a comfortable middle-class manner—remains our master political narrative. The longing for a restoration of the Eisenhower Settlement can be heard on Right and Left, from Donald Trump to Elizabeth Warren. What they long for is not the median household income (which was in inflation-adjusted terms about half what it is today[19]) or the tax burden (in practice almost exactly what it is today, despite the radical changes in statutory rates) but the certainty that Tannenbaum writes about, the situation in which an American could understand himself as "a member of an integrated society" that "protected and raised the dignity of the individual and gave each person his own special role." The deficit that our populists perceive is a social and spiritual one, not a fiscal one. When they speak of their desire to Make America Great Again or to build "an economy that works for everyone," what they are speaking to is the longing for solidarity. The Trump movement, like the "welfare chauvinists" in Europe who are its fellow travelers, have made this desire more explicit and presented it in a more dramatic way, and they have successfully connected it to the sense of a unitary national interest, whereas the populists on the Left are somewhat hobbled by their politics of universal particularism: Make Partially Disabled Lesbians of Color Employed in the Public Sector Great Again is a different kind of proposition. The Democratic

---

19 To the extent that income is a large factor here at all, it almost certainly is a question of *relative* income rather than one of absolute standards of living. Albert O. Hirschman of Harvard described the "tunnel effect" in his article "The Changing Tolerance for Income Inequality in the Course of Economic Development." (*Quarterly Journal of Economics*, 1973.) When drivers are stuck in traffic in a tunnel, they originally are encouraged when they see the cars in the lane next to them begin to move, because they assume this presages their own coming advancement; but, if the other lane continues to move while they remain stuck, their encouragement will soon turn sour, and they will begin to suspect that they are being disadvantaged in some way that they cannot yet perceive. Inevitably, their thoughts will turn to breaking the traffic rules and crossing the yellow line into the adjacent lane in the tunnel.

party's conundrum is the tension between the historical liberal concern for the rights of minorities and the modern progressive emphasis on the masses; as it stands, the Party of the Masses is on the rise and the Party of the Minorities is in decline, not because the masses have more votes but because the unarticulated project of populism is the pursuit of conformity and homogeneity. The minorities—especially the Smallest Minority—must, in this view, conform themselves to the masses.

Our nostalgia has precedent. Fromm believed that the wrenching transition from the stable and predictable (if poor and miserable) economic life of the Middle Ages to the first grasping Renaissance attempts at constructing something that we might recognize as modern capitalism caused a spiritual and political crisis in Europe, as the economic status—and, probably more important, the *social* status— of everybody from serfs to the bourgeoisie to the aristocracy (secular and ecclesiastic) was suddenly up for renegotiation. The newly liberated people of Europe were in reality terrified by their new liberty, because it caused them to be disconnected from their familiar modes of life and introduced them to new kinds of economic and status anxiety. Fromm concluded in *Escape from Freedom*: "The individual was left alone and isolated. He was free."

Those lonely and isolated, *involuntary* pioneers of modernity sought new life-defining values from alternative sources, and new kinds of community in which to dissolve their individualism and relieve themselves of its burdens. In Fromm's view, the Reformation was as much a reaction against the Renaissance as it was an indictment of deficiencies in Catholic doctrine and practice. The Protestant emphasis on submission to God in His complete sovereignty offered a new kind of lordship, a new North Star by which to navigate the mysteries of a newly cosmopolitan world. "Protestantism was the answer to the human needs of the frightened, uprooted, and isolated individual who had to orient and to relate himself to a new world," Fromm wrote, noting that Protestantism, especially its more fanatical expression, found its strongest purchase in the urban bourgeoisie, the most thoroughly deracinated Europeans of the time.

Hayek picks up the ball a few centuries later, faced not with the birth of capitalism but with its evolution into its twentieth-century form, dominated by large, complex organizations—big corporations in the private sector, big bureaucracies in the public and semi-public sectors. The critical change in Hayek's view was the displacement of small-proprietorship and other forms of self-employment by the rise of salaried corporate employment as the norm. (William Whyte would explore this phenomenon at great length in *The Organization Man*.) Hayek, with his characteristic astringency and intelligent anti-majoritarianism, argues that the vast masses of salaried workers need the independently wealthy propertied classes in ways that they do not understand:

> The increase in population during the last two hundred years has been made up mostly of employed workers, urban and industrial. Though the technological change that has favored large-scale enterprise and helped to create the new large class of clerical workers has undoubtedly assisted this growth of the employed section of the population, the increasing number of propertyless that offered their services has probably in turn assisted the growth of large-scale organization.... Since it is now their opinion that largely governs policy, this produces measures that make the employed positions relatively more attractive and the independent ones ever less so.
>
> That the employed should thus use their political power is natural. The problem is whether it is in their long-term

interest if society is thereby progressively turned into one great hierarchy of employment. Such a state seems to be the likely outcome unless the employed majority come to recognize that it would be in their interest to ensure the preservation of a substantial number of independents. For if they do not, we shall all find that our freedom has been affected, just as they will find that, without a great variety of employers to choose from, their position is not as it once was.[20]

Hayek here is less interested in how societies are designed to work than in how they actually work. (His famous proverb: "The curious task of economics is to demonstrate to men how little they know about what they imagine they can design.") Hayek's conception of society is the opposite of the cartoon version of libertarianism often put forward by opponents of the philosophy. Hayek's society is not a cloud of hermetically sealed-off individuals who interact with one another only when they need something but a complex network of delicate relationships, many of which have benefits that are not immediately apparent to their beneficiaries. Hayekian society is an organic whole in which the constituents need one another and benefit from one another—and go terribly wrong when they ignore or misunderstand this arrangement. Hayek continues:

The problem is that many exercises of freedom are of little direct interest to the employed and that it is often not easy for them to see that their freedom depends on others' being able to make decisions which are not immediately relevant to their whole manner of life. Since they can and have to live without making such decisions, they cannot

---

20 *The Constitution of Liberty*, 1960.

see the need for them, and they attach little importance to opportunities for action which hardly ever occur in their lives. They regard as unnecessary many exercises of freedom which are essential to the independent if he is to perform his functions, and they hold views of deserts and appropriate remuneration entirely different from his.

Ask a class-war populist what it is that a private-equity firm *does* and you will see this observation illustrated in dramatic fashion. The only thing he is likely to know is that some financial firms enjoy certain tax advantages, and that these seem to him unfair and indefensible. People who do not understand the role of finance in the larger economy cannot connect the enormous paychecks earned on Wall Street with anything that looks familiar to them in their own experience as *work*, and it seems to them self-evidently unjust (and it may *be* unjust; that is beside the point) that income earned from investment is taxed in a way that is less rapacious than is income earned from salaried work or hourly wages, i.e. the kind of work they most likely do. And, for those reasons, they assume that finance is all[21] some sort of a scam. Hayek concludes:

> Freedom is thus seriously threatened today by the tendency of the employed majority to impose upon the rest their standards and views of life. It may indeed prove to be the most difficult task of all to persuade the employed masses that in the general interest of their society, and therefore in their own long-term interest, they should preserve such conditions as to enable a few to reach positions which to them appear unattainable or not worth the effort and risk.[22]

---

21 "All" is where they go wrong.
22 *The Constitution of Liberty*, 1960.

Hayek's capitalism is still evolving. The twentieth-century model of capitalism typified by IBM and its aggressively conformist culture—the firm used to mandate specifically the wearing of *white* dress shirts, no gingham or pencil stripes for you, Salaryman!—is dying off, with corporate life expectancies declining quickly and new models of work and employer-employee relations evolving. Its instruments of communication already have been largely displaced, as the illiterate and incontinent logorrhea of social media takes its place at the commanding heights of discourse while newspapers and books decline. This, too, represents a radical break from what had seemed like settled arrangements, though Americans' expectations about economic and social life have been shaped by the profoundly abnormal period that directly followed World War II.[23] The displacement of the postwar economy and its norms by the digital world and its norms may not be a break comparable to the end of the medieval period and the birth of capitalism, but it brings with it the same kind of anxieties, which, if you concentrate, you can smell beneath the fecal stink of our popular-culture substitute. And those who suffer the most[24] from these anxieties seek, as peons always have sought, a new master to which to submit in order to be relieved of the burdens

---

23 For a fascinating and educational exploration of this subject at length, consult Yuval Levin's *The Fractured Republic* (2016).

24 That's an interesting thing to noodle on. The lives of very poor people have not been much disrupted by recent technological and social changes, and most of their sources of status and security, such as they are, remain unmolested. The very rich and the famous—increasingly overlapping groups—have enjoyed economic and cultural gains sufficient to offset much of the discomfort associated with this social evolution. The hardest-hit are the college-educated mediocrities, typically white, suburban, and middle-class—and male. Young women are less disadvantaged by the failure to thrive in the modern marketplace because women are less dependent upon their professional prestige and income for status. They are the sexual gatekeepers, which is bad news indeed for the young men who end up playing with spreadsheets all day for $42,000 a year when that college recruiter promised them so much more. These are your hardcore tweet-with-one-hand boys. Generalize from the sexual impulse to a whole sad *Weltanschauung* and the psychological nexus between late-night Twitter rage-monkey and school shooter will come into considerably clearer focus.

of individuality, that strange new thing whose meaning and use remain mysterious to them.

Hayek was restating in expressly *economic* terms Mill's more general *political* observation that a healthy society required cultural prophylactics "against the tyranny of the prevailing opinion and feeling; against the tendency of society to impose, by other means than civil penalties, its own ideas and practices as rules of conduct on those who dissent from them; to fetter the development, and, if possible, prevent the formation, of any individuality not in harmony with its ways, and compel all characters to fashion themselves upon the model of its own." The Old Testament insists that mankind was made in God's image, and Mill is here describing nothing less than the apotheosis of public opinion, a new kind of god and a jealous one—a blind idiot god as H. P. Lovecraft might have imagined.[25]

The American founders understood what democracy really is, which is why they feared and loathed that blind idiot god. John Adams famously made the case:

> I do not say that democracy has been more pernicious on the whole, and in the long run, than monarchy or aristocracy. Democracy has never been and never can be so durable as aristocracy or monarchy; but while it lasts, it is more bloody than either.... Remember, democracy never lasts long. It soon wastes, exhausts, and murders

---

25 "Once his groping hands encountered a pillar of stone with a vacant top, whilst later he found himself clutching the rungs of a ladder built into the wall, and fumbling his uncertain way upward toward some region of intenser stench where a hot, searing blast beat down against him. Before his eyes a kaleidoscopic range of phantasmal images played, all of them dissolving at intervals into the picture of a vast, unplumbed abyss of night wherein whirled suns and worlds of an even profounder blackness. He thought of the ancient legends of Ultimate Chaos, at whose centre sprawls the blind idiot god Azathoth, Lord of All Things, encircled by his flopping horde of mindless and amorphous dancers, and lulled by the thin monotonous piping of a daemoniac flute held in nameless paws." How in the holy McFuck did H. P. Lovecraft know about Twitter?

itself. There never was a democracy yet that did not commit suicide. It is in vain to say that democracy is less vain, less proud, less selfish, less ambitious, or less avaricious than aristocracy or monarchy. It is not true, in fact, and nowhere appears in history. Those passions are the same in all men, under all forms of simple government, and when unchecked, produce the same effects of fraud, violence, and cruelty. When clear prospects are opened before vanity, pride, avarice, or ambition, for their easy gratification, it is hard for the most considerate philosophers and the most conscientious moralists to resist the temptation. Individuals have conquered themselves. Nations and large bodies of men, never.[26]

The Founding Fathers[27] understood the dangers of democracy from the Roman example, among others. They were, unlike their dipshit epigones,[28] well-read in the Greek and Roman classical literature, in which many of them no doubt encountered the concept of "ochlocracy," (ὀχλοκρατία[29]), or what we call today "mob rule."[30]

One of the important lessons of the Roman example is that the formal arrangements of government do not matter greatly compared to the political norms and cultural habits of the time. Constitutions

---

26 Letter from John Adams to John Taylor, December 17, 1814.

27 If you happen to be the sort of person who objects to purportedly patriarchal phrases of perfectly good English such as "Founding Fathers," you might want to go ahead and fuck right off around this point. You just ain't going to enjoy this.

28 Senator Ben Sasse is a very intelligent man, a man of genuine liberal learning with a genuinely humane mind. But he seems even more remarkable than he is, because he is surrounded by debased men who have substituted Sean Hannity for Cicero.

29 John Stuart Mill began his instruction in Greek at the age of three, and if he muffed a translation, his father denied him lunch. I am not saying that's how education should be conducted today, but I'm not not saying that, either.

30 *Mobile vulgus*, in Latin, which is instructively connotative.

come and go, statutes may be overturned or flouted, but the mob is eternal. Ochlocracy is ochlocracy is ochlocracy, whether it arises from an Athenian democracy, a Roman republic, a Roman empire,[31] a French revolutionary regime, or the avuncular mass-murder/mass-psychosis rape junta of Chairman Mao and his wild bunch. Ochlocracy sometimes comprises illegal and non-governmental actions (e.g., lynch mobs) or using threats or violence to intimidate private parties into compliance with the mob's political demands, but it often consists in non-governmental actors' bullying or intimidating the official organs of government or public institutions into following some particular course of action, frequently murderous[32] throughout history, though it generally stops well short of that in the tepid times in which we live. Its main efforts in the early years of the twenty-first century have been focused on the corporate employment and institutionalist mindset that so concerned Hayek and Fromm. Their project is the conversion of businesses—and the university, University Man being Salaryman in larval form—into *disciplinary corporations*, agencies deputized to enforce political and intellectual conformity

---

31 Students of the increasingly imperial American presidency must savor the fact that the word "emperor" is derived from the Latin term meaning "commander-in-chief."

32 E.g. from Edward Gibbon's *Decline and Fall of the Roman Empire*: "The people demanded with angry clamors the head of the public enemy. Cleander, who commanded the Praetorian Guards, ordered a body of cavalry to sally forth and disperse the seditious multitude. The multitude fled with precipitation towards the city; several were slain, and many more were trampled to death; but when the cavalry entered the streets their pursuit was checked by a shower of stones and darts from the roofs and windows of the houses. The footguards, who had long been jealous of the prerogatives and insolence of the Praetorian cavalry, embraced the party of the people. The tumult became a regular engagement and threatened a general massacre. The Praetorians at length gave way, oppressed with numbers; and the tide of popular fury returned with redoubled violence against the gates of the palace, where Commodus lay dissolved in luxury, and alone unconscious of the civil war...Commodus started from his dream of pleasure and commanded that the head of Cleander should be thrown out to the people. The desired spectacle instantly appeased the tumult." But also see the Salem witch trials, the Cultural Revolution, etc.

on subjects ranging from the most high-profile business executives and intellectuals to the most obscure fast-food managers.

As Whyte argues in *The Organization Man*, the prime directive of the Organization—be it a corporation or a church—is to avoid internal conflict. Conflict interferes with the smooth functioning of the Organization in pursuit of its secular aims, but it also inhibits the Organization's metaphysical purpose—providing meaning and belonging in an uncertain world, acting in effect as a society in miniature in which the deracinated individual may strive after a life that is integrated economically, intellectually, socially, and, inevitably, politically. In that sense, the corporation becomes an analog for what the church was and what the state—especially the totalitarian state—has been: a welder of wills, an aggregator and deputy of the general will, an organization that is dedicated not only to the pursuit of particular secular business goals but to a transcendent and all-encompassing mode of life: "For a great state, qua state, is not one which embraces a great population or an extensive territory, but one which achieves a great intensity of social unity. And in this matter we must bear in mind that unity means unity of purpose and will, and not merely unity of action and result."[33] The purpose of corporate life is the same as the Christian sacrament of confession: *reconciliation*.

The Organization incorporates the reconciled individual and conforms him to itself to remove conflict—sanctification by bureaucracy. In *The Organization Man*, Whyte notes that the same quasi-religious striving after belonging has characterized organizations ranging from labor unions to churches to corporations:

> Spokesmen in other areas have similarly bewailed the lack
> of an encompassing, integrated life, and in an excess of

---

33 *Early Political Writings 1925–1930*, Michael Oakeshott, 2011.

good will have asked that their group take over the whole messy job. Many a contemporary prescription for utopia can be summarized if you cross out the name of one group and substitute another in the following charge: Society has broken down; the family, the church, the community, the schools, business—each has failed to give the individual the belongingness he needs and thus it is now the task of ——group to do the job. It is fortunate there are so many groups; with such competition for the individual psyche it is difficult for any one of them to land the franchise.

A particularly fruitful point of comparison here is the university, with its ancient imperative to educate the "whole man." Universities are hothouses of ochlocracy not only because they are the antechambers to power and influence but because of the nature of the institution itself, which is dedicated to the cultivation of holistic flourishing—and the goal holistic flourishing provides the pretext for holistic *discipline*. Hence the arrogation of quasi-police powers to various campus inspectors and committees of inquiry. Moral and intellectual homogeneity is a precondition of the comprehensively holistic communion with the organization—the cultivation and ensuring of which is the organization's transcendent purpose. As Whyte argues, the fact that more than one communion may make a claim on an individual's allegiances may complicate his life but does not enter into the organization's account of itself or of the individual's obligations to it:

> Ideologically these pleas do not cancel each other out. For there is always the common thread that a man must belong and that he must be unhappy if he does not belong rather completely. The idea that conflicting allegiances safeguard him as well as abrade him is sloughed over, and for the

> people who must endure the tensions of independence
> there is no condolence; only the message that the tensions
> are sickness—either in themselves or in society. It does not
> make any difference whether the Good Society is to be
> represented by a union or by a corporation or by a church;
> it is to be a society unified and purged of conflict.

For "sickness" above, one might well read "sin," particularly in light of the more modern Christian emphasis on sin as separation and separateness—a choice the individual makes that cuts him off from the communion.

The individual—the smallest minority—is a constant source of conflict. The individual cannot be assimilated into the Organization entirely because resisting such assimilation is in the individual's nature. The mid-century firm was a creature of bureaucratic capitalism, and it differed from its nineteenth-century predecessors in its generically bureaucratic character, which is distinct from that of the earlier corporations that were in effect a mere legal and administrative apparatus attached to a single entrepreneur, often a charismatic one, whose personality and imagination dominated the corporation as though it were an entirely private enterprise. The turn-of-the-century technology firm represented a partial revival of that earlier model; Bill Gates micromanaged Microsoft in a way that would be entirely alien to a contemporary CEO of Goldman Sachs or Conagra Brands; Steve Jobs's many successes and his messianic return to Apple enabled him to behave in a masterful way, one that was easily erratic and abusive enough that it would have cost him his job had he been a different sort of man at a different sort of firm. The individual may be a company man of a sort, but even when he seeks communion, he seeks it *as himself.*

And that gets up the noses of certain people.

Among people who are morally and (to the modest extent that they are capable) intellectually committed to seeking after belonging and forging "a society unified and purged of conflict," the individual will always—*necessarily*—be the sabot in the Jacquard loom,[34] the sand in the gears, the pebble in the big social shoe. People who dedicate their lives to finding idols before which they may abase themselves—the cult of intersectionality, identity politics, the Make America Great Again jihad, race and/or sex and other demographic features, nationalism, socialism, the Democratic party, the Republican party, organized homosexuality, the Bernie Sanders movement, animal rights, veganism, Crossfit, whatever[35]—cannot abide the presence of those who decline to abase themselves before that idol or, short of that, any idol. The parallel case here is that of the relatively orthodox and observant Catholics and Jews who have in the early twenty-first century discovered that they have far more in common with one another than they do with casual secularists, agnostics, or atheists. True believers believe truly, and what they hold in common isn't that which they believe but *that they believe.*

Fanaticism in politics does not come from a deep and abiding belief in the idol—it comes from the deep and abiding need to submit to *something.* The shame the political idolaters rightly feel at this is reconstituted, through the wondrous interaction of rage and stupidity, as the *takfiri* impulse within Islam, which is focused on denouncing other Muslims as "impure" or as apostates and hence making

---

34 Tragically, the etymology of "sabotage" familiar to members of my generation from one of those awful *Star Trek* movies is false. It comes from a French word meaning to *botch* or to *bungle*, to do something clumsily and gracelessly. The words are related but not in a direct and linear way.

35 Oakeshott was insistent in emphasizing the different and distinct characters of politics properly understood and mere association; in our time, that distinction has broken down in practice, both because of the *totalitarian* bent of our politics (meaning not death camps and jackboots but a politics that seeks to insert itself everywhere, leaving no private sphere of life) and because politics has decayed into a kind of entertainment or hobby, like following a sports team with moral pretensions.

them subject to social or legal sanction.[36] The *takfiri* tendency currently dominates conservative-oriented broadcasting, which is a kind of endless and repetitive radio drama with a single storyline: "They betrayed us!" The strange "antiestablishment" posturing of Washington-based multimillionaire media figures with the White House on speed-dial is one of the milder forms of *takfiri* politics, one that largely contents itself with criticism and political organizing. There are more vicious forms, of course, which generally come into play when the great partisan-cultural divide is crossed, the Sunni-Shia divide of American public life. Sometimes this infidel-hunting is done online, through social-media mobs, and sometimes it is done with fire and blood, as in the case of the literal mobs of blackshirts who enforce political conformity through political violence while declaring themselves—they are absolutely immune to irony—"anti-fascists."

Democracy, properly understood and properly *deployed*, is an exclusively procedural consideration. It is in the Kingdom of Means. It has procedural value not because we believe in equality—the American concept of "equality before the law" describes the functioning of American *institutions*, not the character of the American *people*—and not because we believe that everyone deserves to have his say, that all voices must be heard. There are plenty of people out there who have nothing useful or interesting to say, whose exercise of the franchise is only a great infantile "I want!" endlessly reiterated every four years or so. There is no special virtue in consulting morons and cretins simply because they *exist*. There is no special moral value in bundling together complex problems and policy ideas and asking 50 percent plus 1 of a sprawling and almost pristinely ignorant group of barely improved chimpanzees only a relatively few generations of evolution

---

36 Which, in an unfortunately generous swath of the Islamic world, is indistinguishable from lynching.

removed from habitual public masturbation and ritual poo-flinging[37] what they think about those bundles and which of them they prefer.

We rely on procedural democracy as a substitute for *violence*. It is how we ensure a minimum of accountability in our government: If we do not like how our lawmakers and representatives are behaving, we can relieve them of their duties and choose new ones. Procedural democracy is a *convenience*. It pacifies the chimps in the electorate and gives us an alternative to ritual combat[38] for the chimps in office. It is an important convenience, to be sure, but if there were a better way of ensuring basic political accountability than relying on the whims and resentments of every hillbilly and Brooklyn hipster across the fruited plain, all intelligent people would prefer it. But there isn't.

Democracy kept in its procedural box is a useful tool, one that can do some real good. And its value is most easily appreciated in its absence, as we see as this moment in history with the transnational bureaucratic and political efforts to frustrate the British decision to part company with the European Union. But its moral value consists almost exclusively in its utility as a substitute for violence. Without being situated in the frame of liberalism and the rule of law, democracy is only another instrument for aggregating hatred and grievances and organizing them into repression. The example of Venezuela,

---

37 Obviously, this is not true of all of them. Some of them are still flinging poo.

38 Philip Perry, *Big Think*, July 23, 2017: "Chimpanzees in three West African countries— Guinea Bissau, Côte d'Ivoire (the Ivory Coast), and Liberia, have been observed taking part in strange behavior. They store a great number of rocks in the hollows of trees. Then, usually a male, takes one of the rocks, walks a distance away, grunts an utterance, and hurls the rock at the tree, leaving a mark on it. The rock is then placed back in the hollow to be reused in this manner again. No chimps east of these countries have been observed doing this. What's more, there seems to be no reason for it tied to survival. It has nothing to do with acquiring food, mating, or furthering one's status. Researchers say it might be a unique display of male power, marking the border of their troop's territory, or even a spiritual ritual."

which has descended into political violence even as it maintains democratic forms, illustrates that well enough.

Democracy as a *social ethic* is something else entirely. The implicit proposal that human beings have more value in corporation, that masses grow more valuable and more legitimate the larger they are and the more demanding they grow, and that the individual must always in the end be answerable to the collective is pure barbarism—it is might-makes-right thinking metathesized from authoritarian political principle to authoritarian cult. It is a virtual guarantee of social and cultural stagnation, ugliness, stupidity, repression, bigotry, illiberalism, narrow-mindedness—and, inevitably, violence. It is the cult of the modern primitive, whose object of veneration is the modern primitive himself.

The violence, such as it is, is almost a relief. There is a certain bracing honesty and directness in a black-masked goon firebombing a campus building in Berkeley in order to keep a celebrity-hungry Kentish homosexual from giving a speech. That violence will grow less refreshing and more dreary as it becomes more common, but, for the moment, the authentic mob is marginally less obnoxious than the sniveling one the festers on social media and simpers in corporate offices. A riot is honest.

Foreseeing our current culture, ritually disfigured and lobotomized by everything from social media to the kangaroo courts that mete out "social justice" on college campuses to the intellectual and moral non-entities who run the corporate human-resources departments, Whyte wrote: "Hell is no less hell for being antiseptic."

CHAPTER FOUR

Streitbare Demokratie

The essence of liberty has always lain in the ability to
choose as you wish to choose, because you wish so to
choose, uncoerced, unbullied, not swallowed up in some
vast system; and in the right to resist, to be unpopular,
to stand up for your convictions merely because they are
your convictions. That is true freedom, and without
it there is neither freedom of any kind, nor even the
illusion of it.

—*Isaiah Berlin*, Freedom and Its Betrayal, *1952*

J ohn Adams was not the only man of his time who dreaded
democracy. The word itself was often used as a term of opprobrium in the eighteenth century, when the foundations of what
we now call "democracy" were being laid. The fear of an out-of-
control democracy, by turns anarchic and totalitarian,[1] is ancient,

---

1 We are indebted to Sam Francis, who unfortunately ended his days as a racist crank, for
the very useful term "anarcho-tyranny," the feckless democratic mode in which genuine
crime and violence go unpoliced while the law-abiding are subjected to a regime of ever
more intrusive regulation. The textbook case is the US Attorney's Office for the Northern
District of Illinois, which has for years—as a matter of publicly stated policy—refused to
prosecute most straw-buyer cases, even though those illegal purchases are a main conduit
for firearms deployed by criminals in the bloody streets of murder-happy Chicago. At the
same time, federal law-enforcement agents have called for stricter oversight of federally
licensed firearms dealers and the people who do business with them—one of the least
criminally inclined demographics in the United States. Gun shops have business records,
fixed addresses, and regular business hours, and Chicago gangsters for the most part do
not. Guess which one is easier to police.

going back to Polybius and to Plato before him. That fear of such anarcho-tyranny has been a cornerstone of Anglo-American liberalism and republican government throughout the world. Efforts to contain it represent an intelligent evolution of political thought: The English developed the principle of parliamentary sovereignty, which holds that there were some things that even the king may not do; the American Founders, in turn, built into their constitutional architecture the principle that there are many things that parliament may not do, either. For a couple of centuries, liberalism and constitutional limits on government action helped to keep democracy in its box.

In the twenty-first century, we use "democracy" as a kind of rhetorical shorthand for good and decent and accountable government. But, as I argued earlier, that is an error. In the American settlement, what matters most is not the principle of one-man, one-vote,[2] social equality, or even equality under the law, sacred as those things may be to those gentle souls whose main concern is the infinitely plastic concept of *fairness*. What matters most to a flourishing society is liberty,[3] which is why in the United States we have long cherished deeply antidemocratic institutions such as the Supreme Court and the Bill of Rights,[4] restrictions on the power of the *demos* that are replicated to a greater or lesser extent in all liberal societies as a means of keeping democracy in its box. Senator Huey Long promised a world that made "every man a king." American liberalism, with its antidemocratic limitations on what the people may do through their elected representatives, offers something far better: No man a king— not individually, not corporately, not *en masse*.

---

2 The Swiss canton of Appenzell Innerrhoden didn't give women the right to vote in local elections until 1991, and Switzerland wasn't exactly a totalitarian hellhole.
3 Conservatives sometimes like to put it "well-ordered liberty," which is a redundancy.
4 The Bill of Rights ought to be titled "A List of Things You Idiots Don't Get a Vote On, Because They Aren't Up for Negotiation."

The problem of illiberal democracy—the kingly ambitions of the corporate *demos*—was well-understood, and practically taken for granted, among serious political thinkers in the West for generations.

But in the twentieth century, a new line of thinking about democracy was articulated, first in Europe and largely in response to the burgeoning authoritarian movements the first half of that blood-soaked century, political tendencies which would find their fullest and most horrifying expression in the outrages committed by Germany under the National Socialist German Workers' Party and in the Soviet Union and its satellites under Communism. Adolf Hitler had come to power through means that were, broadly speaking, democratic. Other authoritarian movements partook of democratic opportunities—standing for election, working in parliamentary coalitions—and availed themselves of the full benefit of the liberalism that they despised: freedom of speech, freedom of the press, freedom to organize politically, freedom to petition the government for action. Some of those who witnessed these horrors began to ask what was, at the time, a series of provocative questions: "What if the problem with democracy is not its tendency toward authoritarianism but its unwillingness to engage in enlightened authoritarianism itself, to defend itself from authoritarianism with the weapons of authoritarianism? What if the weakness of democracy is not that it harbors nascent illiberalism, or at least illiberal instincts, but that it fails to act in accordance with that illiberalism when it seems to be necessary? What if the principles of liberal democracy *must* be violated in certain situations in order to prevent deeper and more dangerous violations of liberalism and democracy? What if our tolerant and open societies are too tolerant and too open for their own good?"

Which is to say: "What if we have to destroy liberalism to save it?"

Given the times, the idea was not quite as daft as it sounds: The world had just watched one of the most antidemocratic and illiberal and savage political movements in human history exploit democratic processes to install itself in power—not in some savage backwater but in Germany, arguably the most civilized and intellectually advanced country in Europe at the time. From that dilemma was born the concept of *streitbare Demokratie*—or militant democracy, democracy in arms—described by the German political theorist Karl Loewenstein in his essay "Militant Democracy and Fundamental Rights," published in the *American Political Science Review* in 1937. That essay is not widely read today, but its assumptions and convictions are intuitive to the natural-born ochlocrat[5] and form the moral basis for mob politics in the twenty-first century United States. That should be read as an indictment neither of Loewenstein's thinking nor of the European political practices based on it. While I would not support importing German- or Austrian-style restrictions on political speech and political organizing to the United States, these restrictions are not necessarily unreasonable in the European context, and one can at least understand why they have been adopted.

While this is not the main subject of my argument here, European censorship—and Saudi and Chinese censorship—eventually will have to be dealt with in the context of American politics as US-based global technology firms accommodate the local laws in countries with illiberal speech and press regimes, including both democratic and liberal countries in Europe as well as undemocratic and despotic ones in Asia and the Middle East. The tendency to adopt the most-restrictive demand as a universal standard is a habit deeply embedded in the corporate mind, with its mania for systemization,

---

5 Again, it's not like the members of the mob sit around talking about *streitbare Demokratie* and the structural defects of liberal democracy before they mob up—envy and hatred are enough, and they've always got those in surplus. But we are not going to mitigate the social effects of mob politics without some effort, which means trying to understand it on its own terms.

standardization, and regimentation, which are employed as substitutes for intelligence and prudence, two very expensive commodities. Think of the way in which California's more restrictive automobile-emissions standards became the *de facto* national standard in the United States and then imagine how easy it would be for Chinese norms to come to dominate global free-speech practices as a practical matter if not a legal one. Europe's rules are more enlightened, but even the adoption of a German model would represent a significant loss of free-speech rights for Americans and many other peoples around the world.

The alternative to a free-speech culture is neither principled mediation of political discourse by enlightened philosopher-kings nor the imposition of rational rules governing what can be said and thought and what cannot. The real-world alternative is an endless ad-hocracy dominated by tribalism and social affinity, deployed as a political weapon and subordinate to political discipline. Justice and prudence play only an attenuated role in inter-tribal disputes—and all proposals for censorship or suppression come in tandem with inter-tribal disputes. This much was clear to Niebuhr, who believed that the necessary hypocrisy it entails would certainly prove corrosive to political legitimacy and wider social cooperation. Niebuhr writes:

> The inevitable hypocrisy, which is associated with the all the collective activities of the human race, springs chiefly from this source: that individuals have a moral code which makes the actions of collective man an outrage to their conscience. They therefore invent romantic and moral interpretations of the real facts, preferring to obscure rather than reveal the true character of their collective behavior. Sometimes they are as anxious to offer moral justifications for the brutalities from which they suffer as

for those which they commit. The fact that the hypocrisy of man's group behavior ... expresses itself not only in terms of self-justification but in terms of moral justification of human behavior in general, symbolizes one of the tragedies of the human spirit: its inability to conform its collective life to its individual ideals. As individuals, men believe they ought to love and serve each other and establish justice between each other. As racial, economic and national groups they take for themselves, whatever their power can command.[6]

The tendency that must be defended against is *streitbare Demokratie*'s natural decay: What begins as a principle ends up as an enemies list.

Loewenstein's essay is full of insights that must have been startlingly original at the time and which remain valuable today. He saw across Europe a proliferation of totalitarian movements, some of them openly asserting their fascism and some of them locked in bloody opposition to the self-proclaimed fascist parties,[7] often in what amounted to a turf war over the same sliver of authoritarian real estate, a case of *ote-toi de la, que je m'y mette*,[8] Loewenstein thought. All of those movements were in his view both antidemocratic and illiberal, whatever their *stated* ideological goals. Writing only a few years later and anticipating such frankly fascistic modern mass movements as the one that styles itself "Antifa," Erich Fromm wrote: "The crisis of democracy is not a peculiarly Italian or German problem, but

---

6 Reinhold Niebuhr, *Moral Man and Immoral Society*, 1932.

7 If Joseph Stalin wasn't a fascist, no one was. It wasn't just his mustache that Saddam Hussein imitated.

8 As Senator Kennedy said to Senator Dodd while making a "waitress sandwich" at La Brasserie.

one confronting every modern state. Nor does it matter which symbols the enemies of human freedom choose: freedom is not less endangered if attacked in the name of anti-Fascism or in that of outright Fascism."[9]

Loewenstein insisted that liberal democracy was poorly positioned to defend itself, burdened as it was with toleration, openness, freedom of exchange, and its commitment to open access to the political system. What liberal democracy needed in his judgment was access to the arsenal of authoritarianism, such weapons as banning political parties or shutting down newspapers, using illiberal methods in specific and limited cases to defend itself from illiberalism in its fuller expressions.

Loewenstein argued that fascism was not an *ideology* but a *technique*, which it is—one that is independent of any particular policy content and that can be made to serve any political agenda, from Hitler's psychotic Jew-hatred to Mussolini's romantic corporatism to Stalin's "scientific" socialism to Antifa's self-professed antifascism. The classical technique of fascism described by Loewenstein relied on exploiting nationalism or other appeals to solidarity, together with[10] newly available forms of media and communication that could be harnessed to achieve "a supersession of constitutional government by emotional government." One wonders what he might have made of twenty-first century social media: "The technical devices for

---

9 It should not be entirely surprising that the functional fascists and notional antifascists of our time are the same people—that certainly was the case in the 1930s. And here I will do that weird thing of quoting myself as an outside source, from my *National Review* essay of December 26, 2018: "Antifa has hijacked the name of an earlier German organization, *Antifaschistische Aktion*, a front for the Communist Party of Germany, itself a creature of Moscow and no stranger to authoritarianism, political repression, and political violence. The Communist Party of Germany was banned in 1956 by the same constitutional court that prohibits neo-Nazi organizations."

10 And now this will start to sound awfully familiar.

mobilizing emotionalism are ingenious and of amazing variety and efficacy," he wrote, "although recently become more and more standardized.[11] Among them, besides high-pitched nationalist enthusiasm, the most important expedient, perhaps, is permanent psychic coercion, at times amounting to intimidation and terrorization[12] scientifically applied."

Fascism, in Loewenstein's conception, wasn't founded on corporatist economics, anti-Semitism, or glorification of the military—though it could be put into the service of any of those things, as needed, and put them into its own service as easily. "If fascism is not a spiritual flame shooting across the borders," Loewenstein wrote, "it is obviously only a technique for gaining and holding power, for the sake of power alone, without that metaphysical justification which can be derived from absolute values only."

But whose absolute values provide the metaphysical justification for authoritarian interventions on behalf of liberalism? And what limiting principle, if any, controls such interventions? Without honest and intelligent engagement with those issues, Loewenstein's principle can all too easily degenerate into a pretext.

Karl Popper came up against the same problem in *The Open Society and Its Enemies*.[13] In one much-abused footnote, he writes:

> Unlimited tolerance must lead to the disappearance of tolerance. If we extend unlimited tolerance even to those who are intolerant, if we are not prepared to defend a tolerant society against the onslaught of the intolerant, then the

---

11 Систематическая, you might say.

12 "Of course you have the right to be a Jew or a trade-unionist, but you don't have the right not to be criticized for it, you Semitic vermin who is the source of the suffering of the decent and hardworking common *Volk*..."

13 1945.

tolerant will be destroyed, and tolerance with them. In this formulation, I do not imply, for instance, that we should always suppress the utterance of intolerant philosophies; as long as we can counter them by rational argument and keep them in check by public opinion, suppression would certainly be unwise. But we should claim the right to suppress them if necessary even by force; for it may easily turn out that they are not prepared to meet us on the level of rational argument, but begin by denouncing all argument; they may forbid their followers to listen to rational argument, because it is deceptive, and teach them to answer arguments by the use of their fists or pistols. We should therefore claim, in the name of tolerance, the right not to tolerate the intolerant.

There is something that is alluring to a certain kind of mind about imagining scenarios in which such suppression by force might be desirable.[14] A great deal of effort goes into the construction of hypotheticals; upon examination, it is clear that most of these hypotheticals are not thought experiments aimed at helping us to understand the choices that a liberal society must make but instead are pretexts engineered as justifications for a preexisting desire to engage in suppression.

The easiest and most direct way of beginning to sort this out is to ask the question: What is the goal of the suppression that is under consideration? Is it to prevent the communication of some unpopular idea or point of view on the grounds that suppression is a good in and of itself, because such utterances are inherently evil? Or is the

---

14 Some of my friends in Texas spend a great deal more time talking about the situations in which it is legal to shoot somebody than the facts of daily life in Dallas or Houston require.

goal of the proposed suppression to prevent some concrete evil that is near in proximity to the actual events of the time? This will, I think, at least allow us to consider that there may be no national-security case for asking the POWERS THAT BE AT MOJO BURRITO to act as deputies in the Thought Police. It might, if our interlocutors could muster the honesty for a moment or two, permit us to frankly admit that the campaign to keep Milo Yiannapoulos from publishing books has really nothing at all to do with preventing some hypothetical act of pederasty[15] and everything to do with the fact that many people do not like him. Is there some evil that is likely to come into the world from a Milo Yiannopoulos book other than the book itself? It is a difficult case to make. If the communication itself is the only real objection, then we are not talking about public safety or anything of the sort. We are talking about intellectual and political repression for its own sake, and nothing more.

If we are willing to give a hypothetical evil a moral weight equal to that of an actual evil, then there is no limiting principle at all that is possible, because it is easy to construct an unfalsifiable counter-factual in which practically any particular kind of political communication we find objectionable could contribute to an illiberal or undemocratic outcome, or a criminal one, in some hypothetical scenario. If we allow the publication of *Lolita*, then somebody may be inspired to molest a child; if we allow the depiction of drug abuse in films, then that might inspire drug abuse in suggestible young people and idiots; if we allow too much criticism of the so-called war on terror, then we endanger the protection of citizens' other rights, etc. One of the conclusions that I hope the reader will take from the sum of the arguments in this book is that hypothetical evils are generally preferable to real ones, and that the real evils of censorship and

---

15 I suppose no one reads Gore Vidal anymore.

suppression are considerably worse than the hypothetical troubles that a more liberal attitude toward unpopular speech might risk.

Streitbare Demokratie is today an important German constitutional principle, an idea deeply embedded in the architecture of German government and law. It provides the theoretical basis for German policies that sometimes strike classical liberals in the Anglo-American mode as overbearing and autocratic: prohibiting certain political parties and certain political symbols, forbidding certain candidates to stand for election, criminalizing the communication of certain kinds of political thought, censoring neo-Nazi literature, and treating as criminal offenses acts that would in the United States, and much of the free world, be considered ordinary and unremarkable parts of politics, from giving speeches to holding rallies. For a classical liberal, that kind of suppression is difficult to countenance, but it is not difficult to *understand*, given Germany's recent history. We may not think that Germany *should* do that, but we can at least understand *why* it does that.

What about everybody else? That is less obvious.

The majority of citizens in the United States, like the majority of citizens in most liberal democracies, very much believe that democracies *should* engage in precisely such suppression as a matter of moral and political hygiene, at least in some situations. In the United States, a majority of Democrats support censoring so-called hate speech and prosecuting as *criminals* those who say and think forbidden things, while 43 percent of Republicans support empowering the president to censor news outlets "engaged in bad behavior."[16] A very

---

16 YouGov poll, May 20, 2015; Ipsos poll, August 7, 2018, respectively.

large bipartisan majority agrees with President Donald Trump that US libel laws should be revised to make it easier to take retaliatory legal action against members of the press. The long-term polling on censorship as it relates to national security, privately funded political activism, racial and religious sensitivities, etc., finds a great deal of support for censorship of various kinds, though considerably less if you call it "censorship."[17]

Inevitably, support for censorship and other illiberal policies increases when there is a state of national emergency—real or perceived. "Democracies withstood the ordeal of the World War much better than did autocratic states—by adopting autocratic methods," Loewenstein wrote. "Few seriously objected to the temporary suspension of constitutional principles for the sake of national self-defense. During the war, observes Léon Blum,[18] legality takes a vacation." Here, Loewenstein and Blum both are paying unintentional tribute to Adolf Hitler, who observed that the greatest strength of the totalitarian states is that they force those who fear them to imitate them. That is especially true during times of war, as the United States and the United Kingdom both discovered in different ways.

The problem, here in the United States in sunny uplands of the twenty-first century, is that we are always at war.

---

17 Like much in American politics, this breaks down along class lines. The economist Brian Caplan makes a persuasive case that we should thank our lucky stars that the rich tend to have an outsized influence on American public policy, inasmuch as the rich are slightly less savage in their views than the poor. Surveying the data, he writes: "On distributional issues, there is high consensus. But the rich are noticeably less statist on both economic and social policy. Rich and poor alike favor raising the minimum wage, but the support of the poor is nearly unanimous. The poor are slightly more in favor of extending unemployment benefits. They're much more anti-gay. They're much less opposed to restricting free speech to fight terrorism." ("Why Is Democracy Tolerable? Evidence from Affluence and Influence," The Library of Economics and Liberty). Thank God for Big Money in politics.

18 Three-time socialist prime minister of France.

Or, at least we go to great lengths to convince ourselves that we are.

In a sense we are always at war, the so-called Forever War or Long War that we entered into almost a full generation ago after the events of September 11, 2001. The United States remains, as of this writing, militarily engaged openly in Afghanistan, Syria, Iraq, Pakistan, Somalia, Kenya, Ethiopia, Libya, and elsewhere, with troops stationed everywhere from Germany and Italy to Bahrain, Egypt, Jordan, and Morocco. The paranoia and heightened security—much of it security theater rather than actual security measures—has only grown worse and more expensive in the intervening years. That has provided the suppressors with an invaluable opportunity to train the population in obedience and conformity.

But that is only a small part of the permanent state of emergency in the United States. Every interest group, faction, and policy entrepreneur in the country has a crisis narrative to peddle. The Right blames the rhetoric of the Left every time a cop is ambushed, the Left blames the rhetoric of the Right every time a gay man or a Muslim is assaulted or worse. Traditional protections encoded in the Bill of Rights—not just free speech and freedom of the press but due process and the right ot keep and bear arms—are, we are constantly told, standing in the way of dealing with any number of emergencies. That these "emergencies" are generally cynical fictions and exaggerations constructed on foundations of narrow political self-interest is obvious to anyone with eyes to see—but there do not seem to be very many of us.

Loewenstein was mostly correct about fascism's being a *technique*. What he failed to appreciate is that his *streitbare Demokratie* is a technique, too.

The *same* technique.

Fascism, like many species of authoritarianism, relies on *panic*, and on the related belief that extraordinary measures must be deployed in extraordinary times, that emergencies must be met with unity and—most important—with submission and conformity. The entirety of the American legal doctrine in support of censorship— which goes back to Oliver Wendell Holmes and his "Shout 'fire' in a crowded theater" argument—is founded on the proposition that, during national emergencies, and, especially, during times of war, dissent and criticism will not be tolerated. Justice Holmes, it is worth keeping in mind, first articulated the "crowded theater" standard in a case in which he ruled that the government could ignore the First Amendment and lock up a war protester (Charles Schenk, the sec- retary of the Socialist Party of the United States, was charged with a felony under the Espionage Act for distributing an anti-conscription pamphlet) because the nation was at war. The emergency trumped the constitutional protection, he argued, ruling that "in ordinary times" the defendants "would have been within their constitutional rights. But the character of every act depends upon the circumstances in which it is done." I will have more to say about Justice Holmes and his imaginary theater in subsequent chapters.

If you go looking for an emergency, you will find one. And if you don't find one, you can always make one up: That is the political impetus behind the rash of fake hate crimes on college campuses and the politi- cally charged rape hoaxes advanced by such fabulists as Lena Dunham, *Rolling Stone*, and the accuser in the Duke lacrosse case.[19] The principle at work here is *defining danger down*. If you wish to suppress certain speech or certain points of view, then all that you have to do is construct

---

19 If you doubt that false rape accusations are being deployed as *Kultur*kampf munitions, consider: Lena Dunham fabricated a story about being raped by a College Republican; the rape hoax targeting a fraternity at the University of Virginia was said to illustrate a "larger truth" regarding the problem of "toxic masculinity" and "male privilege" in spite of its being a complete fabrication; the Duke lacrosse case was presented as a matter of both sexual and racial justice; Brett Kavanaugh was said to embody antisocial white male pathologies expressed in a series of gang rapes that never happened, etc.

a crowded theater around it. For example, we might understand and even acquiesce to the suppression of neo-Nazi political propaganda in Germany on *streitbare Demokratie* grounds, especially in the immediate postwar era, when the possibility of a revanchist Nazi movement was far from unthinkable. We might, *arguendo*, accept such censorship in that situation because of the genuine danger that the policy is intended to head off. Likewise, Americans accepted certain kinds of formal and informal censorship during both world wars, and, as Professor Caplan notes, are generally supportive of such measures when they are undertaken in the cause of preventing terrorism. Of course those slopes are slippery—all slopes are. That fact does not liberate us from the necessity of cantering up and down those slopes or relieve us from having to exercise judgment and prudence. The corporate alternatives—such as Facebook's attempt to replace wisdom with the fanatical application of comically malformed rules of discourse—are the product of hubris compounded with a highly cultivated form of stupidity.

The problem for political partisans is that judgment and prudence get in the way of their actual agenda—humiliating their enemies—and the problem for technology firms such as Facebook and Google is that it is too expensive to hire employees who can be counted upon to act with good judgment and prudence, and, in any case, the inevitable failures of those employees would disrupt the organization, hence the emphasis on the mindless and fanatical application of rules that vacillate between the ridiculously vague and the surgically specific.

The rules and laws, and the political assumptions supporting them, are all based on some notion of *safety*. Because abusing those notions of safety creates opportunities for the expression of tribal grievances and hatreds, they are infinitely plastic. But they are not distorted at random in every direction at once. They are distorted almost always in the direction of suppression and restriction. We are constantly *defining danger down*.

Defining danger down consists mainly in elevating the importance of hypothetical evils over real evils. For example, would-be censors argue for the suppression of certain kinds of political speech on the grounds that they might lead to illegal or undesirable behavior: insurrection, sedition, assaults, etc. In order to prevent these hypothetical evils, we are instructed that we must accept real and immediate evils, such as restrictions on speech, invasions of privacy, financial surveillance, limitations on travel to and from our country, and the like.

The hypotheticals in these situations need not be unlikely, though many of them are, owing to the ambient stupidity of life c. 2019 AD; the unlikeliness of a scenario is generally a good indicator of exactly how much intellectual dishonesty went into its construction, as is the distance between the proposed violation of civil liberty and other less invasive and more effective alternatives: "If we don't set aside due-process protections and forbid people on the no-fly list to buy firearms, then we might miss the opportunity to keep a terrorist from carrying out a mass shooting" is a sentiment that is morally and intellectually equal to "If we don't set aside due-process protections and ritually blind all of the people on the no-fly list, then we might miss the opportunity to keep a terrorist from carrying out a mass shooting." To those who generally oppose the right to keep and bear arms, the first sounds reasonable and the second sounds absurd, because they do not take seriously the proposition that the right to keep and bear arms comes under legitimate constitutional protection. Which is to say, the concern about possible terrorism has here been connected to a preexisting hostility toward Second Amendment rights. The proposed limitations on speech work in the same way: If *x* sentiment is expressed in public, then *y* crime is made more likely by some amount, no matter how atomically minuscule or impossible to detect. This is why Caitlyns want to talk about "rape culture" rather than *rape*, and why campus feminists want the job of policing sexual misconduct entrusted to the dean of students rather than to the police, who, whatever their shortcomings, are governed by relatively rigorous standards of evidence, harm, and danger.

These constructions do not take very much intelligence to imagine or to understand (because there is nothing there to understand) and so they are a very popular mode of argument. "Donald Trump is bitterly critical of journalists; journalists sometimes are assaulted and murdered; ergo…"

Defining danger down is, ironically, the basis for a very stupid and destructive line of thinking that is not hypothetical at all, at least in Texas: 40 percent of Americans believe that Islam is *per se* incompatible with American values, and members of the Republican party leadership in Fort Worth have attempted to remove a Muslim officer of the Republican party from his leadership role on the theory that Muslim devotion "is anathema to our Constitution because Islam recognizes no other law but shariah." One could make a notionally plausible if substantively meretricious *defining danger down* argument against both supporting Muslims in public office as easily as against criticizing Muslim beliefs. As political stupidities go, this one is catholic.

Consider the ways in which *defining danger down* can be used in the service of nakedly political goals. For example, transgender people[20] tend to commit suicide at elevated rates and to engage in

---

20 Against my own advice and inclination, I will use this formulation to save myself the trouble of writing "people who believe themselves to be transgender" every time. Suffice it to say for now that I do not believe that the neat little categories into which we try to pigeonhole human sexual behavior and human sexual inclinations have a great deal of explanatory power, and that our classifications are based mostly on superstition and political expediency. I have an essay titled "Alcoholism as a Sexual Orientation" sitting around here, somewhere.

other forms of self-harm.²¹ And, like most people, transgender
people do not much care for criticism or disagreement about things
they feel strongly about, particularly when those things are of a
personal and intimate nature. Trans advocates have argued that
the heightened incidence of suicide in the trans community constitutes an emergency justification for suppressing certain kinds of
speech such as "misgendering" (refusing to cooperate with a transgender person's desire to be socially accepted as a member of the
opposite sex) and "deadnaming" (using the given or legal name of
a trans person who has adopted a new one). In May of 2014, I wrote
a column for *National Review*, subsequently published in the *Chicago Sun-Times*, in which I argued that transgender celebrity
Laverne Cox is not a woman in the same sense that natural-born
women with ovaries and the capacity to become pregnant and give
birth to children are women. This constituted a rare point of agreement between me and a number of radical feminists who hold the
same view.

Transgender advocates argued quite in earnest that I should be
prosecuted as a criminal for writing such things, on the grounds that
my doing so might lead an emotionally fragile transgender person
to commit suicide. Similar pretexts have been put forward for real
and desired prosecutions of thought crimes. Seven Italian scientists

---

21 Sometimes with the assistance of very expensive doctors who have convinced
themselves, their victims, and society at large that ritual genital mutilation is
therapeutic. I do not write that simply to be provocative. What the medical journals call
"gender dysphoria" is no laughing matter, and it is difficult to imagine anybody putting
themselves through the more invasive kinds of surgical transition on a lark. I cannot
help but think that a society that was more generally tolerant of nonconformity—
including sex-role nonconformity—would go a long way toward mitigating at least the
social burdens associated with the condition. Ironically, the self-appointed guardians of
the interests of these people demand a more conformist society on the mistaken belief
that the social power they hold at the moment is likely to be a permanent thing rather
than a temporary vogue.

were charged, convicted of manslaughter (the convictions were later overturned) and given years in prison for having given *opinions* about a certain seismic question in L'Aquila that turned out to be wrong; building on that precedent, American academics and activists have sought to have activists, scientists, policy researchers, and business executives holding nonconforming views on global warming prosecuted as criminals,[22] on the theory that their opinions are endangering the public.

That kind of *defining danger down* is a neat political trick, with the would-be suppressor acting as both hostage and hostage-taker. Irrespective of one's views on transgender-related issues, it is incontrovertible that the prospect of a writer's contributing, however minutely, to a cultural climate that is uncomfortable to transgender people is in a different category of things from shoving Jews into ovens or organizing an effort to shove Jews into ovens. If you cannot understand that, then you should probably stop reading here, because you are not packing the neural gear for either of us to benefit from further conversation.

As a practical matter, *defining danger down* creates an irresistible opportunity for cultural tit-for-tat. If vaguely contributing to a cultural current that might lead to or simply encourage an act of physical violence (self-inflicted violence, in the case of the transgender hypothetical) is grounds for censorship and for setting aside First Amendment protections, then a lot of surly old Protestants in red Make America Great Again caps are going to start taking a keen interest in the sermons at their local mosques and in Antifa communiqués. In fact, some of them already do, but we have been mostly sensible about that kind of thing.

---

22 Adam Weinstein, "Arrest Climate-Change Deniers," *Gawker*, 2016; Professor Lawrence Torcello, "Is Misinformation about the Climate Criminally Negligent?", Rochester Institute of Technology, *The Conversation*, March 13, 2014.

The invention or exaggeration of social threats tends to escalate as institutions grow weaker and populism—acting in the name of "democracy"—overwhelms traditional civil-liberties protections and legal procedure. Consider the case of Rodrigo Duterte's homicidal campaign against drug users in the Philippines. There is a problem with addiction and drug-related crime in the Philippines, but the point of Duterte's terrorism is *terrorism*, not drug control. Like all populists, Duterte is eternally at war with liberal norms and the constitutional protections associated with them. Violating those norms in a dramatic and emotionally vindicating fashion is not a means to some policy end—it is the end itself. As Max Fisher writes in the *New York Times*:

> Populist backlashes, even if they focus on distant elites, tend to emerge as a desire for majority rule, which feels democratic to members of the majority—and, in certain circumstances, like a matter of life and death.
>
> Human beings are tribal by nature. Our instincts are to put our group first and see ourselves as locked in competition with other groups. Liberal democracy, which promises that everyone gains when rights are protected for all, asks us to suppress those impulses.
>
> But this is no easy ask. And tribal instincts tend to come to the fore in times of scarcity or insecurity, when our capacity for lofty ideals and long-term planning is weakest.
>
> When people believe they are at risk of targeted violence, their sense of community narrows.... They grow more supportive of policies to control minorities and less supportive of pluralism or democracy.
>
> Those impulses can be exploited.

The grisly campaign of state-sanctioned vigilante violence by President Rodrigo Duterte of the Philippines pins his country's problems on an undesirable social class—in his telling, a vast army of drug dealers and users—and promises to control them through force. [Jair] Bolsonaro has promised his own extrajudicial war on drugs.[23]

Duterte's drug addicts are his substitute for Stalin's *kulaks*,[24] Elizabeth Warren's "1 percent," Donald Trump's "swamp,"[25] everyone else's "elites," and Antifa's imaginary fascists. They have little or nothing to do with the troubles, real or imaginary, afflicting the constituencies in question. But they provide a pretext for the thrilling violation of legal and constitutional norms. The difference between Duterte's death squads and Antifa is only that the American black-shirts engage in relatively petty violence that generally stops short of murder and more spectacular forms of terrorism.[26] But the principle is the same. The violation of liberal and democratic norms, the abuse of hated minorities or other social villains, the imposition of legal and social burdens on one's rivals as a form of public humiliation— all of these are strategies in yet another status game. Duterte, Trump, and Putin—or such moldering heroes of the Left as Fidel Castro, Hugo Chávez, and Robert F. Kennedy, Jr.—flout the law and the norms of decent government in order to make statements about their

---

23 Max Fisher, "The Weaknesses in Liberal Democracy That May Be Pulling It Apart," *New York Times*, November 1, 2018.

24 "Dekulakization" and the associated campaign for socialist collectivization killed about 11 million people, nearly twice the number of Jews murdered in the Holocaust and sixteen times the number of people who died in the American Civil War.

25 Also his scheming Chinamen, Mexicans, "enemies of the people" in the media . . .

26 But not always. In November of 2012, three Occupy activists were sentenced to prison for conspiring to blow up a bridge in Cleveland.

own high status and about the low status of those who are forced to endure those violations.

Liberal societies do face authentic threats from time to time—the Soviet Union a generation ago, Islamist fanaticism today. Working out what, if anything, to do on free-speech questions in the face of a genuine threat on the order of the Third Reich or al-Qaeda is a difficult enough task for intelligent people acting in good faith. But we are not talking here about good-faith efforts. We are talking about boorish and puerile attempts to use the principle of *streitbare Demokratie* as a pretext to censor political speech, or other kinds of speech, on the grounds that one simply does not want to hear it—or, more accurately, in order to savor the exquisite pleasure that mental and emotional weaklings take in exercising momentary power—declaring their superior status—over the people they hate. No one seriously believes that permitting Ann Coulter to give a speech on a college campus is going to put this republic three tweets away from the Holocaust—and no self-respecting adult with normal mental function should willingly endure being roped into the pretense that this is anything other than mental midgetry and moral absurdity.

But peons must have conformity. The instinct to seek it is in their souls. It is what makes them peons. It is the essence of peonhood.

And if peons are to have conformity, then they must have an emergency—a permanent, eternal, hysteria-inducing emergency that provides them with a notional case for doing what they really want to do, which is to exercise power over people they desire to hurt and humiliate and to use that punitive instinct as an organizing principle for community life. Which is to say: The antifascists are indistinguishable from the fascists.

"Some people will never live comfortably in a modern liberal democracy," behavioral economist Karen Stenner[27] wrote in 2005's *The Authoritarian Dynamic*. "A particular type of person: one who cannot treat with natural ease or generosity those who are not his own kindred or kind, who is inclined to believe only 'right-thinking' people should be free to air their opinions, and who tends to see others' moral choices as everybody's business—indeed, the business of the state.... People who—by virtue of deep-seated predispositions neither they nor we have much capacity to alter—will always be imperfect democratic citizens, and only discouraged from infringing others' rights and liberties by responsible leadership, the force of law, fortuitous societal conditions, and near-constant reassurance." Stenner, who holds a doctorate in political psychology, describes her work as offering "a general account of the conditions under which a large proportion (around a third) of humanity, who harbor (relatively immutable) predispositions to favor 'oneness and sameness' over freedom and diversity, come to find their societies and polities intolerable, and push back with a vengeance. In essence, it is about the limits to liberal democracy. But it is written with a desire to save liberal democracy (from itself)."

Call it *streitbare Psychologie*.

Stenner's model of the "authoritarian dynamic" has two parts: first, the relatively immutable and probably heritable orientation[28]

---

27 Stenner's work tends to focus on the so-called far right and, recently, on the Donald Trump movement, though she sees similarities in the authoritarianism of, say, the Nation of Islam and classic right-wing fantasies about Zionist conspiracies to impose one-world government, which, of course, she would: Jew-hating weirdos are first and foremost Jew-hating weirdos, and racial differences come second. You'll recall David Duke's outreach to black separatists and Louis Farrakhan's footsie-playing with white-power majordomo Tom Metzger. In another paper, Stenner criticizes a scholar for defining "conservatism" in a "manner virtually indistinguishable from authoritarianism," but it seems to me that she slips into the same bad habit from time to time.

28 The authoritarian tendency is, apparently, a preexisting condition.

toward authoritarianism, and, second, a set of social conditions or events that "activates" those tendencies—a disruption. She describes that interaction in a highly regarded paper coauthored with Professor Stanley Feldman of Stony Brook University, "Perceived Threat and Authoritarianism."[29] Essentially, Stenner and Feldman give an account of *authoritarianism* that is substantially identical to Loewenstein's *fascism*, with a focus on the character of the *followers* rather than the strategy of the *leader*. The Stenner-Feldman analysis draws in part on Fromm, whose *Escape from Freedom*[30] I already have discussed at some length. Fromm argued that authoritarianism was rooted in a general and predominant sense of anxiety and in social stresses that are, in his analysis, inevitable features of capitalism.[31] But modern researchers are more interested in the question of how authoritarianism is aggravated by specific events and immediate threats and stresses, such as the Great Depression or the social disorder in the United States (and elsewhere) in the late 1960s. The Stenner-Feldman model (concurring with the views of most scholars on the subject) holds that authoritarianism is a largely immutable personality trait, and those are not supposed to change[32] in the face of transient events. Hence the Stenner-Feldman emphasis on "activation" of those tendencies:

---

29 *Political Psychology*, Vol. 18, No. 4 (December, 1997).

30 Erich Fromm is, of course, up to his intellectual ass in now-discredited (and generally ridiculed) Freudian horsepucky, but there's still a lot of interesting stuff in there—and he had the number of our contemporary social-media celebrities long before there was such a thing.

31 Fromm was a socialist steeped in the thinking of Karl Marx, which tragically deformed much of his political thinking. His "socialist humanism" emphasized the themes of freedom found in Marx and in the early libertarian socialists, but he was perversely unable to see how and where in the world human freedom and human flourishing reached their fullest expression.

32 That's what "immutable" means, Skippy.

Perhaps it is not authoritarianism itself that increases in the face of transient environmental threats, but rather the *relationship* between authoritarianism and its attitudinal and behavioral manifestations or consequences, like intolerance. This implies that the typically observed consequences of authoritarianism result from an interaction between authoritarian predispositions and threat.... Moreover, since even paper-and-pencil measures of authoritarianism[33] are still indirect indicators of an unobserved construct, it is possible that the observed increases in the scale scores reflect an increased salience of authoritarian predispositions—and thereby increased *manifestation* of authoritarianism—in the face of threat, rather than actual changes in the underlying trait.

Without going[34] into the deep and humid and mosquito-infested psychological weeds here, what's essential to understand is that Stenner and Feldman are offering a partial sketch of Loewenstein's fascist "technique" and its psychological basis: *threat*.[35] If

---

33 Some of which are downright hilarious, a reminder that social scientists are generally unable to transcend their times and places and the little human details associated with them. Indicators of authoritarianism in the psychological research have included the themes in comic books and the incidence of attack-dog purchases.

34 (too much further)

35 Considering the case of mandatory loyalty oaths for some government employees and other invasive security measures in the postwar era, peace activist Roy C. Kepler offered a useful approach, and a sensible one: "There is little question that the loyalty and security programs negate many personal freedoms, and are bidding fair to undermine some of the foundation supports of democratic and constitutional government to the degree that it has been achieved in the United States.... I would like to suggest that when we are given these choices between two evils, that we should choose, not in the old sense, the 'lesser one,' but rather that we should choose the *hypothetical* one." *MANAS Journal*, August 1954. NB: The author was apparently still spelling his name "Keplbr" in 1954, but the Bay Area knows him as the founder of Kepler's Books.

there are events and social conditions that can activate the authoritarian tendencies latent in something like one-third of the general
population, then it should be possible to cultivate those conditions—to intentionally and systematically activate the authoritarian instincts within any political group, whether a formal political
organization or a loosely defined coalition of overlapping political
and cultural affiliations. And the easiest and most direct way to do
that—on this we have the testimony of everyone from ancient political philosophers to modern behavioral economists—is to encounter, discover, or fabricate a threat.[36]

The authoritarian political entrepreneur appeals to traditional
in-group–out-group hatred and distrust, economic insecurity and
status anxiety, old-fashioned ethnic and religious bigotry—anything that creates a threat locus that is *exterior, specific,* and *easily
defined*. The most masterly example of that in our recent politics
was Occupy Wall Street's successful effort to make the "1 percent[37]"
the great villains of the world's social drama, though the social-
justice progressives' efforts to make "white male" a term of social

---

36 Which, if you think about it, helps to explain the seemingly insane trend among
young people circa 2019 of fabricating hate crimes, writing racist notes to themselves
or vandalizing their own property or going so far as to injure themselves to falsify
evidence of violent attacks. Of course they want to hurt and discredit their perceived
political and social enemies, but what they are mainly trying to do, in their perverse
and generally batshit crazy way, is to create community. Fascism and its intellectual
cousins, from Buchanan-Trump paleoconservatism to the CAFFEINE-FREE DIET
MAOISM of Occupy and Antifa, is all about community: Who's in, who's out, and
who's fucked.

37 The "1 percent" also has the added attraction of being *imaginary*: The people who
constitute the top 1 percent of income earners are different from year to year, with
turnover rates for high-income groups running pretty high: 75 percent from 1996 to
2005 in a Treasury Department study. The median household incomes of families in
the top 1 percent in 1996 went down over the next decade, even as the median income
of the statistical abstract that is the top 1 percent went up: The income of the category
went up while the income of category members went down *because* their income
went down enough that they were no longer in the category. But the Koch brothers,
or something.

opprobrium have made some headway, too, complicating Stenner's observations on the authoritarian targeting of racial *minorities.*[38]

For the authoritarian *follower,* the villain creates a sense of immediacy, urgency, and solidarity that confers meaning on their lives.[39] For the authoritarian *leader,* the villain provides a way to turn complexity into simplicity, acting as a kind of political solvent by means of which all of a complex society's complex challenges are rendered into perfect simplicity—*Those* problems become *this* problem, and *this* problem becomes: Them—the Jews, the Illuminati, the 1 Percent, the Republicans, the Democrats, frat boys, feminists, whomever. The demagogue always and everywhere speaks to the problem of complexity. As John Harris put it in *The Guardian:* "Their basic approach is: a withering look at the labyrinthine realties of trade, technology, population movement, international agreements, and the rest, followed by the simplest of answers: 'Take back control,' 'Make America Great Again.'"[40]

In the 1930s, the Us-vs.-Them dynamic was made visible through a variety of props, such as uniforms: black shirts, brown shirts, red shirts,[41] etc. The days of jackboots and armbands seem to be mostly behind us, but the red hats of the Trump movement and the black masks of Antifa perform the same function—they are team colors.[42]

---

38 Contextual "minorities," I suppose, though not literal minorities—another way of saying "out-group." But notice that as the power of white men declines and as the white share of the population declines, attacks on white men as such have grown more bitter and more bold, and more plainly racist.

39 And that, dear friends, is sad as fuck.

40 "The lesson of Trump and Brexit: a society too complex for its people risks everything," *The Guardian,* December 26, 2016.

41 Things were pretty shirty, indeed.

42 In practically every American city with a professional sports team and criminal gangs, there is a gang that has adopted the local sports team's jersey as its colors, which is ingeniously efficient from a marketing point of view. Weirdly, though, some of them adopt the swag of out-of-town franchises: The Rollin' 60s in Los Angeles, a Crips affiliate, sport Seattle Mariner caps, which are appropriately Crip blue. The Gangster Disciples wear Georgetown caps and consider HOYA to be an acronym for "Hoover's On Your Ass," a reference to Larry Hoover, their founder.

But our politics have evolved in ways that make those kinds of things less essential. The most important change is the migration of politics away from the public space and onto the Internet, particularly on social media. We still have rallies and protests, and acts of political theater such as Occupy Wall Street and the antics of Gavin McInnes and his estranged Proud Boys. And it *is* theater:[43] The tiki torches at the "Unite the Right" march in Charlottesville were not *incidental*—the ancient ritual of the firelight procession was the whole point,[44] along with the community-building experience of being screamed at by strangers, the age-old adolescent male ceremony of creating a stressful situation for yourselves so that you can congratulate yourselves on your courage after enduring it. As distasteful (and, in the Charlottesville case, murderous) as these events may be, they are very much a part of traditional democratic politics, meaning the democratic politics of human meat physically present in public spaces. But the new militant democracy lives on social media, where the marks of affiliations are hashtags and memes rather than uniforms and banners.

---

43 White-nationalist gadfly Richard Spencer is a major theater nerd. I interviewed him in 2018, and he went on and on about Robert Wilson and experimental theater in the 1980s. I thought about offering to take him to *Hamilton*, which would have made for a fun report/riot, but it was really hard to get tickets, since I was not running for governor of Florida at the time.

44 In the 1990s, I covered a protest by the wonderfully insane Lesbian Avengers, a group of women whose favored form of protest was circus-style fire-eating. "The fire will not consume us!" they chanted. "We will take it and make it our own." They were kicking off a campaign through the South starting at the courthouse in Vidor, Texas, which had been the scene of some Ku Klux Klan activity. They were really, really disappointed that nobody came to counter-protest or spit at them or even offer a drive-by insult. Eventually, a bowlegged little old man got out of a red pickup and approached the group: "You ladies have a right under the First Amendment to protest," he said, "but I'm the local fire marshal, and we try to teach our kids not to play with matches. And I don't think you're setting a very good example." And he tottled off. That "you ladies" made the whole trip worth it.

Political rallies and vexillological exertions require organization, leadership, planning, and institutions. Soft ochlocracy and its most common manifestation—the social-media mob—do not. In fact, contemporary hardcore partisans disdain such things as relics of the hated "establishment," which is regarded by the ochlocrats Left and Right alike—who are inevitably puritanical—as *impure* and morally compromised. ("Compromise" itself has become a term of opprobrium.) This is part of the apparent paradox of our current political climate, which Julia Azari aptly described in *Vox*[45] as the combination of strong *partisanship* with weak *parties*. That combination moves politics away from questions of *policy* and toward questions of *identity*. Identity is more accessible than policy, which requires effort. As Azari observed:

> While party organizations are concrete, partisanship as an idea is abstract. Partisan identity tells us who shares our beliefs, and it helps to make political meaning, conveying important truths about the world through symbols. It is in these cracks of abstraction that truly pathological politics grows.
>
> ... The more abstract party identification is, the more resentment can fester against people whom you do not know or encounter, whose lives you have not considered, but who seem like useful targets for your frustration.
>
> Abstractions allow citizens to ignore the full implications of their views—and to neglect to consider other citizens. This makes it a lot easier to ascribe bad intent to them, or to blame them for your problems.

---

45 "Weak parties and strong partisanship are a bad combination," *Vox*, November 3, 2016.

Here we should probably take a moment to at least try to partly disentangle the historical and rhetorical baggage of *fascism* from the more general *authoritarian* tendency, or at the very least to acknowledge that they are overlapping tendencies and not a single phenomenon. All fascism is authoritarian, but not all authoritarianism is fascist. Those distinctions are important, but they are not really germane to my thesis here. What I am writing about is the intersection of moral, political, and psychological factors that sustains not only the illiberalism of fascism[46] as such but also that of bullying ochlocrats, Antifa arsonists, social-media scalp-hunters, and other similarly sorry specimens of hysteria and emotional incontinence that congeal into real-world and online mobs for the sake of suppressing views and beliefs that they wish to see eliminated, or at least rendered inexpressible. They are single-purpose fascists.

All of them follow the Stenner-Feldman/Loewenstein pattern: The leaders invent, hype, or exaggerate an out-group threat, make appeals to in-group solidarity, and, empowered by the purported emergency they have manufactured, set about on a course of sundry illiberal and authoritarian actions aimed not at persuasion or

---

46 I lived for a while in Bombay, which we apparently are now supposed to call "Mumbai." Do you know why we're supposed to call it that? Because Bombay has long been governed by an actual fascist political party called Shiv Sena, or Shivaji's Army, Shivaji being the Hindu hero who turned back the Muslim invaders and saved his Hindu kingdom from what right-wing Hindu nationalists describe as Abrahamic pollution. (Yes, they hate the Muslims, but they're none too keen on Jews and Christians, either.) Shiv Sena in the 1990s was led by a daft newspaper cartoonist named Bal Thackeray, who liked to pose for photographs with tigers and palled around with Michael Jackson. He set about purging not only English but also Hindi names for local institutions and landmarks, insisting on the regional language, Marathi. Hence, "Mumbai." But if you ask a "Mumbai" taxi driver to take you to Chhatrapati Shivaji Terminus Railway Station, he'll look at you funny, because he still calls it "Victoria Terminus."

argument[47] but at *suppression*, removing the out-group enemy from the public square, cutting them off from the realm of ordinary democratic discourse. The means range from attacking their employment (the main method of keeping gay men out of public life in the 1950s "Lavender Menace" hysteria) to hampering their political communication (Google, Twitter, and Facebook have proved invaluable allies to the mob in this) to carrying out acts of actual political violence and making threats of violence. "Militant democracy," whether they cite the concept or only vaguely intuit it, provides the moral pretext for pursuing vindictive and repressive courses of action that in ordinary times would be considered at least illiberal, and possibly even illegal.[48]

When the threat is perceived to be sufficiently dire, tolerance and intolerance become just another couple of stratagems in the team sport of political rivalry, which is only a proxy for a deeper and more fundamental cultural convulsion.[49] Stenner writes:

> Authoritarians and libertarians are mobilized in defense
> of that which they value only when those valued ends
> appear to be in jeopardy. For each side, this will be when
> they are induced to fear that those ends, and the social

---

47 The Antifa mob that assaulted the home of Fox News personality Tucker Carlson did not stand out there chanting "You're wrong about immigration policy!" They chanted (at his wife, who was alone in the house, terrified and locked in a pantry) nothing but threats: "We know where you sleep at night." It's the twenty-first century version of a cross-burning.

48 Brendan Eich of Mozilla, for example, was chased out of his job over his political views in California, a state in which politics-based employment discrimination is forbidden by civil-rights law. And, of course, fire-bombing college buildings is illegal, too, even when Ann Coulter or some other ghastly hunk of prom-queen jerky is scheduled to speak there.

49 I'll have much more to say about this later, but the short version is this: Social media and the culture surrounding it has, by establishing instantaneous and worldwide channels of communication, forced a great many insignificant people to face their insignificance.

arrangements that serve them, might be at risk, or starting to seem too risky for the collective... Mean levels of intolerance may remain constant or even decline. But it will be a very different world indeed.

The aggregate result of activating this dynamic will be deeply intensified value conflict across the tolerance domain, sharply polarized politics, and enormously increased demands upon the polity: for greater *and* lesser discrimination against minorities and restrictions on immigration; for more *and* fewer limits on free speech, assembly, and association; for stricter and softer policies on common rites, abortion, censorship, and homosexuality; for harsher *and* more lenient punishment.

Examples of this phenomenon are easy enough to cite, i.e. the argument that the same urgent pursuit of justice that obliges us to refuse to tolerate controversial figures' engaging in political *speech* on college campuses also obliges us to tolerate (as acts of legitimate political expression) genuine political *violence* aimed at preventing that dissident speech. Essentially: "*Our* dissidence is the highest form of patriotism; *your* dissidence is a crime against humanity." It is worth reemphasizing that this is not a line of thinking that *could* plausibly be associated with political violence at some point in the theoretical future: the violence is with us already, right here and right now.

How far the followers follow their leaders down that path is not a question of no importance—calling for Tucker Carlson to be fired for his political views is one thing, attacking his wife in their home is another—but that should not obscure the fact that these behaviors are part of a single continuum, one that celebrates *intolerance* as a *virtue*—a wartime virtue for a society in a state of constant if soft civil war: the eternal *Kulturkampf* of twenty-first century politics in the liberal democracies. Embracing intolerance as a virtue is the hallmark of all fanaticism, political or religious. Intolerance and cruelty are advanced as good in and of themselves: "The uniting principle of the anti-fascist front is this: every time fascists announce an event, that event gets cancelled," writes the leftist activist Asaid Haider. "Nazis should be afraid to appear in public. Either you help make that happen, or you're a collaborator."[50] This is familiar sophomoric stuff, the rhetorical scheme (it is not quite an argument) that one's opponents are so uniquely wicked that they must be considered intolerable, that they cannot be permitted even to speak. The hypothetical evil—the risible proposition that these basement-dwelling fantasists are part of an emerging National Socialist regime in the United States—is taken seriously; the real evil—the suppression of speech, the fact that one's fellow citizens are made to be fearful—is transmuted into a necessary social prophylactic.

One of Donald Trump's gifts as a politician runs parallel to Adolf Hitler's observation about the power of totalitarian states: He inspires his enemies to imitate him. If you listen to the advertisements for the programs on SiriusXM's Progress station, home of such left-wing broadcasters as Michelangelo Signorile and Thom Hartmann, Trump's success is confirmed as a matter of political *style*: The rhetoric among his opponents is entirely Trumpified. They boast that they "kick conservative ass," they promise fights and catharsis, and they offer bitter, recriminatory tales of Us against Them. Signorile in particular (perhaps because of his similar New York City background) is pure Trump in his rage. Like Trump—like most demagogues—his language is that of religious deliverance: He is, he says, "converting people from the nasty, vicious, perverted right-wing

---

50 "Those Who Refuse," Verso Books, August 14, 2017.

agenda." *Conversion*—people will always tell you what they are thinking, if you will listen. There can be tolerance of disagreement; there can be no tolerance of sin, because that tolerance invites the larger and more serious sin of *scandal*.

In this rhetoric, Torquemada alternates with the Man of the World, the realist. It is the good-cop/bad-cop act of twenty-first century politics. But even the realism is not understood in purely functional terms: Realism, too, is ablaze with holy fire.

Julian Benda considered the case of these schoolyard ayatollahs in *The Treason of the Intellectuals*. Their litany, he writes, is

> [t]he extolling of harshness, and the scorn for human love—pity, charity, benevolence. Here again, the modern intellectuals are the *moralists* of realism. They are not content to remind the world that harshness is necessary in order "to succeed" and that charity is an encumbrance, nor have they limited themselves to preaching to their nation or party what Zarathrustra preached to his disciples: "Be hard, be pitiless, and in this way dominate." They proclaim the moral nobility of harshness and the ignominy of charity.... We can observe how the modern realists have advanced beyond their predecessors. When Machiavelli declares that "a Prince in order to maintain his power is forced to government in a manner contrary to charity and humanity," he is simply saying that to act contrary to charity may be a practical necessity, but he does not in the least suggest that charity is a degradation of the soul.

The idea of intolerance as a virtue is hardly new—it is part of every puritanical religious movement from the original iconoclasts to John Calvin's bloodlust to the *takfiri* tendency in Islam. The perceived need for ritual communal purification[51] is practically universal and generally murderous: Of *course* the adulteress must be stoned—tolerating her sin once it has become a matter of public knowledge would endanger the entirety of the community. The toleration of some transgression—and not any particular transgression itself—is the threat that animates and empowers the modern illiberal impulse. Ironically, our thoroughgoing secularists and enlightened humanists have, here on the bleeding edge of social evolution, reached back into classical Catholic thinking and rediscovered the concept of "scandal," the intellectual nexus where militant democracy meets the Church Militant. It is, in short, the belief that toleration for nonconforming ideas or actions is a public danger in that the public example will lead to undesirable changes in public behavior—another form of argument from emergency.

There is a certain irony—and familiarity—in the psychological literature on authoritarianism, which in the English-speaking world has for years been largely defined as a right-wing phenomenon; indeed, the popular work on the issue undertaken by Bob Altemeyer beginning in the 1980s explicitly labels the phenomenon "right-wing authoritarianism" and labels it a "personality variable," calling to mind the Soviet psychiatrists who discovered, *mirabile dictu*, that opposition to Communism is a mental disorder, not a failure of "scientific" socialism. Psychologists use an "RWA" scale to measure right-wing authoritarianism.

Altemeyer himself hilariously insists that he doesn't mean to indicate anything right-wing by his use of the words "right-wing"—there

---

51 One of the worst consequences of the laziness and stupidity of the English-speaking news media is its distortion of the language, i.e. adopting the genocidal euphemism "ethnic cleansing" as a term of ordinary political discourse. You can take your Sapir-Whorf hypothesis straight-up and strong or on the rocks with a chaser, but we think in language, and language matters.

are some dumb social scientists in the world, but it is difficult to credit stupidity of that kind in a man who by all accounts is fully capable of tying his own shoes—but instead means something more like "conventional" or "obedient," someone who is inclined to go along with familiar authority figures and their demands. The American Right and Left both have their share of would-be suppressors, censors, and worse, but it is by and large people on the right who are at the moment targeted for their unwillingness to mold themselves—which is to say, to *subordinate* themselves—to what is conventional. As of this writing, I am unable to find a single case of a progressive-leaning speaker being targeted with firebombs on a college campus or a Democrat being fired by a Silicon Valley technology company because of his liberal politics. But we must have our "right-wing authoritarianism."[52]

The activating *threat* of the authoritarian dynamic can take on many forms: economic, military, political, racial, religious, even psychiatric. The abuse of psychiatry to pathologize dissent is of course

---

52 One of the ways you can tell that this theory has a shaky intellectual foundation is that the dumbest people on the staff of *New York* magazine—and there is some pretty fierce competition for that title—see through it. Jesse Singal observed on July 15, 2018, that tests of authoritarianism and intolerance do tend to find more of those vices among conservatives—when the questions are written in accordance with liberal assumptions. Go the other way, get the opposite result. Singal: "According to the rigidity of the right model, conservatives are more intolerant than liberals. But in a *Current Directions in Psychological Science* article published in 2014, a team led by Mark J. Brandt of Tilburg University in the Netherlands poked and prodded that idea—and found that it toppled fairly quickly…Conservatives are more intolerant than liberals of groups *traditionally viewed as liberal*—but what happens when you ask liberals about groups they often view as their ideological adversaries, like members of the military or fundamentalist Christians? The researchers, working in three independent labs, asked respondents to record their agreement or disagreement with statements like 'I think that this group should not be allowed to organize in order to influence public policy,' 'I believe that this group should not be allowed to hold rallies outside of government buildings,' and 'I think that this group should be allowed to distribute pamphlets and other materials on local college campuses.' They did not find any big differences when it came to how willing liberals and conservatives reported they would be to engage in these and other forms of political intolerance."

a classical hallmark of genuine authoritarian regimes. Authoritarian politics is a status game, too, and few enterprises enjoy the status accorded to science at large.[53]

In 1971, the physicist and Soviet dissident Andrei Sakharov made a public statement critical of the Soviet authorities' abuse of psychiatry for political ends—and found himself involuntarily committed as a mental patient suffering from "sluggish schizophrenia," a diagnosis commonly applied to political dissidents. The poet Joseph Brodsky was involuntarily committed as well, and tortured on therapeutic pretexts. Sakharov and Brodsky are known to us because they are famous, and because they lived. Many others died, often horribly—with the blessings of the expert medical opinion of their time and place. The hijacking of scientific prestige is typical of the ochlocracy of our time; some would-be censors propose prohibiting certain kinds of communication because they are "false by consensus."[54]

The Soviet party bosses and the men who ran their gulags and tortured dissidents in their mental wards were committed "antifascists," too. Like those who would invoke the principle of *streitbare Demokratie* to bring the moral equivalent of war to bear on behalf of every scraped knee, they understood themselves to be beset, surrounded on all sides by enemies and—like Martin Luther and Adolf Hitler—to be Hegelian capital-H History's chosen guardians of the one true path for mankind.

I am confident that I am not overstating the case. To stand in the way of founding the Kingdom of Heaven on Earth—the workers' paradise, the millennial *Volkstaat*, social justice, whatever you want to call it—must be considered an offense against the human race and all morality. If not the Kingdom of Heaven, then perhaps the

---

53 Hence such ridiculous neologisms as "political science."
54 "What Europe Can Teach America about Free Speech," *The Atlantic*, August 19, 2017.

German Empire. *Streitbare Demokratie* is an idea with a particularly German character and a particularly German origin, and it is an extension of Germany's Romantic and messianic tradition turned inward on itself, Germans liberating the contemporary Germany that is happy and generally admired from the Germany the Germans would prefer to forget. George Santayana's illumination of the German sense of national destiny[55] is enlightening in the way it captures the messianism and utopianism[56] that has come to define illiberal politics in the foundering liberal democracies:

> The state does not aim at self-preservation, still less is it concerned to come to the aid of those members of the human family that lag behind the movement of the day. The dominion of unorganised physical force must be abolished by a force obedient to reason and spirit.... Natural freedom is a disgraceful thing, a mere medley of sensual and intellectual impulses without any principle of order.
>
> ...If the people are disinclined to obey the Idea, the government must constrain them to do so. All the powers of all the citizens must be absorbed in the state. Personal liberty could be turned to no good use when such individuality and variety of training as are good for the state have been provided for by its regulations. Nor must any idleness be tolerated. An ideal education must make men over so that they shall be incapable of willing anything but what that education wills them to will.[57]

---

55 *Egotism in German Philosophy*, 1916.
56 "The conjunction of ruling and dreaming generates tyranny." Michael Oakeshott.
57 George Santayana, *Egotism in German Philosophy*, 1916.

The above is what Hayek called the "road to serfdom." It does not originate in malice or in the pure desire to dominate for the sake of domination itself unconnected from some greater end. The state has a plan—a five-year plan under Communism, most famously, but liberal states have their own plans, too. And when individuals are found to be incompatible with the plan, the individuals have to be eliminated: off to Siberia, as in the Soviet example, or in the liberal-democratic world simply chased out of work or expelled from school. The conflict in this case is not between totalitarianism and liberalism but between the individual and the collective.

Those who disregard the distinctiveness of individuals also tend to disregard the distinctiveness of nations, believing people everywhere to be raw material to be shaped. Santayana continues:

> ... As to foreign relations, the state, in obedience to its ideal mission, must conquer the surrounding barbarians and raise them to a state of culture. It is this process almost exclusively that has introduced progress into history.

Of course, such messianic aspirations must always and everywhere be totalitarian. With so much at stake, there can be no room for dissent, nonconformity, or heterodoxy. Germany here leads by ironic example: It hopes to neutralize its totalitarian history with a new totalitarian idea: *Streitbare Demokratie*, the very device that is supposed to save Germany—and us nice liberals in the English-speaking world—provides the intellectual basis for a new kind of totalitarianism, one that is not content to dream of a police state but also would impose a police culture. Santayana, again,[58] prophetically:

---

58 "German Freedom," *Soliloquies in England*, 1922.

For liberal freedom, for individualism, these philosophers have a great contempt. They say a man is nothing but the sum of his relations to other things, and if he should throw off one after another these constitutive bonds, he would find his private residuum of a self to be a mathematical point and a naked cipher, incapable of willing or of choosing anything. And they further say that a dutiful soul is right in feeling that the world it accepts and co-operates with is its own work; for, according to their metaphysics, the world is only an idea which each man makes after his own image, and even as you are, so is the world you imagine you live in. Only a foolish recalcitrant person, who does not recognize the handiwork of his own spirit about him, rebels against it, and thereby cancels his natural freedom; for everywhere he finds contradictions and closed doors and irksome necessities, being divided against himself and constantly bidding his left hand undo what his right hand is doing. So that, paradoxical as it may seem, it is only when you conform that you are free, while if you rebel and secede you become a slave. Your spiritual servitude in such a case would only be manifesting itself in a phenomenal form if the government should put you in prison.

The national expression of this kind of freedom is what the Germans call *Kultur*, a word not well understood in other countries. Every nation has certain characteristic institutions, certain representative writers and statesmen, past and present, certain forms of art and industry, a certain type of policy and moral inspiration. These are its *Kultur*, its national tradition and equipment. When by education the individual is brought to understand all these things, to share their spirit and life, and to be able to carry them forward faithfully, then he has absorbed the *Kultur* in his own person. *Kultur* is transmitted by systematic education. It is not, like culture, a matter of miscellaneous private attainments and refined tastes, but, rather, participation in a national purpose and in the means of executing it. The adept in this *Kultur* can live freely the life of his country, possessing its secret inspiration, valuing what it pursues and finding his happiness in those successes which he can help it to attain. *Kultur* is a lay religion, which includes ecclesiastical religion and assigns to it its due place.

German *Kultur* resembles the polity of ancient cities and of the Christian church in that it constitutes a definite, authoritative, earnest discipline, a training which is practical and is thought to be urgent and momentous. It is a system to be propagated and to be imposed. It is all-inclusive and demands entire devotion from everybody.

In this way, *streitbare Demokratie* necessitates the *abolition of private life*. Which is to say, it necessitates the incorporation of everything into the political project: every business,[59] every church,[60] every voluntary organization,[61] every ill-advised tweet by a fourteen-year-old kid who later goes on to win the Heisman trophy,[62] every pronoun,[63]

---

59 "Labor board rules Google's firing of James Damore was legal," *Wired*, February 16, 2018.
60 "Obama Administration Asks Supreme Court to Force Little Sisters of the Poor to Pay for Condoms, Sterilization, and Chemical Abortions," *Catholic Online*, January 12, 2014.
61 "Boy Scouts Lose Philadelphia Lease in Gay-Rights Fight," *New York Times*, December 6, 2007.
62 "Media Attacks Heisman Trophy Winner Kyler Murray for Homophobic Tweets He Sent as a 14-Year-Old," *Reason*, December 9, 2018.
63 "California Threatens Jail Time for Dissenters from the New Transgender Dogma," *National Review*, August 25, 2017.

every word spoken on every college campus and in every coffee shop,[64] every prayer[65,66]—*everything*. Like any parasite, it is opportunistic, and like any cancer, it spreads. The infection is the most severe at the three of the most sensitive inflection points in American life: the university, the corporation, and social media, each of which has been recruited as a disciplinary corporation, an instrument of ochlocracy exogenous to formal state action but correlated to and complementary with campaigns for deeper and more severe state repression.

When William Whyte wrote *The Organization Man* in 1956, he feared that the subjugation of the individual to the bureaucracy would lead not only to an abandonment of individualism but to outright hostility to it as people became convinced of the virtues of Organization life, and that the salaryman's commitment and loyalty to the corporation would produce paralyzing risk-aversion and intellectual stagnation.

His pessimism, in that regard, has proved insufficient.

---

64 "She was expelled from college after her racist rants went viral. Her mother thinks she deserves it," *Washington Post*, January 19, 2018.

65 "Houston subpoenas pastors' sermons in gay rights ordinance case," *Washington Post*, October 15, 2014.

66 "In the lead-up to the 2012 election, agents in the IRS's Tax Exempt Division systematically harassed conservative nonprofit groups, or groups critical of President Obama. Their applications for tax-exempt status were delayed or denied. Their members had their Facebook posts scrutinized, their family members' political ambitions questioned, the content of their prayers examined. Some groups were audited. The National Organization for Marriage had its donor list leaked to political opponents. Then, when this scheme was discovered, IRS agents stonewalled Congress and federal investigators, hard drives mysteriously went missing, and the IRS destroyed tens of thousands of pertinent e-mails under congressional subpoena." *National Review*, May 15, 2017.

CHAPTER FIVE

The Disciplinary Corporation

> Our present-day mini-Nietzsches... are both more
> laborious and more neurotic managers of the self than
> Nietzsche ever was or could be. To his reflexive homo
> faber they are animal laborans, their Democratic-
> Farmer-Labor party full of all-too-human beasts of
> burden, working the yoke beneath preposterously too-
> high piles of individuality. Our craptacular factories of
> self-expression stand to Nietzsche's art of the self as the
> nudie statues arrayed outside The Seventh Veil stand to
> Michelangelo's David.
>
> —*James Poulos, "Hobbes, Hamlet, and Individuality," First Things, 2009*

O chlocracy will, given the opportunity, dominate the formal organs of government and recruit them to its purposes—as indeed the ochlocrats of our time are attempting to do as of this writing, with proposals to limit political speech under the guise of "campaign-finance reform" or "hate speech." But in the case of the United States, the Constitution and, especially, the robust protections encoded in the Bill of Rights makes it difficult to trample over despised minorities. And, if you doubt that this is mainly a question of protecting the rights of minorities, consider that the great villain of the Occupy Wall Street movement, which is very much alive in the circles of Senator Warren and Senator Sanders, was: the 1 PERCENT. If the 99 percent can't boss around and pillage a minority that constitutes a mere 1 PERCENT of the population, then what's the point of democracy, anyway?

When—or, *while*—the apparatus of the state is beyond the mob's reach, the mob must turn to other organizations, grasping other cudgels with which to beat the dissidents and critics into conformity. In many cases, these private-sector organizations are much more effective instruments of suppression than are government agencies. It takes a great deal of effort to have someone convicted and imprisoned for a thought crime; it takes a lot less to bully that person's employer into firing him, but the moral outcome is the same. Hence the arrival of the "disciplinary corporations," some of which are ordinary for-profit business firms and some of which are related institutions such as universities and quasi-government agencies, e.g., the British "Building Better Building Beautiful" commission, whose chairman—Roger Scruton, also Britain's most important living philosopher—was chased out of the position for thinking unapproved thoughts and uttering them aloud in front of people: The philosopher was fired for doing the work proper to a philosopher.[1]

"Corporation" is a peculiar word. C. anno Domini 2018, it is used outside of the legal and business-management contexts mainly as a

---

[1] This particular mob attack was, like so many others, partly an inside job, with Scruton having enraged Britain's keepers of official taste with his retrograde views on architecture: "I want to give the public the opportunity to have the kind of architecture they would vote for," Scruton said, "not the kind that is imposed on them by the disciples of Le Corbusier and Mies." Scruton here is being uncharacteristically generous to the masses in his assumption that what they would vote for would be any good—in a country that just named a naval vessel HMS Boaty McBoatface after choosing the name in an online plebiscite. A more interesting point would be: The problem with the modernists is not that they are undemocratic but that they are not modern—Corbusier and Mies have been around long enough that the aesthetic derivative of their work is every bit as ersatz as 1980s Tudor and those lumpy little "Tuscan" villas they're building all over Texas. If you want to see architecture the people will vote for, visit Las Vegas. The Brexit fight has the British Right rediscovering the virtues of democracy, which is fair enough, but let's not get carried away.

term of abuse, meaning, approximately, "a business that I hate and fear." It is always corporations versus mom-and-pop shops, corporations behind the gentrification of diverse and vibrant neighborhoods, corporations pulling politicians' strings behind the scenes. Science-fiction writers for years have obsessed over practically immortal, galaxy-spanning corporations: Tyrel, Weyland-Yutani, Omni Consumer Products, Cyberdyne.

The sense of corporation as referring exclusively or almost exclusively to a profit-seeking business firm is relatively new and often misleading. National Public Radio is a corporation, too, as are the American Civil Liberties Union, the Salvation Army, the *New York Times*, and Harvard—and these rarely are discussed as corporations with corporate interests. But of course these represent corporate interests, too: Nonprofits, educational institutions, and other kinds of corporations that are not profit-seeking business firms have goals and programs of their own, and these include financial interests, even if those are not realized as profits on a corporate ledger. The Memorial Sloan Kettering Cancer Center is a nonprofit corporation, and its CEO, Dr. Craig B. Thompson, was paid more than $5 million in 2017. Harvard—the oldest extant American corporation—controls an endowment of just under $40 billion, as of this writing. Not all fortunes come from profit.

In the Roman Empire, much business was done in the Piazzale delle Corporazioni, the associated corporations of which had characteristics of both guilds and international trade organizations, as well as having a religious character. In fascist Italy, the lower house of the national legislature was replaced with the Camera dei Fasci e delle Corporazioni. Corporation in the sense of fascist corporatism does not refer to a business firm but to something more like an industrial association, one that is supposed to represent the interests of workers and the state as well as those of business managers and shareholders. Ironically, this model of industrial cooperation has a great deal in common with the so-called stakeholder capitalism advocated by American progressives. Both models assume a kind of benevolent cartelization of business, with labor and social-justice activists given a prominent role in cartel management, under the supervision and coordination of the state. That is emblematic of our time: The Berkeley *squadristi* in their black shirts and jackboots shout "Down with fascism!" and the authentic corporatists complain about the fictitious corporatism of the businessmen who want no part of it.

Catholic religious orders are Europe's prototype corporations, and the canon law governing them is the source of the English common-law conception of a corporation as a persona ficta, a legal person.[2] That the idea of a corporation as a "legal person" should be considered controversial in 2018 is another piece of evidence, as though one were needed, of the failure of our educational system. Without the legal construct of "corporate personhood," a corporation could not, among other things, be taxed or sued or regulated, because there would be no legal entity to tax or to sue or to regulate.

The same people who want to abolish the corporation as a legal person propose to create the corporation as a moral person—and to recruit that moral person into crusades of various design.

Stripped of its dystopian literary and emotional baggage, the modern corporation is a very different thing from what is usually imagined. It is an increasingly fragile and ad-hoc partnership of capital, intelligence, and labor—and a *Kultur*, which is to say, a set of values and a program for realizing those values. The corporation is not merely a form of property: It always has had a mission, and it is part of the mental poverty of our time that we have narrowed the universe of possibilities down to profit.

---

2 W. S. Holdsworth, "History of English Law," 1923.

Perhaps the foregoing seems to you like an awful lot of intellectual window dressing for something as bleach-chuggingly stupid as #HasJustineLandedYet.

If you happen not to know the story of Justine Sacco, the once-and-future corporate-communications executive at IAC, the media behemoth that owns everything from Tinder to the Daily Beast to Angie's List, here is a brief summary: Before an eleven-hour flight from London to Capetown, she tweeted a joke that clearly was intended to lampoon the patronizing and racist attitudes that Americans sometimes express toward Africa: "Going to Africa. Hope I don't get AIDS. Just kidding. I'm white!" She had 170 Twitter followers at the time, but, within a few hours, she became the top worldwide trending topic on the social-media platform. For hours and hours, she was denounced—by tens of thousands of people, practically all of them strangers to her—as a "disgusting racist" and worse. But, being on a long intercontinental flight with no Internet connection,[3] she didn't know, a fact that was mocked with gleeful malice by a hashtag, "#HasJustineLandedYet."

Inevitably, the corporation that employed her got in on the action: "This is an outrageous, offensive comment. Employee in question currently unreachable on an intl flight." The half-literate writing was on the virtual wall: "We are about to watch this @JustineSacco bitch get fired. In REAL time. Before she even KNOWS she's getting fired."

To quote my old friend Jeffrey Goldberg, editor-in-chief of THAT AUGUST JOURNALISTIC INSTITUTION: "Why the fuck do these people care who somebody else hires?" Why do they care who works where and on what terms?

They don't.

Not really. In the case of Justine Sacco, approximately 99 and 44/100 percent of the cretins who joined the worldwide two-minute

---

3 "Round the decay / Of that colossal Wreck, boundless and bare / The lone and level sands stretch far away."

hate directed at this anodyne little corporate-communications monkey had never heard of IAC, had no idea what the firm was and no interest in what it did. All they knew—or cared about—was that it had the power to fire this young woman, and they had begun to intuit that they had the power to push around IAC like the fat kid with glasses on the third-grade playground.

Basically, they decided to take her lunch money: to hurt her financially, and, if possible,[4] ritually humiliate her in public. The corporation that provided her livelihood was to be made the instrument of that humiliation.

Ritual humiliation is always and everywhere a part of ochlocracy, and 21st-century ochlocracy is, for the moment, focused on the corporation—both its business interests and its internal common life.

That is an important change from the twentieth century. The change of preferred ochlocratic venue is a social development that has had real consequences as the sphere of private life is systematically reduced. We are all now "public figures" if at any point our lives intersect with any public-facing institution, which is to say, with any corporation properly understood: religious congregation, government agency, university—and, most often and perhaps most significant, the business corporation. What once was an extraordinary political phenomenon is now an ordinary corporate phenomenon.

---

4 I tend to agree with Eleanor Roosevelt here, that one cannot really be humiliated without one's consent, and I am genuinely mystified by the fact that a few of the gifted and accomplished people I know care about—even agonize over—what's said about them by strangers on social-media platforms and in the comments sections of publications. One writer friend of mine is always constantly writing his own obituary: "How will I be remembered?" The liberating truth is: You won't. And if you were, it wouldn't matter very much, anyway. As Gregory Hays puts it in his rather liberal translation of Marcus Aurelius's *Meditations*: "People out for posthumous fame forget that the Generations To Come will be the same annoying people they know now. And just as mortal. What does it matter to you if they say *x* about you, or think *y*?"

The process has changed, but the underlying social ritual is familiar to those who know their twentieth-century history. Consider the "struggle sessions" of Mao Zedong's so-called Cultural Revolution—which began with the "Anti-Rightist Movement," rhetorically prefiguring our contemporary "antifascists." The Chinese writer Lao She, once a favorite of the Communist Party[5] and one of the leading novelists and playwrights in China, was one of many victims, trucked off to be used as a bloodied up prop in a piece of political theater along with several other nonconforming men of letters:[6]

> About 150 uniformed schoolgirls from the Beijing No. 8 Middle School (renamed the Lu Xun Memorial School) were already there and had been briefed for an hour beforehand on their task. In the inner courtyard, a bonfire was burning, destroying theatrical props taken from Beijing opera groups.
>
> When the writers arrived, they were pushed through a human tunnel of teenage girls screaming 'beat the blackguards,'[7] and waving sticks and fists. For at least three hours, the writers knelt before the fire while the girls beat them with such props as swords, halberds, belts and bamboo sticks. Then, they hung placards stating their crime around the writers' necks as an official photographer recorded the events.
>
> The victims were then trucked back to the Culture Bureau, some say at 5:00 p.m., others say at 8:00 p.m. There,

---

5 Lao She was not selected for public humiliation *in spite of* his having been a giant of modern Chinese literature but *because* he was a giant of modern Chinese literature.

6 "The Mystery of Lao She," *South China Morning Post*, September 27, 2001.

7 This is approximately how they do things at *The Atlantic*, if you were wondering, except that they use Slack.

the beatings continued. Lao She resisted wearing the plac-
ard and this enraged his persecutors, who even attacked a
car that arrived to take him to the safety of a nearby
police station.

Even there he was not safe. The furious crowd climbed
over the wall and continued beating him until midnight.

One wonders what those little girls[8] thought as they were beating
the famous writer. Were they thinking about the precepts of Marx-
ism-Leninism and the necessity of having the peasants as the van-
guard of the revolution? Meditating upon quotations from the Little
Red Book? Pleased that they had the opportunity to beat up a funny
old man who meant nothing to them, or savoring the fact that they
were to be the instrument of bringing down a high-and-mighty literary figure a notch or two? Terrified that if they were insufficiently
energetic in their denunciations and abuse that they would be next?
One suspects that these sentiments were present in admixtures that
varied according to age and education, and congenital meanness.

Similarly, one wonders: Did any young man laboring feverishly
with one hand to see to it that Justine Sacco lost her job really think
that he was helping to fight AIDS in Africa? It is difficult to credit
that notion. It is more likely that they were simply directing rage at,
as one wrote, some "stupid cunt," no doubt one in a long line of them
who had snubbed and excluded them. A great deal of the political
rage of our time is sexual rage redirected.[9] The outcome of the episode had no effect on AIDS in Africa, AIDS policy, or on the more
general discourse on subjects related to AIDS. Justine Sacco was the

---

8 What's Mandarin for "Caitlyn"?
9 "This girl is going to her husband's house. She will rightly order her household. Let the
household be rightly ordered, and then the people of the state may be taught." *The Great
Learning*, Confucius, c. 500 BC.

beginning and the end of the story. It was not a story about AIDS. It was a story about a girl, as so many stories are.

The text and the subtext move in different directions sometimes. But the more obvious public part of the story—the mau-mauing of a corporation by actors external and internal—is familiar enough: James Damore of Google, fired after showing himself dumb enough to give his colleagues an honest opinion when asked for one; Brendan Eich, chased out of his position at Mozilla for taking a policy position on gay marriage identical to the one Barack Obama claimed to hold when he was elected president; any number of media figures, myself included, fired or having their employers pressed to fire them for holding unpopular views.[10] The figures at the center of these controversies may be psychological totems for a little platoon of anime-porn addicts on Twitter, but they are, if you understand what's really going on in these episodes, only incidental to the social-media outrage project. That is something that is rarely understood and needs to be: The stated goals of ochlocracy are seldom if ever the real goals. Politics isn't about policy.[11] That is not to suggest a conspiracy, though people are dishonest enough often enough about their political goals and strategies. Most people do not understand their own motives and assumptions very well when it comes to politics and other things that are outside of their intimate experience.

---

10 Today, in fact, as I wrote this paragraph, some bush-league nobody sought to have me fired from the *New York Post* for gently noting the incontrovertible fact that Alexandria Ocasio-Cortez is not very well informed about things that a new member of the House of Representatives should know, like what the House of Representatives does and how a bill becomes a law.

11 "Politics isn't about Policy," Robin Hanson, 2008: "Food isn't about Nutrition / Clothes aren't about Comfort / Bedrooms aren't about Sleep / Marriage isn't about Romance / Talk isn't about Info / Laughter isn't about Jokes / Charity isn't about Helping / Church isn't about God / Art isn't about Insight / Medicine isn't about Health / Consulting isn't about Advice / School isn't about Learning / Research isn't about Progress / Politics isn't about Policy."

E.g.: The stated goal of having me fired by THAT AUGUST JOUR-NALISTIC INSTITUTION was to prevent my sharing my nonconform-ing views with the reading public, which of course was doomed to be a terrible failure: My next two pieces were in the *Wall Street Jour-nal* and the *Washington Post*, both of which have substantially larger readerships than does THAT AUGUST JOURNALISTIC INSTITUTION, and I became a regular columnist for the *New York Post*, which also is considerably larger in reach.[12] Everybody involved, except for the deeply stupid and the mentally damaged, knew from the beginning that this was going to be the case. It was just a virtual book-burning that, like an ordinary book-burning, was less about keeping the sen-tences in the book from being read in other contexts than making a public judgment on the works and their author.

Likewise, the campaign against James Damore brought his views to many more people than would have seen them without the mob attack. The target was not James Damore—it was the senior manage-ment of Google. Justine Sacco's dumb joke was going to be seen by some of her 170 Twitter followers, some of whom would cringe at it, and that would have been the end without the ochlocratic convul-sion—the target of which was IAC, not Justine Sacco.

As much as the rampant unhinged egoist in me would like it to be otherwise, the fact is: This phenomenon isn't really about me or about people like me. We are props. Seeing me fired is no doubt a kind of perverse moral perk for the sad specimens who get a jolt out

---

12 It also provides me with a direct line to the president, who is a religious reader of the *Post*. My *National Review* colleague Rich Lowry, who also writes for the *Post*, discovered this in a startling and amusing fashion: He wrote a column about the futility of political candidates who tried to imitate Donald Trump—the "Trumpism without Trump" tactic—which ran under the headline, "There Is Only Trump." Later in the week, he received a package in the mail with a copy of the *Post* opened to his column, scrawled above which, in the president's trademark psychotic chickenscratch, was: "Dear Rich. So true! Donald J. Trump." One suspects he did not read much past the headline.

of that sort of thing, but the point of the exercise is to bend the corporation to the will of the mob, repurposing the corporation as an instrument of political and intellectual suppression.

The mobsters would very much like to implement various kinds of censorship through the state and they remain active in that project.[13] But there are other simpler, more direct means to achieve much of the same goal. It is very difficult to take power in Congress, and difficult to exercise that power once it is acquired. But if one can instill in society sufficient terror—you'll recall Karl Loewenstein's formulation: "permanent psychic coercion, at times amounting to intimidation and terrorization scientifically applied"—then such political power is less needful. The current model is single-serving suppression: Hit targets one at a time until those who have not been hit simply keep ducking from instinct.

The little suppressors will still seek after formal political power, if only to silence the few who are willing to pay the price of speaking their minds and to enjoy the act of humiliating the people they hate by exercising state power over them, but the actual political work of intellectual suppression already will have been done.

And Google will do it, along with Facebook, IAC, billionaire dilettantes like Laurene Powell,[14] and less august corporations ranging from Starbucks to Chipotle to (I giggle when I type the words) Mojo Burrito.

The Williamsons,[15] Damores, and Quinn Nortons of the world are almost beside the point.

It is less important to the mob that we be punished for our political speech than that others see the example and never speak in the

---

13 That pathetic cut-rate over-blushed unmusical Liberace imitator in the White House is having a fit about *Saturday Night Live*, for Pete's sake.
14 Just another nobody MBA student until she started banging Steve Jobs.
15 I recommend Paul Robeson's recording of "Scandalize My Name."

first place, thereby rendering certain ideas unspeakable in an ever-widening context, one that now encompasses almost all employment and all enrollment at colleges and universities.

It is not terrorization alone that drives this conformism. The desire to fit in, to be accepted by the people and institutions that one associates with status and with the good life, is natural and to some degree healthy; but as a thousand historical episodes from the Salem witch hunts to female genital mutilation testify, most people will continue to go along to get along even if that means cooperating with evil and horror—and their own intellectual suppression. As Whyte argued in *The Organization Man*, the presence of any conflict between the individual and the corporation is reacted to by the cells in the corporate organism as a kind of moral cancer: "Tensions are sickness," and the moral purpose of the corporation is to be "unified and purged of conflict" so that the integrated life may emerge. Visit the campus of Google or Apple some time: What's going on there isn't just work. It is the evolution of a mode of life. It is communion.

As Mitt Romney says: "Corporations are people, my friend."

That questing after a life that is whole and integrated is how corporate culture becomes Santayana's *Kultur*, an ersatz secular religion whose purpose is conform the subject to its national mandates that he might "live freely the life of his country, possessing its secret inspiration, valuing what it pursues and finding his happiness in those successes which he can help it to attain." (More *Brave New World* than *1984*, yes, yes—but one still must come to love Big Brother, not merely to submit.) The dissident—the heretic—who stands between the corporation and the realization of its *Kultur* must be regarded as a kind of criminal, a spiritual traitor who would inhibit the "life of his country" and stand athwart its "secret inspiration," not valuing what it pursues but questioning it—or holding it in contempt. Our attachment to the corporation is, in that sense, transcendent. But it is also profane: The would-be suppressors desire to dominate corporate *Kultur* for the same reason the Borgias desired to dominate the Catholic Church.

F. A. Hayek foresaw the coercive potential of this in the context of socialism:

> That the freedom of the employed depends upon the existence of a great number and variety of employers is clear when we consider the situation that would exist if there were only one employer—namely, the state—and if taking employment were the only permitted means of livelihood... a consistent application of socialist principles, however much it might be disguised by the delegation of the power of employment to nominally independent public corporations and the like, would necessarily lead to the presence of a single employer. Whether this employer acted directly or indirectly he would clearly possess unlimited power to coerce the individual.[16]

Leon Trotsky intuited the same potential, and savored it in totalitarian fashion: "Opposition means death by slow starvation. The old principle, who does not work shall not eat, has been replaced by a new one: who does not obey shall not eat."

Obedience is what the corporate *Kultur* demands. Not exclusively for its own sake, but because the corporation cannot digest the individual who stands apart from its *Kultur*, which is a politics and an

---

16 *The Constitution of Liberty*, 1960.

etiquette as well as an economy and a faith. Corporations eject[17] undigestible dissidents not in defense of the bottom line or out of some deep principled objection to a political difference but because the individual standing apart disrupts the project of seeking a unified common life that is free from tension and contradiction. Which is to say, the corporation functions as a totalitarian state in miniature. Like all totalitarian regimes, corporations are managed by people who believe they are doing good, and that if a few eggs have to be cracked to make the proverbial omelet, then so be it.

George Orwell asked the relevant question: "Where's the omelet?"

The project to politically cleanse the public square through the medium of the corporation has not produced social harmony, it has not liberated us or nudged us closer to utopia. It has only made the world more dreary, more tedious, and more fearful—a vast virtual Siberia, if a well-fed and tolerable one.

History doesn't repeat itself, nor does it rhyme. It just shrieks like Donald Sutherland at the end of *Invasion of the Body-Snatchers*.

And so we return to a familiar place.[18]

---

17 Like a hairball or a pearl.

18 "One must re-visit a dull but fundamental fact: the highest priority of the top leadership of the Communist Party remains, as in the past, not economic development, or a just society, or China's international standing, or any other goal for the nation as a whole, but its own grip on power. Thus it continues to ban any public expression of opposition to itself and continues to crush any organization that it does not control or could not easily control if it needed to. The fate of *qigong* breath exercises is a good illustration. In the 1980s the Party encouraged *qigong* as an expression of Chinese essence and a symbol of national pride. The central government even set up a national *qigong* association, complete with its own bureaucracy. But in the 1990s, when some *qigong* masters (Li Hongzhi of Falun Gong was not the first) decided to build their own organizations outside Party control, the same Chinese-essence breath exercises overnight became an 'evil cult' and a target for brutal repression. The founders of the Chinese Democratic Party, all of whom are in prison today, ran afoul of the same principle. Their crime was not the word 'democratic' in their group's name (China has long had eight 'democratic parties,' all subordinate to the leadership of the Communist Party); their crime was to declare that their organization was independent." Perry Link, "The Anaconda in the Chandelier," *New York Review of Books*, April 11, 2002.

Socialism, Hayek worried, would leave workers "at the mercy of the most complete monopoly ever conceived." We do not have socialism. And, yet, we have managed to create a strikingly similar situation without it. Adolf Hitler, asked if he intended to nationalize German industries,[19] is said to have replied: "I shall nationalize the people."[20] The historian John Lukacs adds: "which is what he did, alas, quite successfully." That, Lukacs writes, indicates "the essence of Hitler's thinking." What is under way in the United States today is an effort to construct something like Hayek's monopolistic employer, a project that does not require the nationalization of corporations but the nationalization of corporate *Kultur*, recruiting the aggregate power of American employers into the program of intellectual repression. And by "intellectual repression" I do not mean "the repression of intellectuals," most of whom have sufficiently evolved social instincts to remain safe in what Michael Oakeshott described as "warm, compensated servility." Social-media campaigns directed at corporate employers have resulted in the firings of more restaurant workers[21] and office clerks than journalists or college professors.

Some of those burrito-artists and pizzeria waiters did in fact have some very nasty political views, which they put on display at that white-power chimp-out in Charlottesville, VA. But they were not

---

19 The Nazi party's 25-Point Program did in fact call for the nationalization of trusts, mandatory profit sharing for big businesses, expanded employee benefits, and free college educations for all qualified Germans who wanted it. One wonders what exactly it is the contemporary Left dislikes about the Nazi agenda. If the answer is, "Well, there *is* the niggling issue of all that psychotic Jew-hatred," I will want to direct your attention to Louis Farrakhan, the Reverend Al Sharpton, the Reverend Jesse Jackson, Linda Sarsour, Tamika Mallory ...

20 *The Great Terror*, John Lukacs, January 29, 2006.

21 Here is the emblematic sentence of our times, one that no comedic genius could have imagined: "Mojo Burrito does not condone harassment, racism or discrimination of any kind." Of course that sentence was written while the company was engaging in discrimination after knuckling under to a campaign of harassment.

fired for their political views, nor were they fired for anything they did at work. They were fired because the mob demanded their firings. The POWERS THAT BE AT MOJO BURRITO and Pizzeria Uno do not quiz potential employees about their political views before hiring them, nor do most businesses of the sort maintain policies regarding the private political, moral, or religious beliefs of their employees. It is difficult to imagine anything more comically totalitarian than having the POWERS THAT BE AT MOJO BURRITO giving their prospects political examinations as a condition of employment. In some cases, it would be illegal for them to do so under current law. Those on the Left who are enthusiastic about this kind of thing should imagine being asked these questions in a job interview: "Are you now or have you ever been a member of the Communist Party? A socialist? An atheist? Do you believe in private property and the US Constitution?" Eek-a-Nazi! as a justification for conditioning employment on political obedience assumes a rationale without a limiting principle. And, if there is one thing corporations like, it is standardization: The same *streitbare Demokratie* justification for banning far-right parties in Germany and Austria has been used to ban far-left parties, too. It is not exactly blazingly obvious that it would be desirable to have some pointy-headed federal hack commission making decisions about what kind of political views should open an individual up to financial retaliation—it is even less obvious that we want McDonald's or PepsiCo or Procter & Gamble to be deputized as political czars.

And it is strange that the very progressives who claim to be most skeptical of and opposed to corporate power wish to give corporations the remarkable power to decide which political views are acceptable in the public square and which may be excluded. Progressives would not trust corporations with that kind of power if they did not believe that they could control them and thus wield that power themselves by proxy.

And they can—and do.

Calling to mind that infamous crowded theater, this suppression largely happens under the auspices of "safety." Mark Zuckerberg constantly references "safety" when discussing Facebook's suppression of unpopular political ideas, suppression that sometimes is undertaken in concert with both liberal and autocratic governments.

"It's not our place to correct people's speech, but we do want to enforce our community standards on our platform," Facebook News Feed engineer Sara Su told the *New York Times*. "When you're in our community, we want to make sure that we're balancing freedom of expression and safety." The *Times* managed to publish the following sentences with a straight face: "The company's goal is ambitious: to reduce context-heavy questions that even legal experts might struggle with—when is an idea hateful, when is a rumor dangerous—to one-size-fits-all rules. By telling moderators to follow the rules blindly, Facebook hopes to guard against bias and to enforce consistency."[22] The hallmarks of the twenty-first century corporate mind are there: consistency as a good in and of itself, blind obedience to memos, reflexively proprietary preemption (*"our* platform"; *"our* community"; *"we're* balancing"), blatant double-speak (it's not our place to correct people's speech, but here's how we're going to correct people's speech), euphemism ("community standards" for "the elimination of unpopular speech"), and mustelid happy-talk ("balancing").

In a few short years, the Internet has gone from "INFORMATION WANTS TO BE FREE!" to "FOLLOW THE RULES BLINDLY!" And this has

---

22 Max Fisher, "Inside Facebook's Secret Rulebook for Global Political Speech," *New York Times*, December 27, 2018.

been treated as an improvement. Of course Facebook and YouTube can be used to publish propaganda, broadcast falsehoods, and to coordinate crimes. So can a telephone, but there is no push to have T-Mobile tell us what we can and cannot say over its third-rate network. And there is no serious case to be made that online courses from Hillsdale College or Dennis Prager's sanctimonious little videos ("Cops Are the Good Guys") are a *danger* to anybody in any meaningful sense of the word "danger." Facebook has suppressed gospel songs and anti-abortion advertisements, and it has engaged in retaliatory suppression against critics of its suppression; Twitter has blocked communications from pro-adoption groups; Google suppressed videos from PragerU; etc. Of course, these firms are within their legal rights to handle their own platforms in any way they see fit, but none of these things plausibly constitutes a *danger* to anybody, unless "danger" means living in a world in which other people might hear or read something that you'd rather they not hear or read. The corporations that operate these social-media platforms are simply being used as instruments of ochlocracy.

The business corporation is in the early twenty-first century arguably the most important institution in our common life. The Catholic Church is, at the moment, morally handicapped, and the mainline Protestant congregations long ago declined into social irrelevance. Civic engagement has deteriorated as the population—especially the intellectuals, corporate managers, and high-income professionals—has grown more restive and more mobile. Government is at least as morally handicapped as the Catholic Church at the federal level and as attenuated as the Methodist confession at the local level.

That has left the corporation, for the moment, as the bulwark, a place where values get refined and expressed, a source of social norms, and the main theater of social action for a large class of people—a class whose members are as jealous of their positions as they are insecure in them. The tech giants of our time—Google, Apple, Facebook—are in a sense too rich for their own good. Like Babbitt, they are vulnerable to the ailments of affluence, and they suffer from a form of corporate gout, political inflammations in the joints that are least exercised in the pursuit of the actual business of the firm. They form a kind of supplementary welfare state for the white upper-middle class—the denizens of Twitter!—the idiot children of which could not otherwise bridge the financial chasm between an MFA and a hot meal.

Powerful and omnipresent as it may seem, the corporation is a provocatively weak institution. The almighty corporation of the science-fiction imagination is entirely at odds with reality: In the 1960s, the average corporate life expectancy for a Fortune 500 company was about seventy-five years; today it is fifteen years and declining.[23] US Steel never saw its share price decline steeply because of something the chairman said on social media. The value of reputational capital has increased relative to the value of physical capital, especially for corporations such as Twitter and Facebook, whose main products are incorporeal. Smaller, locally owned businesses find themselves the targets of worldwide pressure campaigns involving parties that have no relationship with them or their communities and no direct knowledge of them, while big firms such as Google and Apple are vulnerable to domination by internal political constituencies. A corporation driven entirely and exclusively by the ruthless pursuit of profit would not be vulnerable to that kind of internal manipulation, but that is not what corporations do—they perform a much richer and more complex social role than their critics generally imagine. Corporations are communities within which their members seek after William Whyte's "integrated life." Our houses are where

---

23 Mark J. Perry, "Fortune 500 firms in 1955 vs. 2014; 88% are gone, and we're all better off because of that dynamic 'creative destruction,'" Carpe Diem AEI, August 18, 2014.

we sleep. Corporations are where we live. Corporations are our homes.

James Poulos, writing in *The Hedgehog Review*, argues that our intimate relationship with our employers is only in minor part a matter of compensation. It is also a matter of identity involving questions of status and how we intellectually and socially fix our positions in the world. Poulos writes:

> Partaking of a corporate identity allows us access to the very things that are difficult for us to find as isolated individuals, fortifying us to pursue more productive advancements in social life while shielding us against the loneliness and futility that creep in the minute we sit with ourselves in solitary silence.[24] Encouragement and protection take material form in the basket of perks we've come to expect from any respectable corporation, from health insurance to paid vacations to "life event" leave and beyond. Unlike any other institution in our democratic American life, corporations offer American workers the opportunity to be and feel more sheltered yet less boxed in.
>
> …As much as we fear corporations gone wild, we love corporations that love us. Many of us, from the minute we set foot in the working world, long for nothing more than to establish a stable position in a good corporation. Because money really does matter more in our time than in ages past, as Tocqueville says, we like the steady paycheck. Far more, however, we like how corporations boost our status and purchasing power even if we lack any real net worth; we like how they lift the velvet rope for us, providing us

---

24 Thank God for Instagram, eh, Caitlyn?

with social experiences we couldn't enjoy on the strength of our own name or reputation. And perhaps most secretly, we like the way they lift the burden of having to be ourselves. As good corporate professionals, we are free to stop caring so much about who we are. The corporate identity establishes a fixity that we struggle to find within ourselves or in the consolations of love, faith, or honor.[25]

Colleges and corporations are in effect the gatekeepers of the public square and the good life, which is to say, *status*; holding the power—and showing publicly that you hold the power—to exclude dissidents from college education and a great deal of desirable employment is more valuable as a political weapon than a mere congressional majority. That is one reason why the handful of controversialists who are mostly immune to such leverage—among them, billionaires such as Charles Koch—are hated with such special gusto, and why the top political project of contemporary progressives is to enact legal restrictions on their speech, even if that means gutting the First Amendment as the Democratic party has attempted to do on one occasion[26] and remains committed to pursuing.

These firms of course are subject to pressure from the outside. And they are not immune to that pressure. Indeed—and slightly contrary to Hayek's thesis of the relationship between economic and intellectual independence—the billionaire tech CEOs are among those in American public life who are easiest to shame and to bully.[27]

---

25 James Poulos, "The Last Association Standing," *The Hedgehog Review*, Summer 2017.
26 "Harry Reid Proposes Changing Constitution To Block The Koch Brothers," *Huffington Post*, May 15, 2014.
27 In 2018, I attended an *Atlantic*-sponsored discussion at South by Southwest in which all of the sexist, racist, and colonialist sins of capitalism were laid bare in a feminist forum sponsored by: Google, PepsiCo, AT&T, NBC Universal, Facebook, UBS, JPMorgan Chase, and Deloitte. If you want to know where the corporate power is, you need only look.

Mark Zuckerberg is not the aspy spastic sperg of *The Social Network* but is in fact deeply invested in his social standing and in the high opinion of others. He is manifestly wounded—deeply—by the *New York Times*-led campaign to declare him and his firm responsible for the election of Donald Trump,[28] the undermining of American democracy, the coarsening of our political culture and institutions, and, presumably, genital warts and the lumbago. Facebook's efforts in 2017 and 2018 to reconfigure its internal workings have relatively little to do with Russian bots and troll-farms—whose influence on the actual outcomes of American elections is almost certainly negligible—and still less to do with patriotism. He does not like being held up as an object of ridicule and scorn and, in spite of his billions of splendid fuck-you money, he does not have the sack to follow through with an actual "Fuck you." Facebook is no more responsible for the fact that Donald Trump is a giant gaping asshole adored by a throng of smaller even more incontinent recta who made him president of these United States than Johann Gutenberg is for Bill O'Reilly's literary oeuvre or Jonathan Franzen's novels.

Zuckerberg likes being rich. But he wants to be loved, too. And, as Ross Douthat[29] argues, the overlap between those considerations on the vast Venn diagram of corporate life is considerable:

> Here are two stories about corporate America's current role in our politics and common life. In one, the country's biggest companies are growing a conscience, prodded along by shifts in public opinion and Donald Trump's depredations and their own idealistic young employees, and becoming a vanguard force for social change—with the

---

28 Zuck's guilty of a great many crimes against taste and good sense, but he didn't advise Herself not to campaign in Wisconsin.
29 "The Rise of Woke Capital," *New York Times*, February 28, 2018.

recent disassociations from the N.R.A. by major airlines and rental car companies just the latest example in a trend that also includes recent high-profile corporate interventions on immigration and gay and transgender rights.

In the other story, corporate America just performed another bait and switch at the common good's expense—making a show of paying bonuses and raising wages after the passage of the corporate-friendly Republican tax bill, but actually reserving most of the tax savings for big stock buybacks, enriching shareholders rather than employees in an economy where wage growth still disappoints.

These are not two stories, though; they're different aspects of the same one.

Corporate activism on social issues isn't in tension with corporate self-interest on tax policy and corporate stinginess in paychecks. Rather, the activism increasingly exists to protect the self-interest and the stinginess—to justify the ways of C.E.O.s to cultural power brokers.

What Douthat alludes to here is that these firms are beholden to "cultural power brokers" not only on the outside but within the firm, those "idealistic young employees."[30] Roseanne Barr may be dumber than nine chickens and crazy as any number of bedbugs, but you are even dumber and more disconnected from reality if you think that ABC is making major, multi-million-dollar programming decisions based on the whinging of twelve angry Caitlyns on Twitter. Roseanne's scalp, like mine, was taken by barbarians within the gates. "The masses," as Michael Oakeshott understood, "must be regarded as the invention of their leaders."

---

30 Ross is a good Christian, and is being too charitable with "idealistic."

The corporation is a source of identity and social position, and it is inevitable that interest groups seeking to elevate or reinforce their own socio-economic positions—including positions of relative privilege such as those occupied by college-educated white women, Caitlyn Inc.—will attempt to recruit the corporation and hijack its resources for that purpose. Like the self-serving "diversity" policies that are mainly about reinforcing the positions of people who already are highly paid and well-connected, the project of politicizing the corporation more generally is headquartered not in the C suite but way out there in the corporate boondocks, the non-core functions staffed largely by interchangeable pseudo-professionals with no particular skills or talents other than affability and a cold-fishy knack for detecting minute variables in social currents—marketing, accounting, administrative support, and, above all, human resources, the ninth infernal circle of the tepid and mushy hellscape of corporate culture. The politicization of corporate life is in part a protection racket for practitioners of corporate politics, otherwise unskilled people whose talents in life are ingratiation, wheedling, and middle-school *Mean Girls*-style social maneuvering. For the most part, they are not people who invent new products, engineer new production methods, or manage complicated technical or financial undertakings. They do not deal in ideas; they do not have them or appreciate them, and they would not know what to do with an idea if they had one. Their job titles tend to have the word "relations" in them—human relations, employee relations, community relations, government relations, etc. That is their skill in life: to relate. Which is to say, they are professional players of status games.

Google has a little more than 85,000 employees, about 200 of whom could not be immediately and easily replaced. Caitlyn down in Human Resources, like most of the middling people who play middling roles in departments and business units far removed from the actual business of the firm, knows this—she may not be very creative or insightful, but she is bright enough to comprehend her own professional expendability. This psychologically stressful condition is a very large part of the reason for the push—from HR departments and the administrative staff, not from the creators and entrepreneurs who may nonetheless acquiesce to it—to elevate the importance of demographic features in employment (and in college admissions, which is the template for corporate employment), establishing as an institutional norm the principle that one's value to the firm is not related exclusively to the work you do but to who you are: a woman, an African-American, disabled, etc. This is a project that makes it politically more difficult within the organization to dismiss or discipline a Caitlyn. She may stop performing her job well, but she will not stop being a woman, and she will point to your corporate policy affirming your corporate need for employees with genitals in thus-and-such configuration or thus-and-such ancestry (as the case may be) if she detects that her position is in danger. There are Wall Street firms that quietly set aside money to fund payouts every time they fire an African-American or female employee—it's a racket, but it is less expensive for them and less disruptive than litigation. Note that the top demand of the #MeToo activists was putting more women into executive positions at entertainment companies rather than, you know, that the men employed there stop raping and sexually abusing their subordinates. This is a status game: The Caitlyns complain about "privilege" and seek to have their own privileges encoded into law, university admissions standards, and corporate policy—baked into the social cake.

Having the power to mau-mau a technology company or a magazine into firing an employee for holding unpopular political views is of course attractive to the teacup totalitarians who pursue such projects on social media. Bullies like that they do. But the campaign is bigger and wider and deeper than that. While we are all arguing about what sort of political views justify firing a columnist or a burrito engineer, we implicitly accept the premise that corporations are legitimate venues for the enforcement of political discipline, that policing political thought and political speech is a natural part of the corporate jurisdiction, and that using corporations as penal instruments to exclude nonconformists from common life in order to secure the spiritual blessings of intellectual uniformity is not a regrettably necessary social sanction but a positive good, an exercise in affirming our highest values. Here the rage-monkey Left is united with the rage-monkey Right, who embrace the same *takfiri* thinking but choose different heretics, such as Sarah Jeong or Colin Kaepernick.

They shall nationalize the people.

School life is the prototype of corporate life, and the school day is the corporate work day in miniature: group projects, committee meetings, receiving and returning assignments, action items, quarterly reports. With its bells-and-cells diurnal rhythm, it represents the corporate mode of life in exaggerated and simplified form. The mysteries of the corporate *Kultur* are there on display, for those with eyes to see. Have a look around some time: The institutional architecture of the modern public school is worth noting, with its scrupulous attention to staff security and perimeter controls. As features such as metal detectors, Plexiglass security booths, armed guards, and police dogs have become more common, the underlying character of the educational institution is made visible: It resembles nothing so much as a penitentiary. And it performs much the same social function—preparing unruly and deficient people for entry into a society whose values are the values of the corporation: docility, cooperativeness, punctuality, and, above all, conformism—a willingness to conform that is not dutiful and grudging but joyous, an active embrace of the *Kultur* and its promises. And the one thing that will get you reliably kicked out of a public school is the one thing that will reliably get you fired from a job—and the one thing the corporate titans of Silicon Valley claim to prize above all: *disruption.*

William Whyte did not have it quite right: We didn't all become subordinate salarymen. We became kindergarteners, who know only two sources of justice and social discipline: that of the principal's office, and that of the playground.

CHAPTER SIX

The Lonely Mob

Hatred is the most accessible and comprehensive
of all the unifying agents. Mass movements can rise
and spread without belief in a god, but never without
a belief in a devil.

—*Eric Hoffer*, The True Believer: Thoughts on the Nature of Mass Movements,
1951

Social media is the birth-control pill of political discourse: It has fundamentally changed the nature of an entire broad category of human relationships by rendering those relationships sterile.

The birth-control pill enabled a new kind of sexuality—serial polygamy—in which the absence of the procreative element proved simultaneously liberating and degrading: Sex liberated from the consequence of pregnancy was liberated from many other consequences as well—for a time, that liberation continued under the delusion that contraception together with penicillin had liberated sex from all serious consequences. The shock troops of the so-called Sexual Revolution in the 1960s subsequently encountered horrifying new consequences such as AIDS and fatherless young psychopaths in subsequent decades, and wistfully described their youths as the "PPPP" years: post-pill, pre-plague.

But the biological consequences of sex never stood alone; instead, they were enmeshed in a complex set of social, legal, political, and economic relations founded on that underlying biological reality. Without the mitigating influences of marriage and parenthood—and the social institutions built around them—it was easy, and probably inevitable, that sex would degenerate into a mechanical exercise in self-gratification and exploitation that is mutual but rarely mutual in exactly the same way: Men and women want different things out of their sex lives and out of the relationships built around them. What was once called "women's liberation" has mainly liberated hetero-sexual men at the expense of their female partners, who have been reduced to something not entirely distinguishable from equipment for an advanced kind of masturbation. The consequences of that are everywhere obvious: the undeniable social defects of single mother-hood, the unhappiness that women experience from delaying mar-riage and motherhood until too late in life, the impossible socio-economic expectations laid upon many women, etc.

The current moral panic involving the "epidemic" of sexual assault on college campuses—an epidemic whose existence is to be found nowhere in the actual sexual-assault data—is the revenge young women are exacting for their exploitation and the social blessing that accompanies that exploitation. As Meghan McArdle has eloquently argued, the libertarian approach to sex, which insists that *consent* is the only moral issue of any consequences, leaves women without a moral language to describe their unhappiness with the state of their intimate relationships, and so they attempt to link their regrets to con-sent even in situations in which there was no violation of that consent.

Perhaps it did not occur to the feminists of the 1960s that women themselves, their interests and their happiness, were the principal burdens from which sex was to be liberated, or that the result of this would be more sex with more partners but also more loneliness—a kind of loneliness that did not exist before the twentieth century, one for which we still do not have a precise name.

By connecting everyone to everyone—promiscuously, without the traditional consequences—social media has created another new kind of loneliness. Social-media users are the Casanovas of digital rage: They may have an impressive tally of interactions, but none of them is satisfactory or enduring. They are connected superficially; they are alone more profoundly.

Like sex liberated from responsibility, social-media relationships are divorced from other kinds of human involvement, hence the common observation that otherwise mentally normal adult human beings say and do things on social media that they would never dream of doing in a face-to-face conversation, treating strangers and slight acquaintances with a hostility and brutality that they would not countenance—indeed, that most of them could not muster—in a real-world interpersonal interaction. There are no serious consequences for doing so, in many cases: Popularity-minded people may keep a careful eye on their follower-counts, but losing one follower or potential follower over a harsh or hysterical exchange is no great cost; in fact, it may be a benefit, since shocking and extraordinary behavior draws followers as it draws attention. Emotion sells, and extremism sells—and, on social media, the two are difficult to distinguish.

Extreme behavior and angry extremist posturing are a familiar part of group dynamics, but their role is frequently misunderstood. Deliberation does not, generally speaking, make people more nuanced or charitable or sophisticated in their understanding of their opponents' views—or in their understanding of their own views, for that matter. In-group deliberation generally leads to *radicalization*; which is to say, deliberations within groups of like-minded people tend to move the group toward a more extreme expression of the position the group members already hold, leaving the median group member's views more extreme than they had been.[1] Studies have suggested that the less coherent the group is and the less its members know about the subject of their deliberation, the stronger the tendency toward polarization. This has been observed dramatically in situations in which amateurs are given complex semi-professional tasks that are unfamiliar to them, e.g., when jurors discuss cases among themselves. In one much-cited mock-jury experiment,[2] deliberations among jurors found those who favored more severe punishments became even more severe after discussion, while their more lenient counterparts became more liberal; the effect was present for both types, but the more punitive (the researchers label them "authoritarian," as in the Stenner-Feldman approach discussed earlier) jurors had the more pronounced deepening of their preexisting lean.

Deliberation between members of groups in disagreement, on the other hand, tends to reinforce one's sense of solidarity with one's own group and one's hostility toward the other. Which is to say: Both interactions with like-minded people and interactions with people holding other viewpoints tend to reinforce the preexisting views of those in the conversation and to exaggerate them.[3] For that reason,

---

1 See, for example, "Birds of a Feather: Homophily in Social Networks," Miller McPherson, Lynn Smith-Lovin, and James Cook, *Annual Review of Sociology*, August 2001: "Similarity breeds connection. This principle—the homophily principle—structures network ties of every type, including marriage, friendship, work, advice, support, information transfer, exchange, co-membership, and other types of relationship. The result is that people's personal networks are homogeneous with regard to many sociodemographic, behavioral, and intrapersonal characteristics. Homophily limits people's social worlds in a way that has powerful implications for the information they receive, the attitudes they form, and the interactions they experience. Homophily in race and ethnicity creates the strongest divides in our personal environments, with age, religion, education, occupation, and gender following in roughly that order."

2 "Authoritarianism and decisions of mock juries: Evidence of jury bias and group polarization," R. M. Bray and A. M. Noble, *Journal of Personality and Social Psychology*, 1978.

3 "The idea that men are created free and equal is both true and misleading: men are created different; they lose their social freedom and their individual autonomy in seeking to become like each other." David Riesman, Nathan Glazer, and Reuel Denney, *The Lonely Crowd*, 1950.

the structure of social media makes outraged polarization practically inevitable. Professor Barbara Fields of Columbia is not wrong to call them the "anti-social media."

After the murder of abortionist George Tiller by an anti-abortion extremist, Sarita Yardi of the Georgia Institute of Technology and danah boyd[4] of Microsoft Research undertook a fascinating study of how the conversation about Tiller's murder played out on Twitter.[5] They did not find a great deal of evidence that either opinion polarization or opinion extremity increased during the course of the conversation they observed (the first twenty-four hours after the murder); what they did observe was a significant increase in emotion, particularly anger. Time, reflection, and discussion did not make people calmer, more reasonable, or more willing to entertain the possibility of good-faith disagreement—people just got angry. People grew angrier even as discussion of religion, always a fraught topic in the context of abortion, declined. The authors note: "This resulted in some disengaging from dialogue and debate." What that implies is that those who remain in the debate are the ones most comfortable with—or actively in search of—dramatic displays of emotion: junkies, high on rage. They continue:

> ...some people refuse to speak to people with opposing views and instead direct conversation only toward their co-ideologues. However, the technical constraints on Twitter could exacerbate the effect. The kinds of interactions we observed suggest that Twitter is exposing people to multiple diverse points of view but that the medium is insufficient for reasoned discourse and debate, instead privileging haste and emotion.

---

4 Sic-ly pretentious, like bell hooks et al.
5 "Dynamic Debates: An Analysis of Group Polarization Over Time on Twitter," *Bulletin of Science, Technology & Society*, 2010.

... We observed a handful of extreme views in short periods of time; however, a month later, individual tweeting has largely returned to normative behavior with users' preexisting networks. Indeed, the large spike and subsequent decays in tweets following immediately after any event breaks out on Twitter suggests that people enjoy spreading news that are novel and popular.

Twitter affords different kinds of social participation. In the same way a reader has to skim the front page of a physical newspaper to get to the comic section, most Twitter users will be exposed to varied slices of news. Thus, many people may be witnessing diverse conversations and also participating in topics they otherwise may not have. This can influence how people spread information, how they mutate it, who they talk to, and what they say.

The point of such pseudo-conversation is not discussion—not the exchange of views and ideas. If anything, the actual exchange of substantial ideas would inhibit the desired outcome of the exercise. Outrage is *intoxicating*, and like other intoxicants, it makes people stupid: But there is a reason why the term "social drinker" exists— becoming intoxicated as a group is an almost universal human social-bonding experience. To whip on the metaphor just a little bit, these are people who start the night with a beer or two and then start taking tequila shots, not people sipping a 1982 Latour; they aren't here for the mineral notes of the Bordeaux—they are here to get falling-down drunk on venom as a way of attempting to deepen their connections to their friends, real and mediated.

And when people are drinking, there's always that one guy,[6] whose drunken antics are, in a relative way, reassuring: "Well, at least I wasn't

---

6 His name is on the cover of this book.

the one who got kicked out of a Denny's / got arrested / drunk-dialed his boss / tried to pop a beer open with his dick." The most extreme participants in the conversation—the "fringe"—play a similar important role: They establish a rhetorical boundary, inside of which everyone may assure themselves that they are reasonable, that indefensible extremism lies one step beyond. This happens even as the group grows more extreme on average. "A small number of users were responsible for the majority of the most extreme posts. However, these tweets and users define group boundaries—the occasional extreme post may bind the rest of the group as rational." The extremist fringe is not outside the in-group—it defines the in-group. Group dynamics, rather than reason, argument, or evidence, define what is to be counted as rational.

This has proved corrosive to political discourse—not only online, but in the real world. Because substantive discourse has largely been displaced by gestures of affiliation or disaffiliation, because the model of discourse has been reduced to black-hats/white-hats, and because in-group dynamics tend to encourage and reward extremism, the popular tide has turned very strongly against such old-fashioned liberal institutions as evidence, freedom of speech, and due process. Considering the sexual-assault claims made against football player Jameis Winston and filmmaker Woody Allen, along with the social-media mob attacks on Mozilla CEO Brendan Eich and former L. A. Clippers owner Donald Sterling, socialist commentator Fredrik DeBoer wrote:

> Online liberalism...is not actually a series of political beliefs and alliances but instead a set of social cues that are adopted to demonstrate one's class background—economic class, certainly, but more cultural class, the various linguistic and consumptive signals that assure those around you that you're the right kind of person and which appear to be the only thing that America's twenty-something

progressives really care about anymore. The dominance of personal branding and cultural signaling over political theory means that liberal attitudes change very rapidly and then congeal into a consensus that is supposedly so obviously correct that it does not need defending.

…In the past year, liberalism as an elite social phenomenon has abandoned first the rights of the accused and second the right to free expression. The Jameis Winston and Woody Allen sexual-assault cases saw the rise of resistance to any discussion whatsoever of due process and rights of the accused…[And those] mentioning those rights at all were immediately and angrily denounced, and accused of insufficient resistance to (if not outright support for) rape and rape culture.[7]

Online politics is from this point of view more accurately understood as an etiquette than as an ideology. Etiquette should not be written off as something trivial: A society expresses its most basic character in its manners. Etiquette tells us more about social norms for how we interact with others than the law ever could.

Social media, given all the preceding, is of no practical value as a tool of discourse. It also makes people miserable. Researchers at the University of Pittsburgh found that the young social-media users who checked their accounts most frequently were nearly three times as likely to suffer from depression; those who spent the most total time on social media were almost twice as likely to be depressed than those who spent the least.[8]

---

7 A similar attitude punishes lawyers for defending politically unpopular clients, as in the case of Ronald Sullivan, who, following campus protests, was dismissed as a dean by Harvard for serving on Harvey Weinstein's defense team.

8 "Association Between Social Media Use and Depression among U.S. Young Adults," *Depression and Anxiety*, April 2016.

Social media has made a perverse contribution to public life: By giving everyone an equal opportunity to speak, it has revealed how little of interest most people have to say—and how little the content of what they say actually matters when set against in-group tribal affiliation. That this comes as a revelation to the speakers rather than their auditors is significant even if obvious. Boring people are easily bored by others, but most of them harbor in their souls the belief, explicable and without any support, that they are uniquely interesting, gifted, funny, witty, intelligent—qualities that would become apparent if only they could get in front of the right kind of audience.[9] Finding out how boring they are—and how little the world actually cares about them when given the opportunity to pay attention—is a jolt. Even the embrace of the tribe is only lukewarm, sterile, and superficial: a four-second online hook-up, not a genuine intimate relationship.

Small wonder they are depressed.

For its lonely and atomistic constituents, the social media mob—like the racist's race, the nationalist's nation, the socialist's proletariat—performs two functions that may seem contradictory on the surface but which are in fact entirely complementary: The in-group dissolves the individual identity, relieving the stressed and anxious pleb of an identity that was more a burden to him than an asset; at the same time, it provides a new and larger sense of identity as a member of the in-group. To join a mob is simultaneously an act of self-abasement and self-aggrandizement.[10]

---

9 Most writers meet the occasional person who believes he would enjoy "being a writer," which he takes to mean attending a lot of literary soirees, wearing black turtlenecks, and signing books. The writing part—sitting alone in a room—does not come up so often.

10 "We are proud when we identify ourselves with an imaginary self, a leader, a holy cause, a collective body of possessions. There is fear and intolerance in pride; it is insensitive and uncompromising. The less promise and potency in the self, the more imperative is the need for pride. The core of pride is self-rejection." Eric Hoffer, *The Passionate State of Mind*, 1955. Here's something weird and hilarious: Anna Popova's "Brain Pickings" blog attributes the above quote, and a great chunk of a Hoffer essay, to…Bruce Lee. I cannot tell if that's supposed to be a prank, or what.

Historically, this has been more obvious, owing to the more demographically discrete forms of mobbery, such as racism and nationalism. The racist in glorifying the race as a collective diminishes himself as an individual but lifts himself up as a constituent of the object of his glorification. Julien Benda noted the peculiarity of this phenomenon in *The Treason of the Intellectuals*, specifically in the context of artists and writers, whose abdication of individuality serves "to increase the enjoyment of himself by himself, since the consciousness of the individual ego is doubled in profundity by consciousness of the national ego."[11] Benda was especially put-off by his detection of this tendency in artists, whose profession demands individualism—to be individuals is, in a sense, the business of all artists. His explanation for this abdication was, in part, careerism: The artist needs material, and the glory of the nation provides opportunities for the exercise of lyricism. Social media has not made us all artists, but it has made us all pundits, a creative occupation that combines the general professional talents of preacher and clown. Social media gives people the worst parts of being a writer or performer without any of the ancillary benefits—and, for the vast majority of social-media users, without any pay.[12]

Depression, anger, banality: Why do people subject themselves to this?

Fame. Of a sort.

---

11 In this sense, "nation" need not mean only that: generations, races, religions, political factions, etc. What are the first words Lena Dunham puts into her alter ego's mouth in *Girls*? "I think I might be the voice of my generation." But no such ambition made stand without its being laundered through ironic detachment: "Or…at least, *a* voice of *a* generation."

12 "No man but a blockhead ever wrote except for money." Samuel Johnson, as quoted by James Boswell, *The Life of Johnson*, 1791.

CHAPTER SEVEN

Cage Matches

You might consider how escape from a cage must surely
require, foremost, awareness of the fact of the cage.

—*David Foster Wallace*, Infinite Jest, *1996*

S ocial-media users are lonely, isolated, and in search of significance. They seek to associate themselves with people who are
significant, and significance is a criterion that is easy enough
to conflate with fame, celebrity, or some kind of public profile, which
is a proxy for status. Fromm traces the modern longing for fame to
the end of the medieval period, as Europe's fixed status hierarchies
gave way to the disruption and uncertainty of early capitalism. We
are in the midst of a similar disruption as globalization upends longstanding economic arrangements and communities while Instant
Culture erodes the traditional bases of social relationships. What is
happening in the early twenty-first century is a kind of reemergence
of capitalism: twentieth century postwar capitalism shedding its skin
as the new organism emerges, and much of what Fromm saw at the
end of the Middle Ages has returned in high-tech form. From *Escape
from Freedom*:

This underlying insecurity resulting from the position of an isolated individual in a hostile world tends to explain the genesis of a character trait which was...characteristic of the individual of the Renaissance and not present, at least in the same intensity, in the member of the medieval social structure: his passionate craving for fame. If the meaning of life has become doubtful, if one's relations to others and to oneself do not offer security, then fame is one means to silence one's doubts. It has a function to be compared with that of the Egyptian pyramids or the Christian faith in immortality: it elevates one's individual life from its limitations and instability to the plane of indestructibility; if one's name is known to one's contemporaries and if one can hope that it will last for centuries, then one's life has meaning and significance by this very reflection of it in the judgments of others.

Bishop Berkeley insists: "To be is to be seen." By whom? By as many people as possible, and, especially, by as many significant[1] people as possible.

Everyone now has the theoretical opportunity to connect with everyone else, including celebrities, politicians, and other high-profile people, with whom any social connection, no matter how trivial or ephemeral, is considered desirable. This is the Golden Age of Fame Whores. And any connection will do: Fans of this or that celebrity rejoice when the second-tier college sophomore who operates that celebrity's social-media accounts follows, likes, or retweets them—a great many social-media profiles begin with a rapturous "followed by x"—but the boring, the intolerable, the trolls, and the late-night incel porn masturbators have to settle for boasting about who blocks them.

---

1 You can just assume the asterisk here and elsewhere.

Example from personal experience: A person whose name means nothing to me and appears nowhere in my work maintains a Twitter profile that reads: "Kevin D. Williamson once called me a petty criminal," followed by a disclaimer regarding which class of pronouns he prefers. Google does not bring up any instance of my having written anything about him or having mentioned him in any capacity, but whatever I am supposed to have written or said about him is, apparently, the first thing he wants you to know. I'm a pretty big Kevin D. Williamson fan, and even I think that's sad. But I take comfort in the knowledge that I'll be cast aside as soon as Howie Mandel blocks him.

Journalism and its not-very-bright kid brother, television punditry, offer a weird kind of minor celebrity. At the very high end, television pundits are proper celebrities: Tucker Carlson may not be as well-known as a minor Kardashian—and he is in the same business as the Kardashians—but he is as publicly recognizable as a middle-range movie or television actor, a Jason Bateman or a J. K. Simmons with his beard grown out, a Howie Mandel-level celebrity at least. My *National Review* colleague Kat Timpf, who is better-known as a Fox News regular, is famous enough that she gets attacked in public from time to time, most recently having been chased out of a Brooklyn bar by a raving lunatic who had had either too many cocktails or too few. But even an obscure print dinosaur like me has one of those awkward encounters they call "getting recognized" about once a month.[2]

---

2 A while back, I was in an Academy sporting-goods store in Houston when a young man approached me with his hand out in a friendly gesture. "Love your stuff!" he said, shaking my hand and smiling...but never bothering to interrupt the telephone conversation he was having simultaneously. That's kind of my sweet spot, really: Well-known enough that people sometimes want to come and introduce themselves, but not so much that anybody gets too weird about it. Fortunately, I was in Academy that day buying a couple of boxes of 6.5 Creedmoor ammunition, so I was in character. But I intend to use this episode as an excuse if my wife ever tries to send me to the store for feminine products.

The slight penetration of the world of celebrity by journalists and commentators has combined with the trends discussed above to produce one of the truly peculiar phenomena of our times: the media hate-fuck. A media hate-fuck[3] is what happens when someone who disagrees with a certain media figure follows that person obsessively, like it is his job.[4] It climaxes in a series of moral orgasms, each more intense than the one before, as the onslaught of outrages from the object of his disaffections continues relentlessly. Why anybody would want to be hate-fucked by a stranger who doesn't even know he is hate-fucking you is difficult to understand. But Eros, too, is a jealous god.

I have always found this perplexing, and a little bit embarrassing when it comes to my own case: It seems unfair, and more than a little sad, that there are all of these people who hate me but take an intense, energetic, occasionally erotic interest in my career, while I hardly ever think about them at all unless something shows up in my feed.[5] I have been on Fox News a few dozen times, but I have never watched a single Fox News program all the way through, including those programs that I have been on all the way through. And some of those shows I like. Investing that much time and energy in something I hate—for no compensation other than the pleasure

---

3 It is appropriate here that the first name appearing in Urban Dictionary's usage examples for "hate-fuck" is that of Ann Coulter: "'Man, I would like to hate-fuck Ann Coulter,' said Jeff, a staunch liberal." I guarantee you that Ann Coulter does not think about Jeff at all, one way or the other.

4 Which, sometimes, it is. I once read some tweets from the poor little Caitlyn over at Media Matters for America assigned to the Kevin D. Williamson file. She complained that it was dreadful work, and I do not doubt that it was. But she never seemed to wonder why she didn't have a better job. *National Review*, my journalistic home, used to maintain a blog dedicated to correcting the errors and distortions of Paul Krugman. For a while, I edited *NR*'s "Media Watch" blog.

5 Searching for one's own name on the Internet is supposed to be some sort of embarrassing faux pas, but I do not see why: When people write about me, I respond, if what's been written is worth responding to. People who sell thoughts to the public used to consider that a part of their job.

of hating—is inexplicable to me. I am not above reading the *New York Times*[6] op-ed page on a slow news day looking for a fight to pick—those endless digital column-inches are not going to fill themselves—but it is not the sort of thing I'd make a hobby of.

David Foster Wallace argued that aspiring amateurs who envy professional athletes suffer from the "delusion that envy has a reciprocal." They believe that if only they could get themselves on the other side of the envy equation, then all of the loneliness and dissatisfaction they feel in their current situation of envy would be transubstantiated into joy and contentedness equal in weight and scope. Envy and spite are two cocktails with a heavy pour of the same brand of hatred—and both are methods for trying to make that interior pain exterior.

The ochlocrats have many deficiencies, personal, intellectual, sexual, social, hygienic, and otherwise. But their most pressing deficiency is their lack of someone to hate other than themselves. They are not in need of an enemy merely for the purpose of psychological distraction, welcome as that might be to many of the members of this cohort. The antagonist serves a much more important social purpose—he is the purpose-pretext around which the personal and social identity of the ochlocrat is constructed.

Perhaps you find it difficult at this stage in your life to imagine being so mentally impaired and emotionally besotted that you cannot function without the crutch of some great fiction. But all of you know what it is like to be stone-cold stupid and high on rage: All you need to do is remember what it felt like to be a child.

When I was a boy in the 1970s, a few of us friends from the neighborhood formed a gang. None of us had ever seen a gang in

---

6 My fellow conservatives seethe about this on purely tribal grounds, but I subscribe to the *New York Times* and read it every day. Its op-ed page is terrible, and its national political news is hit-and-miss, but it is an otherwise excellent national newspaper, though of course inferior to the *New York Post* as a New York City newspaper.

action or met a member of an actual gang, but we knew the word and understood the concept, as all boys instinctively do—Us and Them. Our gang grew up out of the same Cold War cultural ferment and thin-spread paranoia that would produce *Red Dawn* a few years later, and, indeed, we spent a fair amount of time planning which sporting-good stores we would loot for guns and ammunition come the Soviet invasion and the need to head for the hills.[7] We had a name (I cannot remember what, and it may have changed a few times), military-style ranks and a chain of command (there may have been five of us), colors, insignia, etc. What we did not have was something to do. I grew up in a peaceful, sedate Texas college town. I am sure that it had its share of crime, addiction, and violence—in fact, I know that it did; my home was a constant crime scene—but none of that really touched us elementary-school kids. Such horrors as we actually knew were ordinary and domestic, and hence hardly noticed.

What the drama we were enacting in our gangster play-acting lacked was an *antagonist*. Most of the kids in my neighborhood and at my school got along pretty well; poor Keith Black and I once got into a desultory fistfight in my front yard simply because we were the two biggest kids in the school, and it was understood to be inevitable that we would. (I am happy that we got that out of the way when we did, while I had the advantage and acted on it, rather than a few years later, when Keith would have proved a much tougher opponent.) We did not have an enemy, so we were obliged to invent one: a rival gang with a name, colors, and insignia of its own, and a dastardly leader with an involved backstory and a penchant for remarkable cruelty, feeding his victims feet-first into the lawnmowers that were the most dangerous things any of us had much real experience with. We would sometimes catch a glimpse of him and his henchmen, spying on us from a tall tree in someone's backyard or exiting the park or

---

7 Heading for the hills is a hard thing to think on the Texas Panhandle, where the nearest hills are a few hundred miles away.

schoolyard just as we were showing up. The game lasted only as long as it had complete psychological and literary buy-in from our little gang—such fantasies are as delicate as soap bubbles and collapse immediately when someone is rude enough to shove them roughly into reality.

Such childhood games cease to be charming around the time one's age reaches the double digits; by the time *Red Dawn* came out in 1984, we were still planning for insurgent warfare against the Russkies—you can imagine the way in which we sagely nodded our sixth-grade heads at one another in the theater during that movie and the strategy session that followed afterward at Mazzio's Pizza—but we had given up the imaginary gangs and the imaginary enemies. We didn't talk about that, and it would have embarrassed us if someone had brought it up, something like the way we'd have felt if our grandmothers reminded us that only a few years before we'd talked about being cowboys or explorers when we grew up. Our attention had begun to turn, in an adolescent way, toward the real world, and toward politics. In the real world, there were real enemies: the Soviets preeminent among them at the time, but also Leopoldo Galtieri, the ayatollahs in Iran, the PLO, IRA, etc. None of these related to us in an immediate and intimate way—not like the invaders in *Red Dawn*—but we were immaturely and imperfectly beginning to come to grips with the world as it actually was and is, and to understand, in spite of our Wolverine fantasies, that we were not in fact at the center of the drama.

Shedding these self-centered illusions marks the beginning of the end of childhood. In retrospect, I would not have been worse off if I had waited just a little longer.

It is Christmas as I write these pages, and my wife is wearing a T-shirt with an image of Santa Claus over the caption: "Don't Stop Believing." (Another member of the family is wearing the same shirt but with a Spice Girls-derived caption: "Tell me what you want, what you really really want.") I would not be the one to tell a little kid that there is no Santa Claus or Tooth Fairy, or that the Easter Bunny is a perverse cultural vestige of an ancient fertility cult that never failed to give the proper due to the legendary fecundity of the *Lepidorae* clan. But someone should break the bad news to Antifa and their imitators online and in the real world: There isn't any Nazi menace lurking in the United States. And the play-acting on that score would be embarrassing for thirteen-year-olds—for thirty-two-year-olds, it's delusional and neurotic. There is no secret cabal of Cultural Marxists out there; *patriarchy* is a figure of speech; white supremacy is not the American zeitgeist.

Even with the shadow of President Donald Trump falling across these fruited plains, this happy republic is not three tweets away from the Holocaust or one bad-hair day away from cattle cars. Melania Trump may very well wish that she were isolated in a bunker as the world crumbles around her, but she is not so lucky as that.

So why all the fantasies about the rising Nazi menace—the strangely welcoming and *celebratory* hysteria about the dark shadow of fascism that is, as Tom Wolfe wrote, always falling across the United States but always landing on Europe? On the subject of Nazis, P. J. O'Rourke once observed that no one fantasizes about being tied up and sexually ravished by someone dressed as a liberal, and I suppose the same thing extends to such ordinary Republicans and figures of the Right as Mitch McConnell and Lou Dobbs.[8] The most infamous practitioner of white racial-solidarity politics as of this writing is Richard Spencer, a well-heeled and gormless suburban kid from Highland Park.

Nazis should be made of sterner stuff—or at least less fabulous stuff.

---

8 Odontophiliacs notwithstanding.

Eric Hoffer, the American social critic and author of *The True Believer,* had our ochlocrats' number way back in the 1950s: "Passionate hatred can give meaning and purpose to an empty life. Thus people haunted by the purposelessness of their lives try to find a new content not only by dedicating themselves to a holy cause but also by nursing a fanatical grievance. A mass movement offers them unlimited opportunities for both."

If the fanaticism and the mass movement is to serve its purpose, then these causes and grievances must be matters of public performance rather than matters of the private soul. They must be occasions for the pursuit of glory, and only the most cultivated kind of mind can comprehend the idea of a private glory. "Glory," Hoffer wrote, "is largely a theatrical concept. There is no striving for glory without a vivid awareness of an audience.... The desire to escape or camouflage their unsatisfactory selves develops in the frustrated a facility for pretending—for making a show—and also a readiness to identify themselves wholly with an imposing spectacle."

A particular form of *spectacle* is *ritual.* And that is what the social-media mob attack actually is: a purification ritual, analogous to the scapegoat ritual described in Leviticus.

CHAPTER EIGHT

Antidiscourse: High-Frequency Trading in the Status Market

Simulacra of simulacra of simulacra. A dilute tincture of
Ralph Lauren, who had himself diluted the glory days
of Brooks Brothers, who themselves had stepped on the
product of Jermyn Street and Savile Row... There must
be some Tommy Hilfiger event horizon, beyond which it
is impossible to be more derivative, more removed from
the source, more devoid of soul.

—*William Gibson*, Pattern Recognition, *2005*

P olitical discourse is not about discourse because politics is not
about politics. Contemporary political discourse—what I
describe here as *antidiscourse*—is political only in the mutant
sense described by Michael Oakeshott, misused as "an instrument
of passion." In its perverted form, he writes, "the art of politics is to
inflame and direct desire."

Desire for what? Social standing, connection, context, belongingness—and *revenge*, which consists in trying to deny those first four
goods to rival social groups.[1]

---

1 No matter how lopsided the rivalry. Anti-Semitism, for example, is strangely prominent
in many communities where there are no Jews.

Politics is about *status*, and antidiscourse is a tool for attempting to raise and lower the status of different social groups or individuals taken as representative of those groups. Social-media mob attacks are not arguments—they are rituals of humiliation[2] that perform the tripartite function of lowering the status of an out-group, raising one's own individual status within the in-group through obedience and enthusiastic conformity with group regulations, and, by doing the foregoing *together*, reinforcing the sense of belongingness and solidarity within the group.

The timing of such mob attacks is one clue that these are status rituals rather than political negotiations. The views of Bret Stephens and Bari Weiss were well-known before they were hired by the *New York Times*; the campaigns against them were activated not by their having written or thought this or that purportedly horrible thing but by their joining the *New York Times*—which is to say, by their elevation in status. (Many of my fellow conservatives are vocal and indeed vehement in their sneering at the *New York Times*, but I have never known one of them to turn down an offer of work there.) The mob attack unfolded on plainly tribal lines, as one can see in Glenn Greenwald's account of the matter:

> Controversy erupted on April 14 over the *New York Times*'s hiring of neoconservative climate-skeptic and anti-Arab polemicist Bret Stephens as the paper's newest Op-Ed page columnist, hired away from the *Wall Street Journal*'s right-wing op-ed page. But just two days after it unveiled him, the paper's op-ed page, with much less fanfare, announced that it had also hired a carbon copy of Stephens named Bari Weiss, also from the *Wall Street Journal* op-ed page, to "write and commission the kinds of quick-off-the-news pieces" that will "amplify the section's already important voice in the national conversation."

---

2 "Jon Stewart destroys . . . x, y, z!" etc.

In her short tenure, Weiss…has given the paper exactly what it apparently wanted when it hired her. She has churned out a series of trite, shallow, cheap attacks on already-marginalized left-wing targets that have made her a heroine in the insular neocon and right-wing intelligentsia precincts in which she, Stephens, and so many other NYT op-ed writers reside.[3]

Which is to say: "Egad, Buffy! One of *those* people!" Greenwald here is unusually obvious[4] in his attention to the relative status of in-group and out-group, and, of course, he is more than willing to tell himself a story—an obvious fiction—to justify this as a moral necessity: that left-wing targets are marginalized by "insular neocon and right-wing" elements in the context of the opinion section of the *New York Times* is preposterous.

The situation was the roughly same with me and THAT AUGUST JOURNALISTIC INSTITUTION: No one at the *New York Times* or the *Washington Post* had any interest in my views on abortion prior to my being hired there; my views about public affairs are reasonably well-known, having been explored at some length in *National Review*, by far the largest and most-read opinion journal of its kind, as well as in outlets ranging from the *New York Post* and *New York Daily News* to *Academic Affairs* and *Playboy*.[5] I had shared those views on Fox News, MSNBC, the CBS *Evening News*, in books, in *Mad Dogs &*

---

3 "The NY Times's Newest Op-Ed Hire, Bari Weiss, Embodies its Worst Failings—and its Lack of Viewpoint Diversity," *The Intercept*, August 31, 2017.

4 *Unusually obvious* is, unfortunately, what the gifted Mr. Greenwald does these days.

5 In one of the more Orwellian moments of the *Atlantic* episode, *Playboy* quietly scrubbed my work from its web site and archives. Pornographers apparently don't have the balls they once did. A book editor who had already offered me money—that's how you know they're serious—suddenly went silent and could not be reached by email or telephone. I apply to my circle of friends and trusted colleagues the same logic that Saint John Paul the Great applied to the Catholic Church during his papacy: I am comfortable if holding to my principles leaves a smaller but better congregation.

Englishmen, the podcast I record with Charles C. W. Cooke, etc. My views were public, having been, you know, *published*,[6] and discussed in public so extensively that I often get sick of the sound of my own voice.

The remarks that purportedly made me too radioactive for employment at THAT AUGUST JOURNALISTIC INSTITUTION predated my employment there by years and generated relatively little controversy at the time they were made, just a few predictably tendentious misrepresentations in a few marginal left-wing blogs.[7] Only a few weeks before the *Huffington Post* began denouncing me as a monster with ideas "not worth debating," the editor-in-chief of that publication, Lydia Polgreen, had contacted me seeking recommendations for a new national political correspondent. Strange, that a black lesbian former *New York Times* editor should have sought out the opinion of an allegedly racist, misogynist, homophobic monster and bad journalist to boot, but, of course, no one took seriously any such proposition at the time. Of course, I haven't heard from her since.

As long as I was at *National Review,* and as long as Bret Stephens and Bari Weiss were at the *Wall Street Journal,* we were only ordinary players in the antidiscourse game: rivals, to be sure, but rivals who

---

6 I will confess to having been slightly annoyed by certain headhunters' claims to have "uncovered" this or that thing I said or wrote. I believe my podcast is available right there on the iTunes store. Even your mom can work that.

7 "Occasionally, I'll get an e-mail from some blogger on the left, and the e-mail will contain nothing but a link. The link will lead me to some slam he's written about me. A day or two will go by, and he'll e-mail again. This time, he'll say, in effect, 'Hey, don't you see that I've slammed you? How come you're not responding to me? What's the matter with you? Why won't you play?'…About ten years ago, a Solzhenitsyn son told me something about his father: He almost never answered his critics (who were numerous and fierce), and he didn't even read them. He preferred to write *The Red Wheel.* 'He could have written *The Red Wheel,*' said his son, 'or he could have dealt with his critics. There wasn't time to do both.'" Jay Nordlinger, *National Review,* July 23, 2012.

knew our places. Affiliation with the organizations that the Left regards as its own private status preserve is what rendered us intolerable. The status shift, and not anything having to do with our work itself, is what aroused the mob. The minute reordering of status hierarchies is the "activation" that Karen Stenner wrote about in *The Authoritarian Dynamic*. It is remarkable that a society that is so crude and oblivious in so many ways[8] is in other ways so careful, so scrupulous, so carefully attentive to the smallest of details and the most obscure disputations.[9] They may not know which countries have nuclear weapons or how federal finances work, but they know who is up and who is down—and, more to the point, whom they want to see up and whom down.

"Occasionally the real force behind a political ideology is the subconsciously held desire that a certain group of people should not be allowed to rise in relative status," the economist Tyler Cowen argues. "Take the so-called 'left wing.' Some of these people favor a kind of meritocracy. They feel it is unfair that money so determines access in capitalist society and they do not want the monied class to rise in relative status, certainly not above the status of the smart people and the virtuous people. It is important to fight for the principle that the desires of this monied class have a relatively low priority in the social ranking. Egalitarianism is the rhetoric of the day, and readjusting the status of other Americans to the status of this monied class often receives more attention than elevating the very poorest in the world to a higher absolute level.... Inequalities which do not raise the status

---

8 A young American girl seeing the sights in Rome with her parents witnessed a terrible scene and asked, with terror in her voice, "What are they *doing* to that man?" at which point her parents, in the dignified quiet of the basilica, tried to explain to her Caravaggio's *Crucifixion of Saint Peter*. They did not seem to know who Peter was, exactly, or what was his connection to Rome.

9 "Madonna Sparks Butt Implant Debate Following Stonewall Performance" is an actual headline of January 2, 2019.

of this monied class, such as inequalities in the sphere of beauty or teenage sex, don't come under so much criticism."[10]

The status-adjustment project can never be directly confessed. The mob's explanation of its rationale is essentially a reconstitution of the Catholic idea of scandal, i.e. that by allowing certain words to be said and thought to be thought in high-status venues, wickedness is implicitly valorized in a way that will lead more people into sin— i.e. that referring to Bradley Manning as "Bradley Manning" will through the flapping of rhetorical butterfly wings lead to the murder of a transgender prostitute working the Third Avenue Bridge in New York City.[11] But even this explanation acknowledges the centrality of status to the concerns at hand; it simply attaches a very tenuous hypothetical evil to the project in order to provide a pretext for the pursuit of an actual evil, the suppression of free speech.[12]

I do not wish to be laboriously bipartisan here, but it is the case that this is a phenomenon that manifests in nearly identical ways on both sides of the political divide. No one was very exercised about Sarah Jeong's crude racial sentiments until she joined the *New York Times*. With apologies to Gavin McInnes, nobody gives a fully processed bolus about *Vice*.[13]

---

10 "Move on—this isn't true here," Marginal Revolution, July 26, 2008.

11 Shout out to Mott Haven.

12 Because we live in morally illiterate times, you sometimes hear this argument: "Suppressing the free speech of Nazis is a moral good, because we want a world in which Nazis are afraid to say what they think in public." The only way that is defensible as a logical proposition is if you deny that there is value in freedom of speech *per se*, in which case, we don't have anything to say to one another.

13 Except for organized transsexualism. Those people care about *everything* and tried to have McInness shitcanned from one of the companies he founded after he published an essay titled "Transphobia Is Perfectly Natural." Sample rhetoric: "You're not a man; you don't even know what TurfBuilder is." Not very funny, really, but what's less funny is the message you get if you try to access the essay on Thought Catalog, where it originally was published: "The article you are trying to read has been reported by the community as hateful or abusive content." "Reported by the community" is CAFFEINE-FREE DIET MAOISM at its most insipid.

The *New York Times*, thankfully for its columnists and to the credit of its owners, for the moment has enough confidence in its own very high status that it could not be mau-maued into reversing its own editorial judgment. The same, unfortunately, cannot be said for THAT AUGUST JOURNALISTIC INSTITUTION, which had been edited by Jeffrey Goldberg but now is edited by the mob. But the *Times* faces the same cultural and economic pressures associated with the tribal culture of social media. It simply has enough self-respect (and paying subscribers) to bear the related opportunity costs. That is not broadly true across the traditional media, which is now economically subordinate to social media and, hence, well on its way toward becoming culturally subordinate as well.

Because status is relative, it is understood as a zero-sum game. If a member of the Red Tribe is elevated to a position at the *New York Times*, then it follows that all of the members of the Blue Tribe are, however marginally, diminished in their status.

In primitive societies—and we are here dealing with modern primitives, tribesmen of an emergent high-tech barbarism—status games and status rituals are typically brutal. Status-raising and status-lowering concerns are why conquering armies engage in mass rapes or in massacres that serve no military or political purpose.

Revisit, for a moment, the *ur*-case.[14] Justine Sacco, though an obscure person from a public-profile point of view, was an attractive target for a mob attack. Set aside the problem of *envy* as a sin and a vice and consider it in purely mechanical terms as a factor in group dynamics, as a stand-in for status anxiety. A nice-looking blonde with a big and slightly dopey smile, a thirty-year-old woman in a high-profile job on a glamorous vacation trip to an exotic locale, Sacco naturally attracted envy, and that envy inevitably was sexualized, something that can be clearly seen in the nature of the insulted directed

---

14 There is a good argument that the ur-case is the Gamergate controversy, but that seems to me different in character—more obviously a cabal than a mob. Plus, no one cares about these nerds.

her way: "dumb bitch," "stupid cunt," etc. And that, of course, is what that episode was really about: The Sacco mob, whose angriest and most profane members were overwhelmingly male, saw an opportunity to hurt a young woman whom its members wanted to hurt for reasons almost entirely exogenous to the social-justice pretext put forward, and they acted on that opportunity. Her status was not related to celebrity; it was rooted in her looks, occupation, and social position.[15]

It is the status dynamic familiar from cat-calling: None of these Midtown Manhattan proles thinks that the pretty young woman in the expensive workday outfit going off to her job doing...whatever it is people like that do...is going to respond to their hoots and invitations with a wink and a smile, much less with a blowjob—that this is so obviously and undeniably the case is why she

---

15 Some very interesting stuff on this subject was written by none other than Sarah Jeong, who ended up experiencing a great deal more of it first-hand than she probably ever expected to. "The US National Violence Against Women Survey estimates that 60 percent of 'cyber stalking victims' are women. The National Center for Victims of Crimes estimates that women actually make up 70 percent. Working to Halt Online Abuse (WHOA) collected information from over 3,000 reports of 'cyber harassment' between 2000 and 2011 and found that 72.5 percent of reporters were female. The Bureau of Justice Statistics reports that 74 percent of individuals stalked online or offline are female. From 1996 to 2000, the majority of the NYPD Computer Investigation and Technology Unit's aggravated cyber harassment victims were female. In 2006, researchers placed silent bots on Internet Relay Chat. The bots with female names received 25 times more 'malicious private messages' (defined as 'sexually explicit or threatening language') than the bots with male names. Casual, non-academic, less-controlled experiments bear out similar results. As described in the next section, Twitter users have experimented with changing their avatars to reflect different genders and/or races. Male users masquerading as female users were rudely awakened to find that they were now subjected to a constant buzz of malicious or just plain obnoxious remarks. One man created a female profile on the dating app Tinder that did nothing but silently match. In less than a few hours, men had called the bot 'a bitch' and also told 'her' to 'go kill [herself].'" "Is Harassment Gendered?" *The Internet of Garbage*, (Vox Media, Inc., 2018). The book is worth reading in its entirety, even if the general takeaway—i.e., that Internet life is a lot like non-Internet life, made more brutal by immediacy and anonymity—is unsurprising.

must be ritually humiliated to begin with. What Aristotle said about envy is true of covetousness[16] and resentment: They hate that which is near enough to them to reach out toward but which is still just out of reach.

The Sacco affair had all the frenzy and brutality of a gang rape, which of course is what it was in stylized electronic form.[17] Gang rapes are a common tool of group solidarity-building, especially in warzones or in martial honor societies.

But why target Justine Sacco? Because she was vulnerable, for one thing, and abusing her was an easy way to fortify group identity. But lowering Sacco's status, however delightful to the mob, was only part of the exercise. As I argue above, the more important part of the ritual from a status point of view was raising the mob's status by establishing its lordship over an important corporation, in this case Sacco's employer.

What met Sacco was not political or social discourse but *antidiscourse*, which is to say, communication intended to prevent the exchange of ideas and views rather than to enable it. The particular form of antidiscourse directed at Sacco began with a familiar and sophomoric rhetorical scheme: treating a joke as though it were a serious proposition. This is not an honest error: It is an intentional strategy adopted with malicious and dishonest intent. These kinds of rhetorical schemes—many of which are simply images intended as insults—are not the exception in social-media political communication but the rule, at least among those who are not using social

---

16 Cf. Lecter, Hannibal, MD, first lecture on Marcus Aurelius, 1991.

17 "The ties that bind: How armed groups use violence to socialize fighters," Dara Kay Cohen, *Journal of Peace Research*, September 2017. "Violence directed at people outside of a group can increase individuals' identification with the unit. Gang rape is a stigmatizing, public, and sexualized form of violence, which can serve to sever ties to fighters' pasts, communicate norms about life as a fighter, and signal commitment to the new group."

media in a professional capacity as journalists or politicians.[18] Not that journalists and politicians are entirely immune from that, either: Cable-news pundits, who by the nature of their profession and its business realities, are obliged to constantly reassure the group that they belong to it, have adopted much of the worst of the etiquette of the commonalty.[19] And, most infamously, President Donald Trump continues to tweet like a deranged high-school sophomore who has been failed, entirely, by his English instructors.

Trump's is the most instructive case—by far. Once you understand that politics is about raising and lowering the status of competing social groups, the unlikely career of this quondam game-show host, serial bankrupt, and occasional performer in pornographic films[20] becomes easier to understand: Trump's boobishness and boorishness did not make him less likely to secure the Republican nomination and to win the general election but instead made it more likely. Trump is a cretin and an ignoramus, a deeply corrupt buffoon who does not appear to be able to go twenty-four hours without lying in public about something, but he is a master of humiliation. He coasted through the Republican primaries on the strength of his penchant for demeaning nicknames and other acts of petty humiliation. It is his gift. He made himself into a minor celebrity by publicly humiliating his first wife in the pages of the New York tabloids and, seeing that it worked, continued doing it.

There is a kind of genius to that: When someone is presented an outrageous insult, there are two possible courses of action, *each*

---

18 One of the deficiencies in the academic literature on social media's relationship to political discourse is that much of it is focused on the communication of politicians and elected officials, political professionals, and other non-typical users. Compounding that, much of the scholarship on non-professional social-media users is concentrated on atypical events, such as live-tweeting presidential debates or reacting to fresh news as in the George Tiller assassination study mentioned earlier.

19 As much as I used to enjoy "Sean Hannity Twitter After Eight," what with the eccentric spelling and the promises of deadly kung-fu action.

20 *Playboy Video Centerfold: Playmate 2000 Bernaola Twins.*

of which lowers the relative status of the insulted party. First, the insulted party can respond, which raises the issuer of the insult in relative status, confirming him as someone whose opinions, no matter how unserious or outrageously presented, must be responded to, while lowering the relative status of the insulted party by forcing him to engage the insulter and "go down to his level." Second, one can ignore the insult, which lowers the status of the insulted by establishing him as the sort of person who must simply stand there and be humiliated while raising the status of the insulter by showing that he not only can issue an insult but has the standing to force his target to stand there and endure it. When Marco Rubio decided during the Republican primary to lower himself to Trump's level and attempt to use Trump's own weapons against him, it had the opposite of its intended effect. Rubio abandoned his own dignity, debased himself, and, in doing so, effectively ended his own candidacy while raising Trump's standing.

Making obscene gestures, "mooning,"[21] flinging excrement,[22] ordinary insults, profanity, demonstrative rudeness, etc., all work precisely the same way. The childishness[23] of this need not be pointed

---

21 Which used to be a thing.

22 A behavior common to both Antifa goons and monkeys in the zoo. It is notable that the signaling I am talking about here is so heavy on scatological themes and images: the poop emoji, the "pig poop balls" meme, etc.

23 Memes and social-media clichés perform much the same antidiscourse function. It's the twenty-first century version of "I Know You Are But What Am I?" for the precise species of dumb fuck who once would have been relegated to writing on the wall of a toilet stall in an Arby's in Bridgeport, Connecticut. E.g.: Chauncey de Vega of *Salon* once wrote a hilariously wrongheaded article in response to a *National Review* report of mine on poverty in eastern Kentucky. He argued that it was terribly clever of *National Review* to send its one black writer to Appalachia to transfer the negative stereotypes conservatives hold about urban blacks to poor rural whites, the one group conservatives obviously hate almost as much. Deviously clever, except for the fact that I'm not black. When I pointed this out, his response was predictable: *Touched a nerve! Doth protest too much!* Etc. (I sometimes get the same thing when right-wing critics mix me up with the screenwriter Kevin Williamson, who is a gay.) Shouts of "racist!" or "rape apologist!" or "George Soros!" or "cultural Marxism!" all do roughly the same work.

out to any mentally functional adult, but the childishness is part of the appeal of antidiscourse, which appeals to the same atavistic emotions as schoolyard bullying.

Antidiscourse is the noise that overpowers the signal.

Professor Whitney Phillips of Syracuse University, a scholar of online extremism and disinformation, points to a version of the same problem: Publicly pointing out that a lie is a lie, or that a conspiracy theory is daft, may be necessary for setting the record straight, but it amplifies the noise as much as it amplifies the signal. "Just by calling attention," to the fact that "a narrative frame is being established means that it becomes more entrenched," she told *Wired*. "And in a digital media environment it becomes more searchable. It becomes literally Google search indexed alongside whatever particular story" it corrects or debunks. "It's not that one of our systems is broken; it's not even that all of our systems are broken. It's that all of our systems are working—toward the spread of polluted information and the undermining of democratic participation."[24]

The economic mastery of social media over traditional news media ensures the power of antidiscourse, and the problem is deepened by the current business model of online media, which increasingly is oriented toward serving its audience *as social-media users* rather than as *readers*. Michael Luo, the editor of *The New Yorker*'s web site, describes the economics: "For digital-media organizations sustained by advertising, the temptations are almost irresistible. Each time a reader comes to a news site from a social-media or search platform, the visit, no matter how brief, brings in some amount of revenue.... As Facebook and Google have grown, they have pushed down advertising prices, and revenue-per-click from drive-by traffic has shrunk; even so, it continues to provide an incentive for any

---

24 "The Existential Crisis Plaguing Online Extremism Researchers," *Wired*, May 2, 2019.

number of depressing modern media trends, including clickbait headlines, the proliferation of hastily written 'hot takes,' and increasingly homogeneous coverage as everyone chases the same trending news stories, so as not to miss out on the traffic they will bring." What editors subsequently prize, he writes is "any content that is cheap to produce and has the potential to generate clicks on Facebook or Google."[25]

Given what we know about online tribalism, what this means is that online news media increasingly serves tribal status-competition purposes rather than the traditional purposes of information, insight, and exchange. Traditional media operations are not only captive to the business model of the Internet but to its culture, which is tribal, puerile, and status-obsessed—which would be all but good and fine for *The New Yorker*, except that it is also illiterate. It is *The New Yorker* with nothing except the cartoons, and those shorn of their captions.[26]

Which is to say: The internal psychological and political mandates of mob politics in our time, compounded with the economic mandates of the media business, make genuine political discourse almost impossible: *From the point of view of status competition, genuine political discourse is undesirable because to engage in serious and respectful conversation with a member of the opposing tribe elevates the relative status of that individual and his tribe while lowering that of you and yours.* It is only with great effort that one can separate one's self from the partisans and the true believers and begin an actual conversation.

If Donald Trump, e.g., had attempted during the 2016 Republican primary to engage Ted Cruz or Marco Rubio in a serious and substantive debate about immigration or foreign policy, or if he had tried to seriously engage Rand Paul or Rick Perry on entitlements or

---

25 "The Urgent Quest for Slower, Better News," *The New Yorker*, April 10, 2019.
26 Just an endless series of half-assed ink drawings of vaguely educated-looking people staring at one another across restaurant tables. And sometimes dogs.

criminal-justice reform, he would today be only a laughingstock instead of a laughingstock who is also, incredibly enough, president of these United States. Antidiscourse may be the weapon of the stupid, the dull, and the weak, but most people are stupid, dull, and weak. The famous riposte from Adlai Stevenson—a supporter told him he had the support of all thinking people, and he replied, "That's not enough, I need a majority!"—may be apocryphal, but it is nonetheless true. Henry Adams was substantially correct: "Politics is the systematic organization of hatreds," and those hatreds are based on *status*.[27] Status is at the root of envy, jealousy, covetousness, spite, *ressentiment*, and—consequently—politics.

The dynamic has always been the same; the organizational structure of social media (which is to say, the design of the social interactions, not the underlying technology *per se*) only serves to exaggerate the tendency and to speed up its timeline. Status is a stock, and social-media is high-frequency trading.

The use of antidiscourse as a tool for inflicting status violence is not by any means limited to campaign rhetoric or to communication involving political contests and debates. It shapes everything related to the conversation: what gets talked about, how it gets talked about, who speaks, ideology, even the length and volume of conversation. For example, there is relatively little discussion in US social media about foreign affairs relative to domestic ones. Part of that is the historic insularity of this continental republic,[28] but part of it is that most Americans do not have a status stake in, say, India-Pakistan relations. As Professor Cowen puts it, "So much of debate, including

---

27 Henry Adams also had it right when he observed: "There is no such thing as an underestimate of average intelligence."

28 It is tempting to think that the United States does sometimes go abroad seeking monsters to destroy because we only have two neighbors, one of which never does anything and the other of which we treat as a kind of nightclub/vacation rental.

political and economic debate, is about which groups and individuals deserve higher or lower status. It's pretty easy—too easy in fact—to dissect most Paul Krugman blog posts along these lines. It's also why a lot of blog posts about foreign countries don't generate visceral reactions, unless of course it is the Greeks and the Germans, or some other set of stand-ins for disputes closer to home. Chinese goings on are especially tough to parse into comparable American disputes over the status of one group vs. another."[29] The Donald Trump movement took an interest in Brexit mainly because they, and their candidate, understood it as part of the same phenomenon as they.

Well-being is absolute; *status* is relative. And status is local. As Aristotle put it in his *Rhetoric*:

> Envy is pain at the sight of such good fortune... We feel it towards our equals... and by "equals" I mean equals in birth, relationship, age, disposition, distinction, or wealth. We feel envy also if we fall but a little short of having everything; which is why people in high place and prosperity feel it—they think everyone else is taking what belongs to themselves. Also if we are exceptionally distinguished for some particular thing, and especially if that thing is wisdom or good fortune. Ambitious men are more envious than those who are not. So also those who profess wisdom; they are ambitious to be thought wise. Indeed, generally, those who aim at a reputation for anything are envious on this particular point.... If we desire the thing ourselves, or think we are entitled to it, or if having it puts us a little above others, or not having it a little below them.... We envy those who are near us in time, place, age, or reputation.

29 "What kind of blog post produces the most comments?", Marginal Revolution, August 3, 2015.

Envy takes many mutant forms: spite (which is envy pointed downward rather than upward), what the Australians call "tall poppy syndrome" and the novelist Aksel Sandemose called *janteloven*, the "law of Jante" after the fictitious small-minded bourgeoise village in *A Fugitive Crosses His Tracks*,[30] based on his home town. These concepts represent different modes of policing relative status. *Janteloven*, which describes real-world attitudes and social mandates in the Nordic countries, has its own Ten Commandments, each of which juxtaposes the individual *you* against the collective *us*. That is not only a grammatical point: The comparison here is not between the individual and a *rival* social group but between the individual and his *own* social group:

> One: You're not to think you are anything special.
> Two: You're not to think you are as good as we are. Three: You're not to think you are smarter than we are.
> Four: You're not to imagine yourself better than we are.
> Five: You're not to think you know more than we do.
> Six: You're not to think you are more important than we are.
> Seven: You're not to think you are good at anything.
> Eight: You're not to laugh at us.
> Nine: You're not to think anyone cares about you.
> Ten: You're not to think you can teach us anything.

Under *janteloven*, individualism itself—which is to say, any social distinctiveness outside of the proscribed boundary—is understood as a declaration of superiority. To the Nordic mentality under *janteloven*, eccentricity and individualism (especially if that individualism involves ambition) produce the same emotional reaction that an Englishman

---

30 *En flyktning krysser sitt spor*, 1933.

feels at queue-jumping: It is a personal affront, one that is implicitly based on status, i.e. the queue-jumper believes that he is important and entitled to cut in line, and, by implication, those standing in line are lower-status. Cutting in line isn't about time—it's about status.

Status worms its way into everything: politics, of course, but also etiquette, journalism and academic discourse,[31] education, and, perhaps most important for our discussion here, *ideology*. As Michael Oakeshott explains, political ideologies are almost always reverse-engineered: practice precedes principle:

> Far from a political ideology being the quasi-divine parent of political activity, it turns out to be its earthly stepchild. Instead of an independently premeditated scheme of ends to be pursued, it is a system of ideas abstracted from the manner in which people have been accustomed to go about the business of attending to the arrangements of their societies. The pedigree of every political ideology shows it to be the creature, not of premeditation in advance of political activity, but of meditation upon a manner of politics. In short, political activity comes first and a political ideology follows after; and the understanding of politics we are investigating has the disadvantage of being, in the strict sense, preposterous.

Antidiscourse is the throne and face of that preposterousness.

---

31 "A major role of political ideology is to attempt to adjust the relative status of various groups…. One outcome of this is that every adherent to an ideology seeks to elevate the status of those who share that ideology and to downgrade the status of those with different ideologies. That is why it matters that journalists and academics are overwhelmingly on the left. This means that the institutions of the mass media and higher education are inevitably and relentlessly going to seek to lower the status of conservatives." Arnold Kling, "Current thoughts on neo-reaction," June 8, 2016.

CHAPTER NINE

Shouting 'Fire' in a Crowded Feedback Loop

It is not actual suffering but the taste of better things
which excites people to revolt.

—*Eric Hoffer,* The True Believer: Thoughts on the Nature of
Mass Movements, *1951*

"You can't shout 'Fire!' in a crowded theater" is an abominably stupid cliché that has empowered more mob rule than Huey Long[1] or the AK-47. The cliché and its invariable companion—the primly truistic proclamation that the right of free speech is "not absolute"—together constitute the *sine qua non* of authoritarian mantras. It is generally misunderstood and almost always misconstrued.

And it provides the intellectual[2] link completing the circuit in the feedback loop between the culture of non-government speech suppression and formal governmental censorship: Government looks to the culture when it is calculating what speech is permissible and

---

1 After one of his wealth-distribution schemes was rejected by the Senate, Long exclaimed: "A mob is coming here in six months to hang the other ninety-five of you damned scoundrels, and I'm undecided whether to stick here with you or go out and lead them." Senator Long was a good deal more honest about his politics than Senator Warren is.
2 The word is barely permissible here.

what must be censored, and culture looks to the state as the och-locrats and would-be censors undertake to define the scope and scale of their efforts. Government prohibits certain speech because it out-rages politically powerful interest groups, and non-state actors pro-hibit speech on the grounds that it may run afoul of legal prohibi-tions. Facebook, for example, prohibits political speech that is illegal in Germany and Austria as well as speech that might under the right circumstances be considered illegal in Germany and Austria, and it incorporates German and Austrian standards in its evaluation of speech that is not generated in those countries nor targeted specifi-cally at their residents.

Legal standards inform evolving cultural norms, which inform evolving legal standards. That is the feedback loop of suppression.

Mila Versteeg, meet Charles Schenk.

Professor Versteeg, who teaches at the University of Virginia Law School, is a native of the Netherlands and a descendent of Dutch Nazis. Writing in THAT AUGUST JOURNALISTIC INSTITUTION,[3] she describes "armed militias and others waving and wearing swastikas" in Charlottesville and reports that "many of my European friends and family messaged me to ask why the government was allowing this to happen." She argues that both the European model of regulat-ing political discourse and the American model of leaving it relatively uninhibited have their particular virtues, and that each may be more appropriate to its own context: "This trans-Atlantic difference is largely the product of Europe's own history with Nazism,"[4] she

---

3 "What Europe Can Teach America about Free Speech," *The Atlantic*, August 19, 2017.

4 Which is of course the strongest part of the argument: Local history matters, and should inform whatever exceptions we make. The United States, for example, would have been much better off if it had established a set of legal and political processes for the exclusive purpose of mitigating the injustices suffered by African Americans rather than creating a new and clumsy abstraction of civil-rights laws and "social justice" mandates that lump Caitlyn Jenner and Frederick Douglass into the same category.

writes. Being a professor at a law school, she writes in the familiar banal and pusillanimous mode: "Free speech is important but not absolute, and must be balanced against other important values, such as human dignity.... Whatever its merits, the European position is rooted in its experiences that the free market of ideas can fail—disastrously. Dangerous ideas can catch on quickly, especially when people holding power or influence endorse them." She adds that, in the American context, it is necessary for private parties to step in and perform the policing function when the state declines to do so.

There is some jarring naïveté in her essay: "I believe that in a system where government does not police vile ideas, as in the United States, a larger burden falls on ordinary citizens and other private actors.... Americans are already doing this. Americans who express objectionable views face harsher community judgment than Europeans who do so.... I have occasionally found myself surprised to learn that there are some things that I absolutely cannot say here, or that people can lose their jobs for what they say off-hours."

Surprise.

The scene in Charlottesville was indeed ghastly and depraved, but it is not the scene that Professor Versteeg describes, and her Dutch friends seem to have been sharing a mass hallucination. Far from being a sea of swastika flags, the Unite the Right march was notable for its absence of them. The photo illustrating Professor Versteeg's essay shows none. The news photos of the event that include a Nazi flag all seem to have captured the same one, being carried by a sad-looking misfit in an olive-drab T-shirt. I am not the only one who noticed this. Rick Hampson of *USA Today* reports:

> When Hitler's political heirs rallied in Charlottesville, Va., his "torch"—the swastika—was not as conspicuous. Instead, most of the neo-Nazis and white supremacists

who helped turn Jefferson's town into a battleground used other symbols, from the Confederate battle flag to the Detroit Red Wings logo.... The organized hate groups and committed race ideologues trying to seize the political moment have begun to shun the swastika on the assumption that its infamy distracts from their message.

Those who would embrace either the European regulatory model or the American mob-retaliation model, assuming they are acting in good faith—a pure hypothetical; we already have established that they are not and really cannot—would be obliged to do as Professor Versteeg suggests and balance the virtues of free speech against other considerations which by definition must also be other than absolute: If they were absolute, then there would be no need for "balance" at all, and they would simply trump free speech on absolute moral grounds.

And if the presence of a mass of Nazi flags is your moral criterion for invoking the censor's powers, then the imagination can always supply a great red field of them when reality cannot.

Professor Versteeg is an intelligent woman proceeding in a sober fashion, not an intellectually challenged and morally stunted rage monkey trying to fling excrement and masturbate at the same time, and even she—a professor of law, a field dedicated in part to questions of fact—cannot even establish with anything approaching reasonable accuracy *what actually happened*, including *what kind of speech was made and which symbols deployed in what proportion*.

She is hardly alone in that failure, which is nearly universal among our intellectuals. Given that she also raises the possibility of prohibiting certain speech that is considered—here is a nice Orwellian phrase for the books—"false by consensus," it is more than fair to ask whether those invested with the coercive powers she contemplates can be expected to achieve a reasonable accuracy. If the facts cannot even be accounted for satisfactorily, what chance does judgment or proportion have?

And *proportion* is at the heart of this kind of thinking, as Professor Versteeg herself argues. Quoting European standards, she writes, "freedom of expression can be restricted proportionally when it serves to 'spread, incite, promote or justify hatred based on intolerance.'"

It is remarkable that she writes this in an essay that is dedicated to justifying intolerance of unpopular political ideas. Of course these are ideas that *should* be unpopular. That does not mean that they are being suppressed or censored for any other reason than their unpopularity. This is the moral conundrum of the would-be censors: If freedom of speech is to mean anything at all, then it must protect speech that is unpopular, hated, offensive, marginal, and associated with people of low social status—i.e., it must be precisely the sort of speech that is the only thing censors really ever want to censor other than military secrets. There is no such thing as principled censorship. Censorship is an exercise of political power, and, hence, a status game—even when it is undertaken with the best of intentions, as in Germany and the Netherlands.

Systems based on the fanatical adherence to blindly enforced rules, as in the Facebook model, have as their most obvious weakness that they are easy to game. (Systems based on *complaints* are even easier to game—the ochlocracy is build in.) If the rules plainly state where the line is, then it is easy to walk up to the line without crossing it or to configure one's expression in such as way as to keep the content the same while changing the form. That tiki-torch Nazis in Charlotte and elsewhere already have done that: The Detroit Red Wings logo means to them the same thing as the swastika—"We're us, you're you, and fuck you!"—but it gets around the prohibition (formal or informal) on swastikas. Street gangs do much the same thing and in fact frequently employ exactly the same kind of camouflage: the logos of sports teams. With the exception of a few transgressive ones such as that belonging to the Washington Redskins, there is no effort under way to abolish the logos of multi-billion-dollar sports franchises or to socially sanction the wearing and display of those logos. A blue star can stand for the Dallas Cowboys or for a sect of American witches.[5] The Flash in the comic books and the Union of Fascists in Britain use similar symbols, which has not been lost on media-savvy admirers of fascism. Street gangs commandeer sports-team colors and mascots. Members of Hells Angels sometimes wear sports regalia with the number 81; Nazis prefer jerseys with 18 or 88.[6]

Systems that are not based on the rigorous enforcement of well-defined rules must instead be based on judgment and prudence, as indeed all decent government must be, scarce as those commodities are. But the power of status-seeking is not to be ignored. Consider, for example, the enormous social difference between an American who embraces Communism and one who embraces Nazism. One of these is a tolerated eccentricity, and one of them is the lowest thing you can be. Trying to balance the moral ledgers of National Socialism and international socialism (which most often in practice is national socialism) is a fool's errand, but there isn't anything obvious that should make us so much better inclined toward Communism: Communism has a higher body count than does Nazism, though it has had more time to pile up the corpses; Soviet Communism was not founded on anti-Semitism in the way Nazism was,

---

5 "Blue Star" wicca was founded in the United States in the 1970s.
6 H is the eighth letter of the alphabet, A the first, hence 81 = HA = Hells Angels, 18 = Adolf Hitler, 88 = Heil Hitler, etc. Cf. Combat 18, the neo-Nazi terrorist group in the United Kingdom.

but it employed anti-Semitism at times as a political measure, and many other Communist movements have been founded principally on racial identity, as in China and North Korea; the United States has been at war with both Nazis and Communists, etc. The real difference between an American Communist and an American Nazi is that American Communists historically have been intellectuals and American Nazis have been rednecks. The nickname "tanky" has made a recent comeback; it refers to apologists for Soviet authoritarianism and brutality who cheered the Soviet tanks sent into Hungary to crush the rebellion there in 1956. It is difficult to imagine an American's being expelled from college or fired from a service job because it was discovered that he belonged to a Marxist reading group—as one of Barack Obama's nominees to a high-level homeland security post had. It was a mini-scandal for about five minutes when she was nominated to the Supreme Court—even if he was one of its more radical members. Imagine the related case of a young person with fascist or National Socialist interests, even if those leanings were devoid of anti-Semitism and other related kinds of bigotry. It is difficult to imagine that person's not being expelled from college or fired from a service job unless he kept those views a secret. That does not have anything to do with the content of the views or their morality—it has to do with status. This is very much of a piece with the "right-wing authoritarian" views of the progressive psychologists mentioned earlier; of course, they know that there exists such a thing as left-wing authoritarianism, but it is not quite the same to them. It is easy for them to imagine a nightmare scenario of right-wing authoritarianism, however hypothetical. It is less easy for them to imagine a nightmare scenario of left-wing authoritarianism, because an authoritarian regime of the Left would have for them many attractive features, however earnestly they deplored its authoritarianism.

Any effort to police speech on substantive political grounds will run up on those rocks. "Yes, okay, I've heard you, for the ten thousandth time, say that freedom of speech is not 'absolute.' But, why *this* restriction? Why on this speech and not that speech?" There is no evidence, really, that these questions can or will be answered according to principle rather than according to politics and status-seeking or that the project will not be dominated by the desire to punish—by retaliation against real and perceived social rivals—rather than by the desire to prevent some real evil. Both government and private actors reliably elevate the hypothetical evil as a matter of concern over the real evil of suppressing speech and thought when the opportunity to do so arises and there are advantages. This is particularly troubling when one understands that it is the mob, and not the state, that takes the lead morally and politically—because government assumptions about which speech can be suppressed and under what conditions are mainly predicated on notions of "safety."

One cannot "Shout 'Fire!' in a crowded theater" because that jactitation might lead to a deadly stampede. But there is no controlling what people will stampede over, and no end to it, either. Can you shout, "This war is immoral!" in a crowded theater?[7] How about a crowded street corner? Justices Holmes says, "No." And he says "No" because the mob says so.

Government-enforced speech controls ranging from the so-called Fairness Doctrine to the outright prohibitions of political speech that masquerade as "campaign-finance" regulation provide an intellectual[8] and political framework for non-state speech suppression efforts such as the silencing campaigns against conservative

---

7 Please do not shout in theaters. Especially into your phone, you gormless little barbarians.
8 See Footnote 3.

talk radio and independently financed political communiques, efforts that in turn provide a political locus of support for further formal and legal prohibitions on speech. For example, the successful campaign for social-media bans on users who do not conform to conventional etiquette in the matter of writing about transgender people is complemented by partially successful demands to prohibit or restrict such communication as "hate speech." California's LBGT Senior Bill of Rights imposes criminal penalties on misgendering,[9] as does similar Canadian legislation.[10] Gordon Larmour, a Christian preacher in Canada, was jailed[11] after sharing his views on homosexuality with a young gay man who asked him about his views on homosexuality.

As in the example of Professor Versteeg above, the simple fact that there is no government action to censor unpopular speech can be taken in itself as an argument for private suppression. "If the

---

9 PolitiFact California challenges me here, not on the facts but on my disinclination to deploy the word "Orwellian" so frequently. The intellectually dishonest fact-checking feature proclaimed that conservative commentators criticizing the California bill on the grounds that it would criminalize "misgendering" and send speech criminals to jail were "misleading" their audiences about the legislation's content. The fact-checkers also wrote: "Violations of the bill could, under limited circumstances, be treated as a misdemeanor with punishment of up to one year in jail and/or a $1,000 fine." Which is to say, the purported fact-checkers deployed an outright lie as a weapon against an incontrovertible fact. This is part of what I mean by *antidiscourse*.

10 Apologists for Canadian censorship argue that Canada's law censors only "extreme" speech—which is, of course, the only kind of speech that actually needs formal protection. Inoffensive speech is…inoffensive. Professor Brenda Cossman of the University of Toronto, displaying the characteristic alloy of dishonesty and stupidity that can only be expensively cultivated in graduate programs, argued that the law doesn't criminalize speech because it only imposes fines rather than jail time. But, of course, many government prohibitions impose fines rather than jail time. And what happens to people who refuse to pay those fines? A fine is only a bit of financial camouflage between you and the guy sticking a gun in your face saying: "You will do x, and you will not do y." Canadians may be nicer than Americans, but they are on average at least as stupid.

11 "Preacher locked up for hate crime after quoting Bible to gay teen-ager," *The Telegraph*, February 5, 2017.

government won't act, then We the People must!" is a very population form of begging the question.

This has been true since the first invocation of the crowded theater, a phrase[12] introduced into the legal and political discourse by Supreme Court Justice Oliver Wendell Holmes.[13] Senator Dianne Feinstein,[14] writing in the *Wall Street Journal*,[15] invoked the crowded theater while arguing for bringing charges against WikiLeaks and Julian Assange for publishing information that the federal government did not wish to see published. A columnist in the *Los Angeles Times*, Sarah Chayes, invoked the phrase when arguing for the censorship of a film called *The Innocence of Muslims*, which was blamed, risibly, for the attack on US interests in Benghazi on the anniversary of the September 11 terrorist spectaculars. It is even more omnipresent than your average cliché.

What those who invoke that proverbial theater almost always omit from their account is that Justice Holmes used it in the course of deciding that the government could lock up Charles Schenk, the secretary of the Socialist Party of the United States, for simply criticizing the Wilson administration's policy of involuntary conscription during the First World War. Which is to say, "You can't shout 'Fire!' in a crowded theater" was first used to justify precisely the thing the First Amendment exists to prohibit: the official censorship of political speech by the state. Schenk was prosecuted under the Espionage Act for distributing a pamphlet containing nothing more controversial or subversive than an exhortation to "Assert Your Rights."

---

12 Originally: "The most stringent protection of free speech would not protect a man in falsely shouting fire in a theatre and causing a panic."

13 The second-place finisher in gems from this giant of American jurisprudence is, "Three generations of imbeciles are enough," offered as a justification for upholding the involuntary sterilization of "mental defectives."

14 Who at the height of her power might have made a justifiable claim to being the Dolores Umbridge of American politics.

15 Which really ought to know better.

Justice Holmes knew this, but ochlocracy was on the upswing and there were ochlocrats afoot—which almost always is the case during times of war and other episodes of moral panic—and so he set out with malice aforethought to torture law and language both in order to come up with a pretext for quashing an unpopular political opinion, writing:

> We admit that, in many places and in ordinary times, the defendants, in saying all that was said in the circular, would have been within their constitutional rights. But the character of every act depends upon the circumstances in which it is done. The most stringent protection of free speech would not protect a man in falsely shouting fire in a theatre and causing a panic. It does not even protect a man from an injunction against uttering words that may have all the effect of force. The question in every case is whether the words used are used in such circumstances and are of such a nature as to create a clear and present danger that they will bring about the substantive evils that Congress has a right to prevent. It is a question of proximity and degree. When a nation is at war, many things that might be said in time of peace are such a hindrance to its effort that their utterance will not be endured so long as men fight, and that no Court could regard them as protected by any constitutional right. It seems to be admitted that, if an actual obstruction of the recruiting service were proved, liability for words that produced that effect might be enforced. The statute of 1917 punishes conspiracies to obstruct, as well as actual obstruction. If the act (speaking, or circulating a paper), its tendency, and the intent with which it is done are the same, we perceive no ground for saying that success alone warrants making the act a crime.

We haven't seen any "ordinary times" since then.

Note that the real basis of Justice Holmes's case is cleverly hidden in plain sight there in the middle: "their utterance *will not be endured.*" That's a logical tautology: "We will not allow this, because this will not be allowed by us." "This will not be tolerated, so it must not be tolerated."

This political strategy is what is sometimes described with too much gentleness as the "heckler's veto." Tom Wolfe described its use as a tool for political shakedowns in his classic essay "Mau-Mauing the Flack-Catchers,"[16] a stratagem employed by activists who would not threaten violence but only lament that violence inevitably would be done by...someone...if the right kickbacks were not paid. It is a particularly cowardly mode of political violence, one that holds the violence itself at arm's length and redirects culpability toward some vaguely defined and vaguely menacing unknown third party. Another way of putting Justice Holmes's argument: "In a perfect world, we wouldn't have to lock up the war protesters, but if we allow them to exercise their free-speech rights, there will be riots, and we can't have that, so in the name of public safety, we have to preemptively give the rioters what they want." The heckler's veto is rioting on the cheap.

You'll immediately recognize Holmes's argument as substantially identical to the argument Berkeley and other colleges have made for shutting down speeches by the likes of Ann Coulter and Milo Yiannopoulos: *public safety.* Never mind that the threat to public safety comes from their opponents, who threaten public safety for the very purpose of pressuring gutless and detesticled university administrators into forbidding unpopular speech. Mark Zuckerberg, the founder of Facebook, invokes "safety" when he's talking suppression as a business policy. Google, Twitter, et al. invoke the same concerns when

---

16 "Mau-mauing brought you respect in its cash forms: namely, fear and envy."

justifying their prohibition or suppression of political and educational videos put together by Dennis Prager, a mild-mannered radio host, and flagging online courses from Hillsdale, an intellectually rigorous Christian college in Michigan. Any conception of "safety" that requires protecting people from college professors lecturing on the Bill of Rights has simultaneously been enlarged beyond right proportion and made utterly empty.[17]

This is particularly galling when the threats of actual violence—the actual attacks on public safety—are coming from the side of the suppressors. Justice Holmes, being an intelligent man, would no doubt see the kinship between his own cynical sophistry and that of those in our own time who seek to suffocate dissent employing the same meager pretext.

Consider the wider historical context of that "crowded theater" horsepucky.

During the Great War, the American people were (see if this sounds familiar) beset by a moral panic—one whipped up intentionally by the Woodrow Wilson administration and its newly formed ministry of propaganda, the Committee on Public Information, which was overseen by progressive journalist George Creel of the *Denver Post*.[18] Creel announced a campaign of publicly demanding "100 percent Americanism," meaning 100 percent support for the Wilson administration and its military (and militaristic) ambitions. Fear, he argued, was "an important element to be bred in the civilian population." Propaganda posters threatened and hectored dissidents and non-joiners alike: "I am Public Opinion," one poster for war bonds read. "All men fear me! If you have the money to buy and do not buy, I will make this No Man's Land for you!"

---

17 It occurs to me that "enlarged beyond right proportion and utterly empty" is a pretty good description of Sean Hannity's head.
18 And, hilariously enough, *Cosmopolitan*.

That sort of strategy is typical of the American[19] mob-rule mentality. The idea is to walk right up to the line of actual physical compulsion and then stop just short of it, which enables the suppressors to say, "See, no violation of the First Amendment here!" as though the formal prohibition of forcible state censorship were the only relevant consideration. There are many variations on that stratagem: "Sure, you have the right to express unpopular thoughts—but you don't have the right not to be criticized for them!" That sentiment—which is almost always in fact invoked in an effort to suppress the thoughts in question—usually forms part of a pincer maneuver: Like the little suppressors at Berkeley, the Wilson administration combined the appeal to public opinion on one hand with open violence on the other. The administration created the American Protective League, which provided the model for the *squadristi*[20] who served Benito Mussolini's fascist government in Italy. They were American "patriots" who were sent around to beat up and intimidate war protesters, dissidents, troublesome journalists, and nonconforming intellectuals. There were more than a quarter of a million of them at one point, carrying badges issued by the government. The administration closed unfriendly newspapers and magazines. Lynchings "developed into a programmatic ritual of torture and murder,"[21] a program that continued after the war to include the lynchings of black veterans.

"You can't shout 'Fire!' in a crowded theater." And the theater grows ever more expansive and ever more crowded until it is rhetorically expanded to encompass society as a whole. The specific context of the crowded theater becomes the general social context; the threat of a panicky stampede in a specific defined context

---

19 As opposed to your more exotic hack-'em-up-with-machetes versions of mob rule.
20 The Blackshirts.
21 David A. Davis, "Not Only War Is Hell: World War I and African-American Lynching Narratives," *African American Review*, 2008.

becomes a vaguer threat of undefined disorder (including strategic threats of creating disorder) in the general social context; the public-safety argument for limitations on speech in a discrete context with defining physical characteristics becomes a general license for censorship in the general social context.[22]

Official acts of suppression and unofficial (or at least not officially sanctioned) acts of terrorism fed off one another. The Wilson administration's programmatic pursuit of authoritarian presidential powers was sustained by—and worked to sustain—a political culture marked by paranoia, by xenophobia, and, above all, by coerced conformity to both the official agenda of the federal government and the social norms supporting that agenda in the name of patriotism and "100 percent Americanism."[23]

World War I was advertised as a "war to end wars," and President Wilson went to Congress to demand a declaration of war on Germany in order that the world might "be made safe for democracy." And for decent government to thrive abroad, it must be abandoned at home—*streitbare Demokratie* as foreign policy.

A censorship regime that is based on mass hysteria and panic is a censorship regime that creates incentives to cultivate mass hysteria and panic.

The project of hunting down those who hold unpopular political opinions in order to subject them to harassment and humiliation was never going to end there. As a matter of the facts of American political life, it cannot. On the day of this writing, the new Democratic majority in the House of Representatives has introduced a piece of legislation that would place substantial new burdens on political speech and political organization, a "radical expansion of the

---

22 A great many critics of the Cuban government have been imprisoned on charges of "social dangerousness" or "pre-criminal dangerousness."

23 My friend Jonah Goldberg tells the story at fascinating length in *Liberal Fascism*, a book more often reviewed than read by its oddly defensive left-liberal critics.

regulation of political speech" as David Keating of the Institute for Free Speech put it. It is aimed at cultivating mob attacks on the financial supporters of non-campaign political groups and activist organizations, would force social-media companies such as Facebook to disclose parts of their customers' political activity, prohibit certain kinds of groups from engaging in political communication, etc. All of these provisions are designed to harass, denigrate, and suppress individuals and organizations whose political inclinations are at odds with those of the Democratic party. There is barely any effort to conceal it: Some of the measures are plainly directed at the current president of the United States. It is part of a larger power grab that would strip all fifty states of the right to draw their own legislative districts and impose vague "ethical" limitations on members of the Supreme Court.

True to totalitarian form, it is called the We the People Act.

If you ask what evil some proposed restraint on speech is designed to prevent, you will get one of two responses: the hypothetical danger of varying degrees of absurdity, or the concrete threat of "scandal," though the would-be censors rarely if ever use the word or acknowledge its religious basis. From the point of view of scandal, the fact that certain ideas and opinions are expressed at all is an evil in and of itself, and that they may be expressed in public without severe legal or social sanction is an evil of an even more expansive character because the example contributes to the corruption of public morals—the crime for which Socrates was given the hemlock.

The Catholic Church's philosophy of sin is without a doubt the most refined body of thought of its kind in the history of organized human moral reasoning—irrespective of whether one agrees with the church's conclusions. The catechism describes the sin of scandal in a way that is very commodious to censorship and suppression. Try reading this from the point of view of someone who believes that his political rivals are not merely wrong or in possession of temporal values and priorities at odds with his own but are in fact evil.[24]

> Scandal is an attitude or behavior which leads another to do evil. The person who gives scandal becomes his neighbor's tempter. He damages virtue and integrity...Scandal takes on a particular gravity by reason of the authority of those who cause it...Scandal is grave when given by those who by nature or office are obliged to teach and educate others.
>
> Scandal can be provoked by laws or institutions, by fashion or opinion. Therefore, they are guilty of scandal who establish laws or social structures leading to the decline of morals and the corruption of religious practice, or to "social conditions that, intentionally or not, make Christian conduct and obedience to the Commandments difficult and practically impossible." This is also true of business leaders who make rules encouraging fraud, teachers who provoke their children to anger, or manipulators of public opinion who turn it away from moral values.
>
> Anyone who uses the power at his disposal in such a way that it leads others to do wrong becomes guilty of scandal and responsible for the evil that he has directly or indirectly encouraged.

---

24 You may need to temporarily take off a few IQ points. Options here include Jack and Coke, reading *Vox*, or spinning around in a tight little circle until you feel like you are going to vomit. All of these end up providing very similar sensations, if you really commit.

We are again faced with the problem of the mob's failure to understand its own political assumptions. The idea of scandal as an inherent evil is not only reasonable but necessary and unavoidable in the context of Christian moral teaching. The Catholic Church makes room for the individual conscience as both a religious and political matter (a bit more than it used to, in fact!) because that freedom of choice is understood as necessary to the Christian project. The Catholic Church, in this regard, does not take one step back from its fundamental position: that there exists one transcendent moral order, that the inheritors of Saint Peter have access to its truth, that they teach this truth with an authority that is not of earthly origin but delegated to them by the Architect of the Universe, that these truths are absolute and universal, that rejection of this truth is the greatest calamity possible.

The theory of liberal democracy is entirely different: Of course there are truths, some of which are absolute—there is good and evil, and knowledge of these is not entirely beyond us. But liberalism—particularly the Anglo-Protestant liberalism of our own tradition—assumes that there exist in a society different kinds of people with different views, different beliefs, different values, different priorities, different conceptions of the good life, different habits of life and of mind, different hopes, and different fears—and that all of these people can and should live together, neither as a family in the old tribal mode of blood-and-soil nor solely as trading and advantage-seeking strangers in separate intersecting orbits, but as friends and collaborators, as fellow citizens together engaged in the great business of being free men under their own government.

The Left (by which I mean the center-Left, Democrats and progressives and so-called liberals) has long had an organizational problem that is at heart a philosophical problem: People who understand themselves to be liberals have a historical commitment to protecting the rights and interests of minorities, an honorable patrimony that survives today in the progressive concern for the rights of sexual minorities, immigrants, poor black people suffering from police excesses, etc. But the liberals, what's left of them, are conjoined to the progressives, whose interest is in "the masses," from whom they believe themselves to derive moral authority. The bigger the mass the better—and, by implication, the smaller the minority, the worse for its members. That is the origin and the genius of "1 percent" rhetoric, which focuses hatred on a small, powerful, rich, globalist minority that is secretly pulling the strings behind every bank, business deal, and war: It's anti-Semitism for nice people. The Anglo-American Left struggles to justify its commitment to minority rights against the demanding masses, and, unless there are obvious issues of tribal allegiance (the masses were not calling for a crusade on the social status of transsexuals) that can be difficult to negotiate. The Right, until recently, had a less difficult time of it, because it historically took a process-based view of justice rather than a substantive one based on identity. If Bob is rich and Sam is poor, and Bob didn't steal what he has from Sam, then there is no injustice. But the Right has lately moved away from that process-based approach and embraced a blood-and-soil nationalism which insists that General Motors— whose shareholders, customers, and workers live all over the world, in dozens of countries—is somehow an "American interest," and that angry white guys in moribund Rust Belt towns have an existential right to a twenty-first century standard of living with an Eisenhower-era culture. The libertarian tendency among Republicans is in hiding.

Properly understood and at their best, both American conservatives and American liberals are—or were until five minutes ago— heirs to and advocates of classical liberalism, however much they disagree about particulars of its application or interpretation. Inherent in the classical liberal model is what Oakeshott called the "politics of skepticism." The easiest way to understand what is meant by "the politics of skepticism" is to consider its alternative, the "politics of faith," in which governing is a "godlike adventure" the goal of which is the perfection of man. Under such a model of government, "the activity of governing in the politics of faith will require not only obedience but express approval and even love; conversely, dissent and disobedience will be punished as error and sin."[25] It is obvious that there can be no tolerance of competing values under such a conception of our common life.

That this mystical and fanatical interpretation of social life should have come to dominate some views of government is unsurprising—it is, in a sense, the Second Coming of the Divine Right of Kings. That this view should have made such advances into how we think about the life of universities and businesses is both dismaying and terrifying, if comical: Who would have thought that Mojo Burrito even had a metaphysics? Or that the Divine Right of Starbucks would be a necessary subject of meditation in the twenty-first century? Howard Schultz, like King James, reigns by the grace of God—in the case of the Starbucks chairman, that god is named Public Opinion.

From that point of view, the social-justice campaigns against obscure nobodies like Jack Phillips (the nonconformist baker whom organized homosexuality wants to shanghai into its service) or to make elderly celibate nuns purchase birth-control coverage (another example of why we used to have the expression, "You don't have to make a federal case out of it!") or to exact retribution on obscure fast-food workers who think bad things, etc., all make perfect sense. If the point of common life is unity in perfection, then dissent and nonconformity must be ruthlessly rooted out. The heretics must be hunted down and either brought to heel or burned at the stake.

---

25 "Michael Oakeshott on Representative Democracy," George Feaver, 2003.

The politics of skepticism, on the other hand, understands the state and its force as necessary rather than divine; it contributes to human flourishing by maintaining order and liberty, a philosophy in which "moral approval and disapproval are no part of the office of government, which is not at all concerned with the souls of men."[26] The politics of skepticism understand a healthy and just society as a greater and more splendid thing, if a more heterogeneous and disunified one.

That is one of the great ironies of our time: that the tribe least interested in traditional religious observance should have made its politics those of seeking the Kingdom of Heaven on Earth in the present—to immanentize the eschaton.[27]

If that slop bucket of totalitarian goo is to be our Heaven on Earth, then the individualist must take up a new slogan: *"Non serviam."*

---

26 *The Politics of Faith and the Politics of Skepticism*, Michael Oakeshott, 1996. "The authority of the state is not mere government and law, nor is it founded upon a contract or any other form of the consent of the people, but resides solely in the completeness of the satisfaction which the state itself affords to the needs of concrete persons. Apart from its completeness, the state has no authority, for that only is authoritative, in the full sense, which is itself complete. Of this authority, and of no other, can it be said: *Non est potestas super terram quae comparetur ei.*" That last bit of Latin means, "There is no power on Earth which can be compared to him," and appears under the illustration of the great prince on the cover of Thomas Hobbes's *Leviathan*.

27 *The New Science of Politics*, 1952. "The problem of an *eidos* in history, hence, arises only when a Christian transcendental fulfillment becomes immanentized. Such an immanentist hypostasis of the eschaton, however, is a theoretical fallacy."

CHAPTER TEN

Of the Devil's Party

Truth never comes into the world but like a bastard, to
the ignominy of him that brought her birth.

—*John Milton,* The Doctrine of Discipline and Divorce, *1643*

J udas is spending eternity in good company, at least according to
Dante Alighieri, who locates him in the afterlife alongside one
of history's greatest heroes: Brutus the Younger, the lead assassin
of Julius Caesar. Dante did not understand Brutus as a hero, instead
condemning him as a traitor.[1] But even Homer nods, and Dante, like
Mike Tyson, Spike Lee, and Taylor Swift, may be forgiven for the
occasional political oversight, having purchased that indulgence with
the greatness of his art. Even Robin Williams had his *Bengal Tiger
in the Baghdad Zoo*, and Alec Baldwin his *Orphans*.[2] We must make
certain allowance for talent.

---

1 If Judas's story were being written today, you can bet that some witless monkey would
insist that those thirty pieces of silver had come from the Koch Brothers or George Soros.
2 You can walk into the theater all ready and amped up to hate a play, as I often have
as a critic, but the play is the play, and if it's good, which is rare enough, you should be
grateful. See *The New Criterion* May 2011 and June 2013, respectively, for those two plays.
The column from 2013 also has that funny story about me getting thrown out of *Natasha,
Pierre, and the Great Comet of 1812.*

Dante's Hell is a full of famous people brooding and waiting around gloomily for...*something*...something that seems to be terribly far off, perhaps even beyond seeing—it's a vast dank cable-news greenroom without the Keurig machine and day-old cookies. Everybody who is anybody is there: Paolo and Francesca da Rimini, the original star-crossed lovers; Minos, the beastly king of Crete;[3] the notoriously corrupt Pope Boniface VIII and his *consigliere*, Guido da Montefeltro; Fra Alberigo, a political rival of Dante's deemed so wicked that his soul is down in the Ninth Circle of Hell before he has even died. It's got the makings of a pretty great party, but each of these big personalities turns out to be only another wan shade in Dante's already shady eternity. They are everlasting disappointments, and Hell itself is basically inert, spinning its infernal wheels and going nowhere.

That is exactly how Dante and many other Christians understand Hell: It is a kind of death in death, a cessation, negation, and annihilation so utter that it transcends even time. Life is action and becoming; death is the absence of those. If Hell's inmates are able to do anything, it is only to suffer and to regret.[4] Only the thief Vanni Fucci, who let an innocent man be condemned for his crimes, has retained something of himself: As Dante departs his company, Fucci curses God and flips the Almighty the everlasting bird.[5] It is difficult to blame him, even though his crimes were horrible: The Author of the torments in Dante's Hell is not Dante's Satan, who has

---

3 Minos was a *Cretan*; Matthew Yglesias is a *cretin*. Cf. the old UPI reporters' handbook: "A burro is an ass; a burrow is a hole in the ground. As a journalist you are expected to know the difference."

4 Two kinds of people habitually say, "I have no regrets"—the invincibly stupid and those who have never done anything of interest. It is of course possible to be both at the same time. I'd add, "You know who you are," but the fact is they don't.

5 Worse, really. Fucci threw Him the double *mano fica*, meaning that he called God a "cunt"—twice.

no real power, but Dante's God. He is the Architect of the Universe, including its torture chamber. In John Milton's *Paradise Lost*, Hell is Satan's own private dominion: "Th' Almighty hath not built here for his envy," Lucifer says. But in Dante's universe, the omnipresence of God's irrestible reach leaves Satan with no room to maneuver. It is God's plan, all the way down like Hindu turtles.

When Dante, the weary middle-aged pilgrim, finally reaches the lowest pit of Hell in *The Inferno*, he encounters Satan, who is, to this reader's great disappointment, a pitiable figure: The once-mighty angel is powerless, inert, frozen in ice up to his chest, incapable of speech or action or motion or even malice. He is a slobbering, jibbering precursor to H. P. Lovecraft's "blind idiot god," more of a force of nature than a personality. He *does* nothing; he just *is*. Like winter and passing time, he is a source of suffering and torment, but there is no will behind his brutality, no intelligence to enable malevolence properly understood. He has no more evil intent than does a tornado or cancer or a swarm of malarial mosquitos. The mindless beating of his chiropteran wings produces the freezing wind that makes Hell so deathly cold—there is fire in Dante's inferno, but it is fundamentally a place of coldness, characterized by the stagnation of that which is frozen rather than the dynamism of that which is on fire—but even that is only animal instinct and reflex. The pit of the inferno turns out to be an eternal Oakland: There's no there there. Father Christopher Ryan[6] details the scene in "The Theology of Dante."[7]

> The silent Satan, then, tells out loud and clear the pain sin inflicts on others. But this wordless figure speaks no less clearly of the harm sin causes to the self, for Satan is a once

---

6 An English priest who, unlike so many others of his time, journeyed from Rome to Canterbury rather than the other way 'round.
7 *The Cambridge Companion to Dante*, 1993.

splendid being (indeed the most perfect of God's creatures) from whom all personality has now drained away. The movement of his jaws, the beating of his wings, are purely mechanical; even the ability to move about, that modest prerogative of animal life, is now beyond him. Dante's last word in Hell on sin is, then, in every sense damning: intended by the sinner to be an assertion of self, a forward thrust, sin in Dante's eyes is the ultimate denial of self, the immobilizing of personality,[8] for at its worst it denies that love which quickens the spirit.

Satan, from this point of view, is neutered, having neither the satanic majesty attributed to him by the Rolling Stones and countless other rock-'n'-roll musicians nor the sex appeal and charisma of great B-movie devils such as Al Pacino's in *The Devil's Advocate* or Peter Stormare's in *Constantine*.[9] Dante's Satan is basically dead Jabba the Hutt in *Return of the Jedi*, choked to death by an anorexic Carrie Fisher in a metal bikini, which is an ignominious way for a big guy to go out. This is the great dramatic flaw in *The Inferno* and in much of orthodox Christianity: Without an adversary—and a worthy adversary at that—the story loses its zest. There's a reason that Darth Vader is the most memorable of the *Star Wars* characters. It isn't *The Saga of Grand Moff Tarkin*, that tedious company man.

At the climax of the 1907 apocalyptic novel *Lord of the World*, the Antichrist, a very familiar kind of politician known to the world

---

8 As T. S. Eliot remarks: "Only those who have personality and emotion know what it means to want to escape from these."

9 Do you know that weird little scene in *Con Air* when Steve Buscemi's depraved serial killer is playing by an abandoned swimming pool with a little girl and her creepy broken dolls? She asks him if he is sick, he answers that he is, and she asks him if he takes medicine. "There is no medicine for what I have," he answers. It's like a whole different little ninety-second film inside a giant craptacular action movie, and I wish they'd made a whole movie out of the little one, instead. I feel the same way about Peter Stormare's performance in *Constantine*.

as Julian Felsenburgh, leads the diabolical forces at the battle of Armageddon, coming on like unholy thunder only to disappear in a harmless puff of smoke.

> He was coming now, swifter than ever, the heir of temporal ages and the Exile of eternity, the final piteous Prince of rebels, the creature against God, blinder than the sun which paled and the earth that shook; and, as He came, passing even then through the last material stage to the thinness of a spirit-fabric, the floating circle swirled behind Him, tossing like phantom birds in the wake of a phantom ship.... He was coming, and the earth, rent once again in its allegiance, shrank and reeled in the agony of divided homage.
>
> ...He was coming—and already the shadow swept off the plain and vanished, and the pale netted wings were rising to the cheek; and the great bell clanged, and the long sweet chord rang out—not more than whispers heard across the pealing storm of everlasting praise ...
>
> ...*genitori genitoque laus et jubilatio salus honor virtus quoque sit et benedictio procedenti ab utroque compar sit laudatio.*[10]
>
> and once more
> *procedenti ab utroque compar sit laudatio* ...
> Then this world passed, and the glory of it.

The End—seriously, that's it. The story may be theologically sound, but, as literature, it is deficient. *Lord of the World* is said to be Pope Francis's favorite novel. Some people say we need a better pope.

---

10 What's left of the Catholic clergy is singing Saint Thomas Aquinas's *Tantum Ergo*.

I say we need a better devil. Enough of these little satans.[11] It is time to Make Satan Great Again.

After all that Dante has been through to get to the bottom of the inferno, his actual encounter with Satan is anticlimactic. Satan is supposed to be the great archenemy of both mankind and God Himself, but an enemy must have power, potency, the will to act and a theater of action. Satan has none of those things—and that, not the metaphorical torments of Hell, is his real punishment.

But he did *once* have the power to choose, and that is why he is in Hell. In his three mouths he is chewing eternally on three men, each condemned for a single choice: Judas Iscariot, who betrayed Jesus, and Brutus and Cassius, who together betrayed Julius Caesar. Dante considered Brutus worthy of eternal damnation because he betrayed his friend, patron, and rightful ruler.[12] But if Brutus betrayed his friend, he did it in order that he might be true to his country—and to himself. Caesar was a dictator who aspired to kingship, and in fact was successful in converting the Roman republic into something like a hereditary monarchy. Brutus tried to stop him, and to save the republic. That he failed does not diminish the glory of the deed.[13]

---

11 I user the lowercase satan here in its common Old Testament sense: an accuser or prosecutor, not an embodiment of evil serving as God's infernal counterpoint. In the Book of Numbers, a "satan" is "the angel of the Lord," who places himself in the road as an adversary against Balaam. In the Tanakh, the satan is a heavenly prosecutor who conducts the case against the people of Judah in God's court. The generic satan as a common noun can refer to any accuser. Satan as a proper noun—and a proper personality—is present in Scripture, but he is something different from our (relatively) modern universal antihero. In both the Tanakh and the Book of Job, Satan seems to be on God's team, doing His dirty work.

12 Possibly his father, according to some legends, though Caesar's affair with Brutus's mother seems to have happened long after Brutus's birth.

13 The opposite idea reigns today: that success is its own justification. Cf. Trump, Donald Clusterfucking. Julien Benda in *The Treason of the Intellectuals* called this the "desire to abase the values of knowledge before the values of action," meaning "the teaching that says that when a will is successful that fact alone gives it a moral value, whereas the will which fails is for that reason alone deserving of contempt." He called this the "cult of success." It is yet another variation of "might makes right."

Brutus, and not Jaime Lannister, was the original king-slayer. On his father's side, he was a descendent of Lucius Brutus, the hero of the republic who had overthrown the last Roman king, Tarquin, and seen off the idea of monarchy entirely and in doing so founded the Roman republic. He launched his assault on Tarquin after gathering the people in the Forum, only a few feet from where Caesar would be stabbed to death. Lucius Brutus's first act after overthrowing the king was to call a public meeting at which the Roman people took an oath never to suffer another king to rule over them. That was Brutus's inheritance on his father's side. On his mother's side he was a descendant of Gaius Servilius Ahala, a hero of the republic who had killed Spurius Maelius, a wealthy pleb[14] who had plotted to install himself as king. On top of all that, he was the nephew[15] of Cato the Younger, who was among the first to detect Caesar's monarchical ambitions and who sought to have him relieved of his military command and brought back to Rome as a civilian.

Brutus's betrayal of his friend and patron was, in Dante's view, an unforgivable transgression, comparable to Judas's betrayal of Jesus. But what is the *purpose* of Brutus? What is a Brutus *for*? Does Brutus exist to serve Caesar and his ambitions? To serve the Senatus populusque Romanus? No: The purpose of Brutus is to be Brutus, and to be Brutus was to be a hereditary enemy of kings and would-be kings. Brutus was charged with a special duty to prevent the return of monarchy to Rome—not by the Senate and people of Rome or by his ancestors but by his own nature. Brutus had a choice, and, like a man, he made his choice—not to be a traitor, but to be Brutus, whole and complete. The Romans saw that as treason, and Dante saw it as sin, but it was the opposite of the "ultimate denial of self, the immobilizing of personality" attributed to Satan by Father Christopher Ryan above. Though the deed was bloody and brutal,[16] Brutus in that

---

14 They didn't have reality shows back then.
15 And posthumous son-in-law; Rome was a little weird.
16 *Brutus* was indeed Latin for "beastly," but not during Brutus's time.

moment expressed his highest form and purpose, true to his own nature in the service of something that is worthy. His nature is at once disobedient and obedient: Disobedient to the lesser thing and obedient to the greater one.

That decision cost him everything: Caesar, like most tyrants, was beloved by the common people, who rose up from their squalor to rage against their liberators, declaring them murderers and traitors. Brutus was driven from Rome and defeated in battle, after which he, in the Roman fashion, honorably ended his own life. In Dante's version, even that was not the end for him: For the crime of going against his friends and the people in pursuit of his transcendent principles, he is condemned to the lowest circle of Hell, stuffed into the ravening maw of Satan himself.

But Brutus enjoys another kind of immortality. Everywhere kings are overthrown, Brutus is implicitly honored. Have a good look at the official seal of the Commonwealth of Virginia: The goddess Liberty, in Roman battle dress, stands over the bloodied corpse of a would-be king, stabbed through his purple garments, his crown cast on the ground, broken. Who is that but Brutus reborn in mythological guise? Even as a transvestite, he is barely disguised. And for those who might otherwise miss the symbolism, Brutus's own legendary words are there as the state motto: "Sic semper tyrannis."[17] That dead king and his cast-down, dishonored crown, and not some silly ichthyophagous buzzard, ought to be understood as the real true symbol of the American Revolution—and the best symbol of the American spirit, too. Brutus was, at heart, one of us: a traitor, and a glorious traitor at that, like George Washington and Thomas Jefferson.

---

17 In the American context, that phrase has an unhappy history. But the American conception of the afterlife is considerably more forgiving than the old Italian once, if we take Tom Waits as our Dante: "There's no eye for an eye, there's no tooth for a tooth / I saw Judas Iscariot carrying John Wilkes Booth." One wonders whether Abraham Lincoln's assassin knew that he was shouting the motto of the United States Colored Troops during his act of homicidal political theater.

The traitor is the monkey-wrench in the machine of society. Every machine exists to do one thing: to run. That is the nature of machines. When I was young, I knew a man who was accidentally pulled through a cotton gin. What was left of him was not recognizable. But the machine did not mean anything by it. They just do what they do. And if what they do is horrifying, someone has to stop the machine.

Shakespeare's histories and tragedies endlessly reiterate the idea of society as machine: Something, somewhere gets out of place in the social order—Macbeth becomes king when he wasn't meant to—and the machine begins to malfunction; no peace is possible, and no life is safe, until the proper order is restored. The gears must grind until they are sufficiently lubricated with blood. Macbeth is a monster because he murders his rightful king, an enormity that is compounded by his violation of the taboo against doing violence to guests in one's home, a moral principle that is more ancient than any extant religion. But what kind of a king was Duncan? Not a very good one. And why *not* Macbeth, who was the greatest man in the kingdom but consigned to doing the dirty work of a complacent and borderline incompetent king? Shakespeare wrote the play in the shadow of his patron, King James—supposedly a descendant of Banquo—at a time when England was racked with uncertainty about the future of the monarchy: King James was the Scottish and Protestant son of the Catholic traitor Mary, Queen of Scots. Shakespeare's understanding of the scenario is straightforward: The case for Duncan's being the rightful king is that Duncan is the rightful king—and Macbeth, whatever his quality, is not.

The mechanical nature of Shakespeare's universe is right there in the text of his plays and sonnets: Hamlet is a "machine," Coriolanus an "engine," and Richard II a helpless "jack of the clock." The clock of Sonnet 12 is a model of the mechanical world and its ruthless inevitability, a *memento mori* announcing: "Nothing 'gainst

Time's scythe can make defence / Save breed, to brave him when he takes thee hence."

King James was a tyrant in theory if not in practice, arguing in *The Trew Law of Free Monarchies* that, because kings rule by divine right, their subjects owe them total obedience irrespective of their character, ability, or any abuse of power. King James believed that the king was always *right* even when he was not *good*. He linked the divine right of kings to the Christian principle of apostolic succession, which holds that properly consecrated bishops are the legitimate heirs and inheritors of Saint Peter even if they are personally corrupt. It is not the character of the *bishop* or the *king* that matters, but the character of the *succession*, which is to say, the orderly operation of social institutions under norms and rules. Like their contemporary Thomas Hobbes, Shakespeare and King James feared disorder—anarchy—above all.[18] Even a despot is preferable to *bellum omnium contra omnes*. The intellectual model of society as a kind of machine—as one big factory, in the socialist ideal—is very old, and it remains very much with us today. The American superstition that the president manages the economy like a foreman manages a factory is a direct descendent of this misconception.

For Dante and others of his time, not only society but the universe itself was an orderly machine, its physical organization and metaphysical organization united in a single harmonious whole. His Hell is composed of morally significant shapes arranged in morally significant ways in a morally significant number.[19] Dante's mental model of the world is an orrery, a clockwork universe in which

---

18 Which is not to suggest that King James the royal absolutist would have agreed with Hobbes's social-contract view of government had he lived long enough to read *Leviathan*; he might very well have judged it treasonous.

19 The association of the number nine with wickedness and the occult goes back at least to Pythagoras.

everything is in its place because it must be in its place, with every course and orbit mechanically determined. The intellectual currents of Dante's age included the early stirrings of humanism (in art, Giotto; in politics, Dante's own White Guelphs, whose defeat Fucci prophesies) and empiricism, an idea advanced in Dante's time by Roger Bacon, an English Franciscan friar (celebrated as *Doctor Mirabilis*) who championed what would later become known as the scientific method. Bacon was famously associated with a machine, the "Brazen Head," a fortune-telling automaton that was the work either of magic or of science—the distinction was not robust at the time.[20] (The machine did not exist, but Robert Greene wrote a play about it.) Bacon was an advocate of educating theologians in natural science and mathematics, believing, as many of the leading men of his day did, that these disparate fields of study described aspects of a single and unitary truth.

The fascination with the motions and character of heavenly bodies during this time was not abstract scientific curiosity but reflected a belief in the principle of as above, so below[21]—"on Earth as it is in Heaven" was not understood as an exclusively *theological*

---

20 Arthur C. Clarke had it right: "Any sufficiently advanced technology is indistinguishable from magic." But in spite of Bacon's reputation as a man of science, it was generally assumed and widely rumored that his brazen head was created in association with the devil himself, in the classical Faustian style.

21 "*Quod est inferius est sicut quod est superius. Et quod est superius est sicut quod est inferius, ad perpetranda miracula rei unius,*" as *The Emerald Tablet*, an alchemical text, put it, "That which is below is like that which is above & that which is above is like that which is below, to do the miracles of one only thing." This principle was considered the master key to all knowledge. *The Emerald Tablet* continues: "It ascends from the earth to the heaven & again it descends to the earth & receives the force of things superior & inferior. / By this means you shall have the glory of the whole world / & thereby all obscurity shall fly from you." If you'd like an indicator of the prevalence and reach of this compound of ancient mysticism and the early scientific sensibility, consider that the above translation was made by Isaac Newton.

proposition.[22] When Copernicus and Galileo challenged the consensus model of the universe, it was not only the religious authorities who were scandalized: The philosophers and scientists were bent out of shape, too, because Galileo's *observed* universe was more disorderly and unruly than the one they *deduced*—and more complex. It was not only biblical astronomy but the Aristotelian taste for mathematical perfection (they mistook *neatness* for perfection) that left them too terrified to consider the truth: The heavens, Aristotle wrote, must be "perfect and unchanging," and to think otherwise was to invite anarchy into the world. And even Galileo wouldn't always believe his own eyes: His contemporary Johannes Kepler, working from physical principles, showed that the sun was one of two foci of an elliptical orbit rather than the center of a circular one, but Galileo himself continued to work from a circular-orbit model, even though it forced him into unlikely explanations for the observed movements of the planets. Why? *Because it is extraordinarily difficult to throw off entirely one's assumptions about the nature of reality and the assumptions of the society in which one lives.*

That is precisely why we need radicals: Milton's Satan, history's Mohandas K. Gandhi, religion's Jesus. Someone has to overturn the tables in the temple of our mind and drive out the corrupt and the complacent.

Metaphor has a way of shaping our thinking until we have trouble distinguishing between the metaphor and the world itself, between the map and the territory. All that Ptolemaic talk of

---

22 It is something more like Nicolas Malebranche's psycho-physical parallelism at a universal scale rather than at the individual one. The same divine love of order that governs the motions of the heavenly bodies governs the moral universe of man—it is God's will alone that keeps the planets in orbit, and, in Malebranche's philosophy, God's will alone that makes human thought possible, man having no cognitive apparatus of his own. The astronomical and the moral move in the same course because they are manifestations of a single principle: twin brothers, one Father.

"heavenly spheres" was understood as both literal and moral.[23] Life on Earth is linked to life in Heaven as the same way the tides are related to the moon. As goes Judas, so goes Brutus—so *must* go Brutus: One betrayed a heavenly kingdom, and one betrayed an earthly one. The conjoining of their fates is an inevitability, an inescapable law of nature like gravity, as predictable as the movements of the stars.

> The Eagle soars in the summit of Heaven,
> The Hunter with his dogs pursues his circuit.
> O perpetual revolution of configured stars,
> O perpetual recurrence of determined seasons,
> O world of spring and autumn, birth and dying.[24]

Dante, and later Shakespeare and Hobbes, lived in a world that feared choice. One wrong choice could mean the end of a career, a life, a kingdom, even the moral order of the universe. John Milton, born in the last years of Shakespeare's life but twenty years Hobbes's senior, helped to give birth to a world that would embrace choice, having the confidence to leave behind the fear of choosing. Shakespeare linked the legitimacy of the monarchy to domestic peace, and Hobbes believed that without the "terrour of some power" mankind would descend into anarchy; Milton was a partisan of the unruly Parliament against the absolute monarchy. Milton was a Puritan who

---

23 From Plato's *Timaeus*: "Wherefore he made the world in the form of a globe, round as from a lathe, having its extremes in every direction equidistant from the center, the most perfect and the most like itself of all figures;...Such was the whole plan of the eternal God about the god that was to be, to whom for this reason he gave a body, smooth and even, having a surface in every direction equidistant from the center, a body entire and perfect, and formed out of perfect bodies. And in the center he put the soul, which he diffused throughout the body, making it also to be the exterior environment of it; and he made the universe a circle moving in a circle."

24 T. S. Eliot, "Choruses from *The Rock*."

stood against the power of the bishops, and also a liberal man who argued—controversially, and at some cost to himself—for toleration, freedom of speech, and circumspection. He himself was censored when he tried to publish tracts in favor of divorce, which scandalized many of his fellow Calvinists. Like Adam and Eve, he was eager to eat of the fruit of the Tree of Knowledge: "Give me the liberty to know, to utter, and to argue freely according to conscience, above all liberties," he insisted.[25]

Which is to say, Milton had some sympathy for the devil. Coming dangerously close to a "poet/know-it" rhyme, William Blake smelled a whiff of sulfur on the old Puritan: "The reason Milton wrote in fetters when he wrote of Angels & God, and at liberty when

---

25 What Milton most objected to was not punishing the authors of books that were blasphemous or libelous but the licensing regime that preempted the publication of controversial material, with the state substituting its judgment for his own. He simply did not believe that a man could be wounded by reading scurrilous material, no matter how unholy. It was clear to him from his scriptural studies that Paul, at least, had read the classical writers—he quoted from them. Likewise, he found the ancient Greeks and Romans to be reasonably liberal in their treatment of controversial works of literature. He argued that censorship was as likely to be used as a tool against the faith as in its service, and he smirkingly celebrates the death of one hated censor. From his *Areopagitica*: "Not to insist upon the examples of Moses, Daniel, & Paul, who were skilfull in all the learning of the Ægyptians, Caldeans, and Greeks, which could not probably be without reading their Books of all sorts; in Paul especially, who thought it no defilement to insert into holy Scripture the sentences of three Greek Poets, and one of them a Tragedian, the question was, notwithstanding sometimes controverted among the Primitive Doctors, but with great odds on that side which affirm'd it both lawfull and profitable, as was then evidently perceiv'd, when Julian the Apostat, and suttlest enemy to our faith, made a decree forbidding Christians the study of heathen learning: for, said he, they wound us with our own weapons, and with our owne arts and sciences they overcome us. And indeed the Christians were put so to their shifts by this crafty means, and so much in danger to decline into all ignorance, that the two Apollinarii were fain as a man may say, to coin all the seven liberall Sciences out of the Bible, reducing it into divers forms of Orations, Poems, Dialogues, ev'n to the calculating of a new Christian grammar. But, saith the Historian Socrates, The providence of God provided better then the industry of Apollinarius and his son, by taking away that illiterat law with the life of him who devis'd it."

of Devils & Hell, is because he was a true Poet and of the Devil's party without knowing it."[26]

Dante's Satan is a dead fish on eternal ice. Milton's Lucifer is on fire. In *Paradise Lost*, Lucifer is not some pathetic figure reduced to an eternal spasm in the service of God's unalterable program. Milton's Lucifer is the hero of *Paradise Lost*, albeit a tragic hero, a lively figure—an *individual*. He insisted upon his own mind and his own judgment, even at the cost of Paradise lost. Lucifer, too, is a partisan of the smallest minority.

> Hail horrours, hail
> Infernal world, and thou profoundest Hell
> Receive thy new Possessor: One who brings
> A mind not to be chang'd by Place or Time.
> The mind is its own place, and in it self
> Can make a Heav'n of Hell, a Hell of Heav'n.
> What matter where, if I be still the same,
> And what I should be, all but less then he
> Whom Thunder hath made greater? Here at least
> We shall be free; th' Almighty hath not built
> Here for his envy, will not drive us hence:
> Here we may reign secure, and in my choyce
> To reign is worth ambition though in Hell:
> Better to reign in Hell, than serve in Heav'n.

Dante's Satan has no will and no individuality; Milton's Lucifer has a surfeit of it. He did wrong, of course, meeting with disobedience the one Force in the universe to Whom his obedience was rightfully owed. But there is in Milton's Lucifer a recognition that there

---

26 *The Marriage of Heaven and Hell*, William Blake, 1793.

is something splendid in the spirit of disobedience. Dante's Satan is a thing. Milton's Lucifer is one of us, alive, a personality, an individual—a traitor.

God made man, but Lucifer made him human. Man was not man before he was a traitor—he was only another piece of livestock in Eden, being fed and cared for and looked after. And if the Serpent made man human, then man made Lucifer what he is, too: There is no mention of Satan anywhere in the Book of Genesis, and scant mention of such a character anywhere in the Bible.[27] Up through the Middle Ages, Satan played only a minor role in organized Christian thinking—he was mainly known as a frolicking, farting clown in mystery plays. The Lucifer we know is a modern literary invention. Our Lucifer is a little bit of the Greco-Roman underworld gods— Hades, Pluto, Dis Pater, and other chthonic deities of the ancient world—a little bit rock-'n'-roll,[28] and a whole lot of Milton. That the Christian world decided that God the Father needed an adversary— a near-equal counterpart who was not provided by the Bible—is something that should be of interest to contemporary Christians: The moral poles of the Christian world in the modern era are not Good and Evil, but Authority and Rebellion. In the first few centuries, the Christians were the rebels. In the next several centuries, they were the empire. Political power was one of the worst things that ever happened to the church. What we Christians will be in this millennium remains unknown. But if there is to be a repository of genuine civilization, a fragment shored against our ruins as high-tech barbarism rises on all sides, it will be in the churches. Whatever else the

---

27 Which is not to say none: Satan is God's partner-in-crime when He is torturing Job to make an obscure theological point, and he later tempts Jesus to forsake His mission. It's not until crazy old John on Patmos that we start to see something like the archenemy of relatively modern Christianity.

28 Of course, Donnie Osmond is the Antichrist. Everybody knows that.

Christian religion may be, it is the seedbed of Western civilization, and not only in vague and abstract ways. Among other things, it is in the Anglo-Protestant tradition that runs from William Tyndale through John Milton to the American Founders that freedom of speech as a legal and ethical principle took root.

Milton's poetic liberties with Lucifer's career were wildly unbiblical, to be sure—but that does not mean that they are *untrue*. Or un-Christian, for that matter.[29]

Rebellion is human. To choose is to be human, even if one chooses disobedience and wickedness. Lucifer sees the clockwork universe of Shakespeare and Dante and wants no part of it. He will not be a cog in anybody's machine—not even God's. Brutus's gang of assassins called themselves the Liberators, and Lucifer might well call himself the same. He is the instrument by which mankind was elevated out of blind obedience and raised to reason. Adam and Eve in the Garden may have been happy and blessed, but they were not entirely satisfied with their state. They were in a sense like Dante's Satan: Without knowledge of good and evil, they were unable to choose. Their obedience to God was like the tides' obedience to the moon: They were simply part of the natural order under the tyranny of natural law. They were immortal—but immortal *whats*? Creatures, to be sure, less than angels but more than goats. They were not immortal human beings. It was only in their disobedience that they became human, for better and for worse.

There is a grudging acceptance of this in the Christian concept of "*felix culpa*,"[30] the theodicean insistence that even the Fall is part of God's great plan for mankind, that our disobedience is a Divine

---

29 The idolatry of the book is still only another idolatry.

30 In the words of the Catholic Easter Vigil Mass: "*O felix culpa quae talem et tantum meruit habere redemptorem*," "Oh happy transgression that earned for us so great, so glorious a Redeemer."

instrument through which we may be brought into an even more profound and intimate union with the Creator by freely choosing him in the person of Jesus, the Redeemer.

To choose is to be human. To be the *first* to choose is to be an outcast. Milton, the great advocate of free speech, understood this all too well: Because he defended the practice of divorce, his enemies portrayed him as a divorcer himself (he was never divorced, though he was estranged from his wife for a period) and a polygamist. The same kinds of low-minded people employ the same stratagem today: If a lawyer defends a white supremacist and then later runs for political office, he invariably will be smeared as a white supremacist or a sympathizer rather than acknowledged as a lawyer performing his professional obligation to provide a legal defense even to those who are least sympathetic—including the obviously guilty. Including, even, Harvey Weinstein, even though providing him with legal counsel cost a Harvard dean his position. Those who defended the free speech of Communists in the 1950s were derided as fellow travelers, and those who defend the free speech of neo-Nazis, pedophiles, or other detestable characters today are smeared in the same way. The case for toleration is never more than an inch away from being suffocated by the desire to punish. And those who will not serve the desire to punish are to be cast out as heretics. The desire to punish comes in many forms—political, religious, social—but it is always and everywhere the same in its demand for obedience and service. Angels come in choirs, and a choir is no place for those determined to go their own way. Harmony is the reason for a choir's existence. Disharmony—disruption—is the one thing that the choir cannot tolerate. As it is in the choirs of angels, so it is in the corporations of men.

"*Non serviam*," Lucifer said, "I will not serve." These are the words that supposedly led to the brightest angel's expulsion from

Heaven. Lucifer's *non serviam* is shared in the same formulation in the Israelites' rejection of God's demands, as in Jeremiah 2:20: "*Saeculo confregisti jugum meum: rupisti vincula mea, et dixisti: Non serviam. In omni enim colle sublimi, et sub omni ligno frondoso, tu prosternebaris meretrix.*"[31] In that parallel we see the principle of the clockwork universe once more implied: As goes the individual, so goes the tribe, God's favorite angel and God's chosen people.

"*Non serviam*" has become, over the years, a battle cry. Aldo in *Planet of the Apes* announces that he has become something more than a chimp with his monosyllabic *non serviam*: "No!"[32] James Joyce has his own variation on that phrase at the end of *Portrait of the Artist as a Young Man*: "I will not serve that in which I no longer believe, whether it calls itself my home, my fatherland, or my church: and I will try to express myself in some mode of life or art as freely as I can and as wholly as I can, using for my defense the only arms I allow myself to use—silence, exile, and cunning."

God confesses that He is a jealous God. The God of Israel is a tribal deity, and he is strangely concerned with dietary etiquette, what with the prohibitions on eating buzzards and short-eared owls and chameleons and other things that it probably never occurred to any hungry Jew of old to chow down on. Indeed, many of those animals almost certainly had never been seen by the ancient Israelites, because they are not native to the Semitic homelands. In *The*

---

31 "For of old time I have broken thy yoke, and burst thy bonds; and thou saidst, I will not serve; for upon every high hill and under every green tree thou didst bow thyself, playing the harlot."

32 The apes went one way, we are going the other: "At first, they just grunted their refusal. But then, on an historic day, which is commemorated by my species and fully documented in the sacred scrolls, there came Aldo. He did not grunt. He articulated. He spoke a word, a word which had been spoken to him time and again without number by humans. He said: 'No.'" *Planet of the Apes*, 1971. On July 15, 2006, Twitter was released to the public, which immediately went back to grunting its disapproval.

White Goddess, Robert Graves makes a persuasive argument that these dietary prohibitions are in fact only codifications of a wider and deeper prohibition against participating in pagan religious rituals. Among ancient Egyptians, for instance, the pig was regarded with a kind of awful horror, and contact with pigs and swineherds was the subject of a strict taboo—except when it wasn't: Once a year, pigs were sacrificed to Osiris,[33] and every Egyptian partook of their flesh as part of the ritual. The biblical prohibition on eating pork doesn't have anything to do with some ancient intuition of trichinosis: More likely it was God once more being obliged to remind His chosen people to keep themselves separate and apart from the Babylonians and Egyptians and other nations with whom they came in contact. "No God before me," and all that.

When it comes to that, God is up for a little rebellion, too: Consider the Maccabees, who insist that the Jews will be Jews and not anything else, no matter what the king says. Jesus is a kind of double rebel who steps into a vipers' nest of mixed allegiances—zealots and collaborators, the Roman Empire and the kingdom of Judea—and He confounds expectations and demands on all sides: He is a stumbling block and a retribution, a sign of contradiction, telling Pontius Pilate that he will render unto Caesar what is Caesar's but nothing

---

33 Robert Graves, *The White Goddess*, 1948: "The conventional epithet *dios*, 'divine,' [is] applied in the *Odyssey* to the swine-herd Eumaeus. Because of the horror in which swine-herds were held by the Jews and Egyptians and the contempt in which, thanks to the Prodigal Son, they have long been held in Europe, the word is usually mistranslated 'honest or worthy' though admitted to be an *hapax legomenon*. It is true that except on one night of the year—the full moon that fell nearest to the winter solstice, when the pig was sacrificed to Isis and Osiris and its flesh eaten by every Egyptian—the taboo on any contact with pigs was so strong that swine-herds though full-blooded Egyptians (according to Herodotus) were avoided like the plague and forced to marry within their own caste; but this was a tribute to their sanctity rather than anything else. The public hangman is similarly avoided in France and England because he has courageously undertaken, in the interests of public morality, a peculiarly horrible and thankless trade."

more and informing the religious authorities that the political salvation they had been expecting was not to be, that His Kingdom was
not of this world, that they misunderstood the entire point of the
Messiah. Of course He had to be put to death. The people love
their tyrants.

Judas misunderstood Him, but perhaps we could consider that
even he believed, at the time, that he was doing the right thing. Jesus
did not want to be a king, not in the same sense as Julius Caesar or
King James. He was on the other side of the barricades. Some modern scholars believe that the original Greek texts of the Bible suggest
very strongly that it was not a commercial inn that Joseph and Mary
were turned away from before Jesus was born but rather Joseph's
family home. You can imagine the scene: Mary is pregnant, and
Joseph has, in the delicate language of the time, known her not. From
that point of view, he was something very familiar to John Milton,
the truth that never comes into the world but like a bastard, to the
ignominy of him that brought his birth. Jesus turned over the tables,
even in the temple—especially in the temple. Was that rebellion?
Against what? To what should He have been obedient?

Jesus was executed as a traitor. Jerry Bowyer describes the scene
in mock-journalistic prose in *Forbes* under the headline "Jesus of
Nazareth, Enemy of the State, Executed for Treason":

> Jesus of Nazareth was executed today on the orders of the
> Roman State. Method of execution: Crucifixion. The
> charge under Roman law was treason, and under Herodian
> law blasphemy against the Temple. The evidence against
> this anarchist was so strong that authorities of both the
> Roman State and the Kingdom of Herod concurred with
> the arrest and execution, and he was subjected to trial by
> both governments. And in a rare uprising of spontaneous

collective justice, the mass of people who were gathered for Passover called for his execution as well. The mob affirmed their loyalty to the state, chanting, "We have no king but Caesar."

Treason? Yes. Glorious treason.

I have been called a traitor to many things: to my class and tribe (poor white trash from the Texas Panhandle), to the political party I left a decade ago, to the political movement with which I have been affiliated for all of my adult life, to the United States, and even, on occasion, to God. But: "I will not serve that in which I no longer believe, whether it calls itself my home, my fatherland, or my church: and I will try to express myself in some mode of life or art as freely as I can and as wholly as I can." Unlike James Joyce's young Stephen Dedalus, I do not have much use for silence or cunning; on the other hand, although I cringe a little at the dramatic connotations of "exile," I do not find myself in any particular hurry to return from my periodic stays in Switzerland. I do not speak any of Switzerland's four major languages, and there is a great peace in being in a place in which the incessant banal telephone conversations and low-minded political hysterics that surround us at all times can be partly banished, and the conversations of others reduced to make only a limited and vague claim on my attention. I am sure that the Swiss answer to American cable-news rage-monkey festivals of ritual masturbation and talk-radio group therapy sessions is almost as insufferable as our domestic product, but it does not mean anything to me. Talk radio and cable news don't mean anything to me, either, at least not on a sentence-by-sentence basis, but the individual words still mean things, despite the best efforts of our commentariat, and so they remain distracting. I do not want these voices in my head. Insane people have voices in their heads, and I am not insane. One voice in my head is enough most of the time, though I will let Dante in from time to time, and Eliot, and Jeremiah, and my wife, and my friends. But I will issue the invitations, and I will let them know when it is time to go. And I will not make myself an instrument of any other voice—not in the name of conservatism, patriotism, or anything else.

If that makes me a kind of traitor, then at least I find myself in excellent company. I will reserve my obedience for that which deserves it.[34]

Obedience is a loaded gun: It matters who is holding it and at whom it is pointed. As V. I. Lenin insisted, the only real question in politics is кто кого?—Who, whom? To what or whom do we owe our obedience. Whom shall we serve—and to whom shall we say *"Non serviam"*? Richard Attenborough's Gandhi was a bit more eloquent than the man himself, and while the film borrows from Mohandas K. Gandhi's own words, the courtroom scenes bring to mind Jesus's wry interview with Pontius Pilate, and I suspect they were in part consciously modeled on that exchange. And Jesus might well have said of the Romans: "They may torture my body, break my bones, even kill me. Then they will have my dead body—but not my obedience."

Nothing like that is being asked of me or you, of course. Not yet, anyway. At the moment, I stand with Cardinal George: "I expect to die in bed. My successor will die in prison, and his successor will die a martyr in the public square. His successor will pick up the shards of a ruined society and slowly help rebuild civilization, as the church has done so often in human history." His Eminence is a traitor, too, a mild-mannered man who is at heart a political radical: "The greatest threat to world peace and international justice is the nation-state gone bad, claiming an absolute power, deciding questions and

---

34 "His servants ye are to whom ye obey." Romans 6:16.

making 'laws' beyond its competence," he wrote. "Few there are, however, who would venture to ask if there might be a better way for humanity to organize itself for the sake of the common good."[35] I like those sneer-quotes around "laws." The cardinal knows the score.

Before Russell Kirk taught him to call himself a "conservative," William F. Buckley Jr. called himself "an individualist." That, and not *conservative*, is how he describes himself in *God and Man at Yale*. That attitude stayed with him all his life. "I will not cede more power to the state," he wrote with Luciferian verve in *Up from Liberalism*.[36] "I will not willingly cede more power to anyone, not to the state, not to General Motors, not to the CIO. I will hoard my power like a miser, resisting every effort to drain it away from me. I will then use my power, as I see fit." And here Buckley departs from Milton's Lucifer, from the adolescent love of rebellion for its own sake, and from the childish conflation of eccentricity with individuality.[37] "I mean to live my life an obedient man, but obedient to God, subservient to the wisdom of my ancestors; never to the authority of political truths arrived at yesterday at the voting booth."

Buckley's juxtaposition of God and the voting booth was prescient.

If the Romans had had popular elections, Julius Caesar surely would have won. The people chose to spare Barabbas and condemn Jesus. Abraham Lincoln didn't free the slaves with a plebiscite—he chose to use his power, and a man shouting *"Sic semper tyrannis!"* killed him for it. If we had waited on a vote to free the slaves, slavery would have lasted another century or more. We might very well have

---

35 *Catholic World*, October 21, 2012.

36 1959.

37 "I am not my own light unto myself. As long as I will look only at myself, I will never find what I am. Because all I can see in myself is darkness." Nicolas Malebranche, *Dialogues on Metaphysics*, 1688.

it still. We have a knack for accommodating evil, and for accommodating ourselves to evil. In Dante's tour of Hell, he mostly encounters people damned for ordinary things: lust, greed, the love of political power. Picayune things. In *The Inferno*, even Satan lacks magnificence.

We have stopped thinking very much about Lucifer in our own time. We do not take Lucifer seriously, because we do not take God seriously. God, in the American Protestant Consensus culture in which I was raised, seems to care a great deal about lottery tickets and the outcome of bingo games. A god that small does not require an adversary so great as the one Milton imagined. Milton's Lucifer is an adversary for a morally and intellectually confident people—and for a confident God, too, one who is willing to let His universe be a living organic thing and not a brazen head. But the God of Milton, Shakespeare, and Dante has almost been forgotten. We do not have Pope Boniface VIII—we have Joel Osteen. And we have a new god.

Like Brutus, this new god sometimes comes to us in the form of the goddess Liberty, helmeted and arrayed for battle, as in the case of the 1918 war propaganda poster that I have here on my desk. The advertisement reads: "I am Public Opinion! All men fear me!" Public Opinion, in this advertisement, is peddling war bonds, and is very fond of exclamation points.

> If you have the money to buy and do not buy, I will make this a No Man's Land for you! I will judge you not by an allegiance expressed in mere words.... I will judge you by the material aid you give to the fighting men who are facing death that you may live and move and have your being in a world made safe.... I am public opinion! As I judge, all men stand or fall!

Hobbes conceived of the state as something like Leviathan, the gigantic sea-serpent from the Old Testament: big and brutal, with a singular *motive* if not a single *mind*: In Abraham Bosse's famous 1651 frontispiece for *Leviathan*, the torso of the great prince is composed of countless smaller figures, a literal body politic, a colonial organism like a Portuguese man-o'-war. But the state is not really anything like that. It is a bureaucracy—sometimes vicious and bloody-minded, but lacking in the cohering will of a mythical monster. No, what the state most closely resembles today is what the church resembled in Dante's time. The state is only an instrument, a professional staff, and a sanctum in which public rituals are conducted—a vast vicarage with nuclear weapons, not for the Vicar of Christ but for the vicars of Public Opinion.

If Milton's Lucifer seems attractive to us, it is because, in our time, Public Opinion is God.

Non serviam.

CHAPTER ELEVEN

Jeffrey and Me

Against him first: He's a very dog to the commonalty.

—*William Shakespeare, Coriolanus, Act I, Scene 1*

A note from the author: I do not think that I am the most important part of this story, or even a particularly important or interesting part of it. To be entirely honest, I've been asked to revisit the episode of my brief career at The Atlantic *so often that it has become a little tedious for me. But the personal context is necessary here. If you already have heard this tawdry little tale, don't feel obliged to continue, though if you're really interested, I do have a couple of new things here.*

"You should know that the campaign to have me fired will start two minutes after you announced you've hired me," I told Jeffrey Goldberg, the editor of *The Atlantic*, who had just hired me away from *National Review*, the conservative political magazine for which I had written for a decade.[1] It had been

---

1 "Standing athwart History, yelling 'Fuck you!'"

something of a whirlwind professional courtship: With Donald Trump in the White House and the neo-nationalists marching out in full ugly and stone-cold stupid force on the Right, I had been looking for journalistic outlets outside of the conservative media ghetto and hence had written to Goldberg offering to do some writing on fiction or theater for *The Atlantic*. I'm mostly known for writing about politics and public policy, but my first interest has always been literature, and I served for several years as the theater critic of *The New Criterion*. By Anno Domini 2018 I had—I think you'll find this entirely understandable—grown a little weary of politics *per se*.

I was surprised and flattered by Goldberg's response: "G-d works in mysterious ways. I was just having lunch with the president of the company and he asked me who I would have write for me if I could. You were on the top of the list." That was a pretty big deal to me,[2] I'm not too proud to admit. But what *The Atlantic* wanted from me wasn't book reviews and theater criticism—it was a great deal more than that. Much of my work at *National Review* over the years leading up to the election of Trump had consisted of traveling reports on poverty, addiction, and dysfunction among the white underclass, especially in Appalachia, in the Deep South, and in my native Texas. Goldberg summed up in six words what he wanted from me: "*The Moynihan Report*[3] for white people." That meant months or years of in-depth reporting—a full-time job.

---

2 But not as big a deal as the time William F. Buckley Jr. asked me for a vocabulary word. "Ah…what is it…means as though it were engraved in stone?"
"Lapidary?"
"Yes, that's it."
I went home and wrote a letter to one of my high-school English teachers, recounting the story and telling her that she should immediately demand a raise.
3 "The Negro Family: The Case For National Action," Daniel Patrick Moynihan, 1965. *The Moynihan Report* may represent the last time an employee of the US Department of Labor did anything useful or had a thought worth recording. If you want two points to define the line tracing the devolution of American politics, consider that Moynihan was succeeded in the Senate by Hillary Rodham Clinton, who is to the Democratic Party what herpes is to a sexagenarian Palm Beach sex party.

After a few weeks of meetings and discussions, I accepted *The Atlantic*'s offer, thanked my friend Rich Lowry, the editor of *National Review*, for his support and encouragement[4] over the past ten years, and told him that I was joining *The Atlantic*. Lowry asked why I would want to do that, and I told him: *The Atlantic* would give me the opportunity to reach a larger audience, including people who were not already committed political conservatives, which seemed to me very much in keeping with *National Review*'s broader mission as an evangelist for right-of-center ideas, and that it would give me the opportunity to pursue long-form, in-depth reporting of the sort that *National Review* simply does not have the resources to support: dedicating six months to a story rather than six hours.[5] Lowry asked me if I had considered the likely outcry over my joining *The Atlantic*—there had only recently been a vicious campaign against the *New York Times*'s decision to hire Bret Stephens, a mildly conservative op-ed columnist with considerably less controversial views than my own and a style much less abrasive and confrontational. Some combination of my vulnerability to flattery and my lamentable weakness for wishful thinking left me with level of confidence that turned out to be woefully unjustified. I told Lowry that I had the full support of *The Atlantic* and its editor. If it was good enough for Ralph Waldo Emerson, it was good enough for me. Lowry wished me the best but, being more politically intelligent than I am, gently counseled caution.

Goldberg, for his part, scoffed at the notion that my hiring would result in a major public controversy, and he wasn't troubled by the

---

4 Rich has no doubt endured a cargo barge of shit from donors, board members, Republican elected officials, and others because of me, and all he ever really did was ask me to stop referring to the Trump boys, Eric and Don Jr., as "Uday and Qusay." A pretty reasonable compromise, I think.

5 Once, when a previously planned *National Review* cover story by another writer fell through, I produced a cover essay in twenty-seven minutes. Having spent much of my life in daily newspapers helped to make me a pretty fast writer, one of the upsides of all the screaming and constant threats of immediate unemployment around the daily copy deadline.

example of Bret Stephens. "*The Atlantic* isn't the *New York Times*," he said. "It isn't the high church of liberalism." *High church*: That would prove to be a prescient choice of words, because what followed was an identifiably religious experience, and a perversely Catholic one at that: a *scandal* in its classical Christian sense, pseudo-episcopal demands by the self-appointed Grand Inquisitors of political discourse that I make a public recantation of my views, suggestions from Goldberg and others for an act of contrition, and my eventual excommunication when I declined to recant or apologize.

And, of course, a book. Goldberg was right about one thing: He[6] does work in mysterious ways. Jesus may be the Eternal King of the Universe, but His book sales probably would have been crap without a public execution.[7] I got the boot from *The Atlantic* around lunchtime, and got my first call from a publisher before boarding my flight at Reagan International later that afternoon.

I don't mention that to boast.[8] There is a more serious consideration: I work in the argument business, laboring fruitfully in the vineyards of controversy. Which is to say: I get paid for this stuff. That is not true for most people who are targeted by the mob.

I love reading *The Atlantic* and think I would have done good work there, but, ultimately, what such institutions provide to a writer such as myself amounts to very little more than administrative support, a marketing department, and shelf space. It is not like I stopped

---

6 One of the things I approve of about God is that He is always pretty straightforward and constant when it comes to His pronouns. (Please spare me the disquisition on the linguistic gender of "spirit" in Hebrew, Greek, and Latin. Feminine, neuter, and masculine, respectively, if you're wondering; the confusion between the grammatic concept "gender" and the biological fact of "sex" is the origin of much modern unhappiness, along with the conflation of metaphysical propositions and physical characteristics.)

7 A note to the Matt Yglesias types who review books without actually reading them: This is the point at which you'll want to say I finish off by comparing myself to Jesus.

8 Not *just* to boast, anyway. But I will note right here that I flew home first class.

writing or stop getting paid for it,[9] or as though that were ever even
on the list of likely outcomes. Before the *Atlantic* affair, what most
people knew me for was a series of reports on white underclass dysfunction in Appalachia and wresting a cell phone away from a rude
theater-goer at a performance of *Natasha, Pierre, and the Great
Comet of 1812*[10] and pitching it out the door of the theater, an act of
vigilante justice against the barbaric peons we all are enforced to
endure in this age of excessive democracy. A few Broadway produc-
ers quietly thanked me for that, and I received a bit of wounded
criticism from a few incontinently gaping Millennial recta who can't
put their phones away for ten minutes and be terrifyingly alone with
a bit of secondhand Tolstoy, much less bear without mediation the
rodential scrape and scurry of their own banal and meaningless
internal dialogue. Win some, lose some. That's my profession—it's
fun, it's lucrative, and it beats the Hell out of working for a living.

But that's just me.

Most of the people who suffer under the ruthlessly conformist
mob mentality that is my subject in this book do not work in the
controversy business. They are Google programmers and Chipotle
managers and public-school teachers who are reckless enough to
say what they think in public without getting paid handsomely for
it. When my outlet at *The Atlantic* was closed to me, I simply moved
on to bigger and better platforms, telling my story and making my
case in the *Wall Street Journal*, the *Washington Post*, and other publications, starting a regular column in the *New York Post* and, eventually, returning to my old position as a reporter and columnist at

---

9 Indeed, the rage-monkeys who sobbed about my having a job at *The Atlantic* were
gnashing their teeth in anguish afterward as they began to mentally calculate the checks
I was cashing after the controversy.

10 If you are the sort of person who can't put away your cell phone for two minutes, then
maybe an opera based on *War and Peace* isn't really your best bet on a Saturday night,
even if it is a nice change from your usual weekend regimen of appletinis and sadness.

National Review, the conservative political magazine launched by William F. Buckley Jr. in 1955 because he knew what a bunch of chickenshit yes-men and monkey-house poo-flingers were then—as now—occupying the commanding heights of American journalism and American culture. That's not how it generally goes for people in the real world, who have to seriously consider the implications for their ability to make the monthly mortgage payment every time they make an observation about current events on their personal Facebook pages or roust a bum camping out in their Starbucks. People sometimes use my name as a shorthand for these sensational Twitter-mob episodes, but who even knows the name of Dominique Moran or Holly Hylton?

The very silly series of events leading up to and following were described by some people as a "lynching," which is of course a grotesque exaggeration and an abuse of a metaphor[11] that should be reserved for sterner stuff than a social-media outrage mob and the more consequential in-house scalp-hunting campaign at *The Atlantic,* where a small group of young women who could not bear the thought of sharing an office with me three days out of the month[12] eventually succeeded in bullying Goldberg into firing me, notionally[13] over my views on abortion—i.e., that it is premeditated homicide and should be treated as such under the criminal code. My views are indeed controversial, even among my fellow pro-lifers, who take the generally patronizing and pusillanimous position that young women in difficult circumstances are basically indistinguishable from thumb-sucking preschoolers who cannot be treated as whole and competent human beings morally accountable for their actions.

---

11 I prefer "Nerf-stoning."

12 I live in Texas. *The Atlantic* is based in the Watergate building, which naturally produces conflicted feelings in a nefarious right-winger such as myself.

13 What actually happened was less about my views and more of an act of class hygiene, and partly about purely internal matters such as my compensation. More on that later.

Muppet News Flash: I'm an extremist. I always have been. It's right there in the *New York Times*, in the headline over a Ross Douthat column.[14]

None of this was unknown to *The Atlantic*, of course. My case was a little like that of Marc Lamont Hill, the mush-brained half-literate ass-clown who was fired from CNN a few months after I was fired from *The Atlantic*, purportedly because of his views on Israel, which run toward the extreme and which he expressed in eliminationist rhetoric borrowed from Hamas. But, as any mentally functional adult who has followed the case knows, Hill was not fired for the *content* of his political views. CNN is full of reporters and investigators: They knew what Marc Lamont Hill believed when they hired him. They knew he was a cretin and an asshole, but they had an editorial opening for a Jew-hating black man and MSNBC already had the Reverend Al Sharpton under contract. Hill wasn't fired for his politics: He was fired for being unpopular enough that his presence was disruptive to the Organization. He was an indigestible little nugget in the corporate alimentary canal, eventually puked up.

Media organizations in particular are put in an awkward position by this new microclimate of sudden (but by no means *ex nihilo*) outrage storms: They embrace controversy to the extent that it drives readership and revenue, but they abhor controversy to the extent that it disrupts the smooth daily flow of memo-writing and committee meetings and executive auto-fellatio. Like idiot children on Christmas morning, they turn up their noses at the gift of genuine intellectual controversy and content themselves by playing with the box it came in.

Like Hill, I wasn't hired in spite of my controversial views but because of them. "You just don't give a fuck," Goldberg said, admiringly comparing me to Caitlyn Flanagan, another *Atlantic* writer

---

14 "Among the Abortion Extremists," April 7, 2018.

who has engendered a fair bit of controversy. Later, that sentiment would undergo a small but significant evolution: "You just don't give a fuck," Goldberg said. "That's what makes you a great writer, and what makes it impossible for you to work at *The Atlantic*."

We were, strangely enough, in agreement at that moment. Weird that I should have received such a high compliment while I was being fired—but that's media life in the early twenty-first century.

I like Jeffrey Goldberg. Goldberg is a veteran of the Israeli Defense Forces, who by all accounts served honorably and courageously, and a lifelong journalist who has taken on the high and mighty from Washington to Riyadh. You'd think a man like that would be difficult to push around like some hapless nerd in *Mean Girls*. But there are discrete and non-overlapping kinds of courage. Who knows—maybe Aleksandr Solzhenitsyn was afraid of spiders or terrified of heights— that wouldn't make him any less of an admirable character. Not that Jeffrey Goldberg is Aleksandr Solzhenitsyn. But if you aren't in media or politics or a similar field, then you probably have no idea how absolutely *terrified* middle-aged white men such as Jeffrey Goldberg are of their young female subordinates, whose tender if occasionally bananas sensibilities represent a kind of Sword of Damocles hanging over the scrota of their male[15] superiors.[16] A couple of hundred thousand tweets from people on the intellectual level of dead-average chimpanzees and a few passive-aggressive threats from a handful of dotty young Millennial women on staff had Goldberg's tackle shriveling up like a couple of unharvested Bordeaux grapes in late November.

Which isn't to say that Goldberg is a coward, full stop. One act of cowardice does not a coward make—journalism isn't *Lord Jim*. Goldberg made a bad call in my case, but if I were to boycott and abominate every publication that made a bad editorial decision, then I'd have nowhere to write at all—including the publications I have

---

15 Formally if not functionally.
16 Formally if not functionally, also.

edited over the years. People make mistakes, and they sometimes make the wrong decision for the wrong reason.

On the other hand, I very much admire the *New York Times* for having enough institutional self-respect to stand by its hires, even when they are people who have views which I myself find distasteful, e.g. Sarah Jeong and her sour racial resentments. The enterprise that our frequently bankrupt president habitually ridicules as "the failing *New York Times*" is, thankfully, making a great deal of money these days, which gives it sufficient confidence to say, "We're the *New York Times*. We'll hire whoever we goddamned well please." Goldberg took the same view...until he didn't. "Who the fuck is Jessica Valenti?" he asked, indicating the *Guardian* columnist who took an unseemly personal interest in my employment status. "And why does she give a fuck who I hire?"[17] Goldberg had the right attitude—he just overestimated himself and overestimated *The Atlantic*'s ability to absorb the kind of controversy that comes when an institution that is not explicitly right-wing publishes someone like me. *The Atlantic* doesn't think of itself as a partisan center-left magazine: It boasts that it is "Of No Party or Clique." In reality, it is a cheerleader-by-default for center-left social and political views, notwithstanding the odd David Frum column. It is much more a clique than a party, of course, but that doesn't change the underlying dynamic. If anything, parties are more tolerant, in their way, because they rely on formal rules, whereas cliques have only the moment's status competition to guide them.

That's one of conservatives' sometimes tedious but by no means untrue complaints about the American media: There are explicitly left-leaning magazines such as *The Nation*, there are explicitly right-leaning magazines such as *National Review*, and there are purportedly nonpartisan "mainstream" publications such as the *New York*

---

17 In retrospect, the fact that Goldberg reads this sort of thing at all should have been a warning of sorts.

Times and *The Atlantic*—at which no conservative is permitted to work except as a token house conservative, and even then only under very tight restrictions and intense editorial supervision. For example, Ruth Marcus of the *Washington Post* is, like me, a genuine extremist on the question of abortion,[18] albeit in the opposite direction: She takes a frankly eugenic view of the procedure and wrote that she would have contentedly inflicted a horrifying and gruesome late-term abortion on either of her children had they been diagnosed with Down Syndrome *in utero*. But Marcus is not only a columnist—she also has administrative and editorial duties at the newspaper, including green-lighting columns and editing them. When I wrote a piece for the *Post* about the possibility of adopting some European-style restrictions on abortion in the United States, it was Ruth Marcus who edited it, and it was her sensibility that had to be satisfied before the piece ever saw print. She's a good enough editor, but imagine the reverse situation: a pro-choice activist being asked to submit a column to the *Post*—but only if pro-life radical Kevin D. Williamson signed off on it. You'd lose your job for that.

Conservatives have often enough rehearsed the fair point about the direction of bias in the media, but insufficient attention has been paid to the way in which the internal dynamics of mob politics make that bias—and the mobbery itself—quite nearly invisible from within the bubble—which is much more a *social* bubble than a political one.

There's radicalism and there's radicalism, and it is social allegiances rather than the degree or direction of radicalism that govern our relationships to political ideas. Slavoj Žižek, the Marxist philosopher and sometime apologist for political violence, is routinely cited in *The Atlantic*'s pages—without so much as an acknowledgment of his views on violence. I mentioned to Goldberg that the late Christopher Hitchens, who was controversial in his own very safe

---

18 She was the other extremist in that Ross Douthat column.

way[19] (nobody gets fired or murdered for taking a rhetorical dump on Mother Teresa), had in the very pages of *The Atlantic* written a very persuasive justification for political violence up to and including murder.

"Hitchens was in the family," Goldberg said. "You are not."

And that, of course, is what all this is really about.

To give you an idea of the social flavor of the deliberations about my employment, Goldberg insisted at one point that the question was whether I was "clubbable," an expression rarely heard outside of early-twentieth-century English novels. I told him that I thought I was as clubbable as a baby seal, but he wasn't so sure.

One must be ever so careful these days.

Goldberg wasn't the only one suffering from delusions of testicular adequacy: This goes up and down the corporate ladder, from technology titans such as Facebook to old-fashioned magazines—and those worlds now frequently overlap. At the time of the controversy surrounding my coming on board, *Atlantic* publisher David Bradley was in the process of handing ownership of the magazine and its related businesses over to a consortium led by Laurene Powell, a billionaire dilettante who inherited a vast and splendid fortune from her late husband, Steve Jobs. Bradley is one of the WASPiest WASPs who ever WASPed, a man who makes Thacher Longstreth look like James Brown. He is a man out of time. He called me into his office on my first day at the magazine to give me a little speech about *The Atlantic*'s values—namely its commitment to the collegial exploration of meaningful ideas—which began with an indecipherable and possibly senescent reverie on his childhood experiences at Sidwell Friends and ended with his putting his hand on my shoulder and speaking directly and confidently to the controversy surrounding me: "We are not wavering," he said. "*I* am not wavering."

---

19 The one time I ever encountered the famous atheist was, oddly enough, in church, at ten in the morning. He was drunk.

I should have just packed up my personal belongings in a shoebox right then and made for the elevators—when an old WASP banker with no ass feels compelled to put on a serious face and promise that he's not about to fuck you, you're already fucked. He wavered like one of those weird pneumatic puppets that gyrate outside of car washes and storefront tax-preparation services.

Like Bradley, Goldberg was very sure of himself—at first. He was confident because he misunderstood the contours of his tribe: His theory was that because I am a conservative who opposed and opposes Donald J. Trump and his odious brand of rabble-rousing politics, I would be accepted, if grudgingly, into the progressive-dominated conversation at *The Atlantic*. And, to his credit, he seemed to sincerely believe that the conversation needed me: We first discussed the likely opposition to my hiring at South by Southwest, the Austin film-and-media festival where *The Atlantic* was hosting an unbearably pretentious discussion of diversity in cultural institutions, which Goldberg cheerfully (if carefully and quietly) mocked all the way through. "I am insufficiently intersectional" for this discussion, he said, describing the event as the "wokiest" thing he'd ever participated in. He savored the idea of injecting me into such an environment. It was sponsored by a feminist group enjoying the patronage of Google, PepsiCo, AT&T, NBCUniversal, Facebook, UBS, JPMorgan Chase, and Deloitte. If you want to know where the great nasties of Corporate America put their power, it ain't the Cato Institute.

I was a little surprised at Goldberg's nonchalance and by the ease of his contempt: The star of the show was Ta-Nehesi Coates, *The Atlantic*'s marquee writer on questions of race, whose goodwill Goldberg was and is self-abasingly solicitous of, a man who gives every impression of taking this kind of thing much more seriously than it deserves. Coates had been one of the main advocates of my joining

The Atlantic, a position for which he would later do public penance. The lines of moral acceptability in Coates's world move quickly, and it is easy even for a gifted polemicist such as Coates to go from politically coddled social-justice mascot to moral deviant: Like those ancient ranching families in Texas, he didn't have to cross the border—the border crossed him.

Shifting borders makes it difficult to stake out a defensible position for men in Goldberg's position—for those who do not have the luxury of not giving a fuck. And there was the tenor of the times: In the wake of the Harvey Weinstein revelations, powerful white men at the commanding heights of culture were being blown away like so many toupees in a hurricane. Goldberg himself remarked that it would be impossible to hire a white man[20] as editor of *The Atlantic* if the position were to come open, that he does not expect to see such a job offered to a man such as himself in his lifetime—and surely he knows that there are a great many people, some of them in his employ, who would very much like to see his position come open. The *Atlantic* episode was less about the question of my losing a job than about the question of Goldberg keeping one.

Between us, I'm not sure he will.[21] The mob is always hungry. It is a ravening maw, and there are many of its members who already want Goldberg out the door feet first on political grounds, owing to

---

20 I should note that Goldberg now specifically denies ever having said any such thing to me—unlike more than a few of my colleagues in journalism, I double-check these things—though I specifically remember being especially surprised by his choice of words: "a white man" rather than "a white male." I am from the South, where a white man talking about the plight of the "white man" is a culturally fraught thing indeed, though I doubt this is known to Goldberg, a Jewish guy from Brooklyn. I'll put it this way: Goldberg and I have different recollections of the conversation, though if you want to know about the "insufficiently intersectional" stuff, I'll be happy to show you the emails.
21 As of June 2019, I'd give 50/50 odds on Goldberg's surviving another two years as editor of *The Atlantic*. I am told that his billionaire mistress in California was unimpressed with his handling of l'affaire Williamson.

his pro-Israel views and his sometimes hawkish posture on US foreign policy. But they also want him gone for other reasons: because he's a white man, because they have a superstitious zero-sum view of public life and believe that his absence would create an opening that one of them might fill, because he's a happy and successful and maybe just a little bit self-satisfied public figure with a slightly smug and eminently punchable face they might seize upon the opportunity to hurt for reasons of envy and pure sadism, a kind of brief opiate high to deaden the pain of their own mediocrity and insignificance— because he, too, is in his way a member of the Smallest Minority.

But you don't need to worry about guys like Jeffrey and me. We're going to be fine.

It's the rest of you poor dumb bastards who need worrying about.

The Emerging American Police State

> Sentimentality was arguably the most modern feature
> of National Socialism, in that turn-of-the-millennium
> politics are permeated, if not from presentiments of
> apocalypse, then by a cloying sentimentality from politi-
> cians hard to distinguish from preachers, and a wider
> culture of self-absorption, sincerity and victimhood. In
> this respect, Nazism was truly ahead of its time, beyond
> its unremarkable fascination with mere technology. This
> was politics as feeling.
>
> —*Michael Burleigh,* The Third Reich: A New History, *2001*

"Sentimentality" is wrongly taken as a synonym for "sweet-ness" or general emotional softness and gooeyness. That is not what the word means. "Sentimentality" is the tendency to be controlled by sentiment. Hatred is a sentiment—an important one, as it turns out. Envy, resentment, self-loathing—these are the stuff of sentimentality, too, properly understood.

James Baldwin analyzed sentimentality in relation to *Uncle Tom's Cabin* and other works of protest literature. For the uncritical mind, the important thing for the book is to be on the "right side" of the issues, not whether it is a good book or a bad book. "It is, indeed, considered the sign of a frivolity so intense as to approach decadence to suggest that these books are both badly written and wildly improbable," Baldwin wrote. "One is told to put first things first, the good of society coming before niceties of style or characterization. Even if this were incontestable—for what exactly is the 'good' of society?—it argues an insuperable confusion, since literature and sociology are not one and the same; it is impossible to discuss them as if they were. Our passion for categorization, life neatly fitted into pegs, has led to an unforeseen, paradoxical distress; confusion, a breakdown of meaning. Those categories which were meant to define and control the world for us have boomeranged us into chaos; in which limbo we whirl, clutching the straws of our definitions." This is not the sentimentality of sweetness but the sentimentality of the "*volk*," the "fatherland," the "proletariat," of "social justice" and "Make America Great Again." It is the sentimentality not only of dishonesty but also indecency. "Sentimentality, the ostentatious parading of excessive and spurious emotion, is the mark of dishonesty, the inability to feel," Baldwin wrote. "The wet eyes of the sentimentalist betray his aversion to experience, his fear of life, his arid heart; and it is always, therefore, the signal of secret and violent inhumanity, the mask of cruelty."[1]

The mask has slipped.

One in five Americans who identify with one of the major political parties told researchers in 2018 that members of the opposing party "lack the traits to be considered fully human." A similar number believe that "we'd be better off as a country if large numbers of [members of the opposing party] in the public today just died." About one in ten report that if they heard that a politician had died of cancer or had been murdered, their feeling about that would depend on his party affiliation. About 13 percent of Republicans and 18 percent of Democrats believe that political violence would be justified in 2020 if their party lost the presidential election. Substantial *majorities*

---

1 *Notes of a Native Son*, 1966.

believe that members of the opposing party "are a serious threat to the United States and its people."[2]

Oh, Sunshine: You didn't think that tribal rage-monkey stuff was going to end with Twitter mobs and "de-platforming," did you? Tell me you are not that stupid.

The authors of the study cited above explored Americans' attitudes along three lines of inquiry: first, "partisan moral disengagement," by which they mean the inclination to rationalize the infliction of harm on political opponents; second, "partisan *schadenfreude*," welcoming death and disease for political opponents; and, third, outright support for political violence. They discovered correlations between aggressive personalities, a strong sense of political identity (a social and cultural identity distinct from support for a particular political ideology), and the basket of dysfunction they describe collectively as "lethal partisanship." The more committed the partisan, the more lethal the partisanship. "We found that large portions of partisans embrace partisan moral disengagement," the authors write, putting the share at 40 percent to 60 percent. Fewer would confess to supporting political violence—but not as few as you might think: The number runs as high as 15 percent. A minority, but "even so, their views represent a level of extreme hostility among millions of American partisans today that has not been documented in modern American politics."

And here Julien Benda's cult of success—the "the teaching that says that when a will is successful that fact alone gives it a moral value, whereas the will which fails is for that reason alone deserving of contempt"—makes another cameo: On the specific question of political violence, the responses varied significantly depending on whether partisans expected to win or lose an upcoming election. The direction of that variation may surprise you, if you have somehow

---

2 "Lethal Mass Partisanship: Prevalence, Correlates, & Electoral Contingencies," Nathan P. Calmoe and Lilliana Mason, 2018.

missed the ugly triumphalism of our contemporary primitives: "Experimental evidence showed that inducing expectations of electoral *victory* led strong partisans to endorse violence against their partisan opponents more than expectations of electoral *loss*." And while only a minority endorse violence *per se*, "many times more embrace partisan moral disengagement, which makes the turn to violence easier if they have not made it already. As more Americans embrace strong partisanship, the prevalence of lethal partisanship is likely to grow."

The Hutu-Tutsi character of partisan tribalism is difficult to appreciate it unless you are able to distinguish the Republican and Democratic parties from Republicans and Democrats as people. The class of people who work as officials and functionaries of the two major parties have much more in common with each other than they do with members of their own parties who are not ordinarily and professionally involved in the direct business of operational campaign politics. That Republicans and Democrats are social grouping distinct from their respective formal party apparatuses is how political scholars solve "the puzzle of how a public that is traditionally skeptical of parties, has little information about their activities, and virtually no contact with them as organizations could identify themselves as partisans," as Donald Green, Bradley Palmquist, and Eric Schickler put it in *Partisan Hearts and Minds: Political Parties and the Social Identities of Voters*.[3] "The conceptual focus is not on identification with the parties *per se* but with Democrats and Republicans as social groups.... Merely asking respondents whether they like a political party, support it, vote for it, feel close to it, believe it to be effective in office, or find its ideas attractive is not the same as asking about self-definition and group attachment."

---

3 Yale University Press, 2002.

People do not choose political parties based on their ideologies; more often it is the case that they acquire ideological orientations through preexisting political affiliations, which is to say, through preexisting social identities. "Ideological self-categorization differs in subtle but important ways from ideology itself," Green et al. write. "It taps not what the respondent thinks about various issues but rather the ideological label he or she finds most suitable. In that sense, it bears a certain similarity to party identification: It is hard to tell from available data whether survey respondents are primarily describing their intellectual orientation of their opinions of the social groups known as liberals and conservatives." That was the view at the turn of the century;[4] perhaps it is a little more clear now that the latter absolutely is the case.

The authors of *Partisan Hearts and Minds* note three aspects of partisanship as a social identity: 1. It is relatively stable among both individuals and groups; 2. It does not respond strongly to current events; 3. It exercises more influence on policy views than policy views exercise on it. The incorporation of the political identity into the broader social identity is demonstrated most dramatically by the case of African Americans, who statistically identify very strongly with the Democratic party irrespective of their policy views or ideological orientations. African Americans who hold very conservative political views are only *slightly* less likely to identify with the Democratic party than African Americans with liberal views. But the melding of

---

4 Innocent times! Green et al. also report: "Identification with political parties is a minor part of the typical American's self-conception. Race, sex, ethnicity, religion, region, and social class come immediately to mind as core social identities; political party does not. The core identities suffuse nearly all of our day-to-day interactions with others; It is difficult to imagine a social gathering in which people fail to take notice of accents, skin color, or secondary sexual characteristics. Partisan stereotypes and self-images, by contrast, are called to mind sporadically.... *It is not unusual for people to be unaware of the party affiliations of their friends.*" Does that sound like your life now?

political identities with racial, ethnic, religious, sexual, and other identities touches every social grouping: If only the votes of white Americans were counted, the last Democratic president would have been Lyndon Baines Johnson.[5] Donald Trump won only 46.1 percent of all votes cast in 2016, but won 58 percent of white voters—more significant: 87 percent of the people who voted for Trump were white. If you are looking for the tribalism, it's there in the numbers.

Democracy, the sentimentalists call it. A more clear-eyed description is this: the emerging American police state.

Ochlocracy and the tribal instincts that enable mob rule are always there; in our time, social media and its products, antidiscourse and Instant Culture, channel those passions in unusually destructive ways, especially vicious in part because they mimic the mechanics of addiction: For the miserable and isolated members of the lonely mob, those little jolts of attention[6] do roughly the same work that cigarettes do for the smoker and heroin does for the junkie. Addiction is not the cause of misery—it is a *strategy* for miserable people. Misery in numbers is an ancient political force, maybe the most ancient of them all. The methods of ochlocracy, the concept of *streitbare Demokratie*, the degeneration of constitutions and the rule of law into crass majoritarianism, the absolutism of Organization *Kultur*—these are all illustrations of the fact that ideas matter, that ideas have consequences, but they are only the conditions on the ground. The French Revolution was carried out with muskets and guillotines for the same reason the Rwandan genocide was carried out with machetes: Those were the tools at hand. The charges of "white privilege" or "rape apologist" are thrown around only because

---

5 Possibly Harry S. Truman if you discount those Cook County election shenanigans that brought John F. Kennedy to power.
6 "You like me! You really like me!"

we no longer accuse people of being witches or communists when we wish to destroy them.

These are the tools for creating and managing mobs. But remember your Gibbons and the example of Cleander: Mob rule does not end with the mob. The mob rarely acts on its own and never for long. Mob rule is not a mere riot: It is what happens when the mob successfully recruits the state to act as its henchman.

In 2009, six Italian scientists were convicted of manslaughter for having thought and said the wrong things leading up to the L'Aquila earthquake. If the scientists had said different things, the argument went, then fewer people would have died. That argument was immediately imported into the American political context, with Professor Lawrence Torcello of the Rochester Institute of Technology arguing in an academic journal that those with dissident views on climate change in the United States could and should be prosecuted as criminals, and that we should not allow "misguided concern regarding free speech" to protect speech that "remains a serious deterrent against meaningful political action." Progressive journalists[7] soon picked up the thread, as did Democratic politicians and progressive activists.[8] Soon afterward, a group of Democrats state attorneys general, including future senator and presidential hopeful Kamala Harris of California, put together a plan to prosecute those with nonconforming views on climate change under a host of pretexts, including securities violations. Subpoenas were issued to research nonprofits and advocacy groups, among others, with Harris et al. particularly

---

7 "Arrest Climate Deniers," Adam Weinstein, *Gawker*, March 28, 2014. "Climate Denialism Is Literally Killing Us," Mark Hertsgaard, *The Nation*, September 7, 2019. Etc. Hertsgaard writes: "Murder is murder … we should punish it as such."

8 Robert F. Kennedy Jr. at the People's (!) Climate March in 2014 accused Charles and David Koch of *treason* for their climate-change views, and, in case that wasn't clear enough, added: "I think they should be enjoying three hots and a cot at the Hague with all the other war criminals." *Reason*, October 1, 2014.

interested in seizing their private donor lists.[9] The First Amendment has long stood in the way of such efforts, but whether it will survive the ochlocracy feedback loop is unclear. In September 2014, all 54 Democrats in the Senate voted to repeal the First Amendment; in May of 2019, Representative Adam Schiff (D., Calif), the powerful chairman of the House Intelligence Committee, renewed the effort. Like the 2014 effort, Representative Schiff's attack on free speech is couched as regulating "independent expenditures" aimed at influencing elections. *The New York Times* is an independent corporate expenditure aimed at influencing elections. So is this book.

Of course bakers with nonconforming views on same-sex marriage must be prosecuted as criminals. Of course films critical of presidential candidates must be suppressed. Of course critics of certain global-warming policy proposals must be investigated as criminals and charged with felonies—the mob demands it.

What the mob hates above all is the individual, insisting on his own mind, his own morals, and his own priorities. The mob hates him less for the content of his views than for the fact that he holds them without the mob's permission and declines to abandon them at the mob's demand. Democracy has always been the enemy of minority rights. It always will be. And the biggest democracies will always be a dangerous place for the smallest minority.

---

9 The matter remains in litigation. The demands are plainly unconstitutional, and law professor Glenn Harlan Reynolds of the University of Tennessee argues that the attorneys general are engaged in an actual criminal conspiracy. "Conspiring Against Free Speech Is a Crime," *USA Today*, April 11, 2016.

Index